# Progressive Business Plan for a Mobile Food Truck

Copyright © 2017 by Progressive Business Consulting, Inc.
Pembroke Pines, FL 33027

# NON-DISCLOSURE AGREEMENT

_____ (Company)., and _____ (Person Name), agrees:

_____ (Company) Corp. may from time to time disclose to _____ (Person Name) certain confidential information or trade secrets generally regarding Business plan and financials of _____ (Company) corp.

_____ (Person Name) agrees that it shall not disclose the information so conveyed, unless in conformity with this agreement. _____ (Person Name) shall limit disclosure to the officers and employees of _____ (Person Name) with a reasonable "need to know" the information, and shall protect the same from disclosure with reasonable diligence.

As to all information which _____ (Company) Corp. claims is confidential, _____ (Company) Corp. shall reduce the same to writing prior to disclosure and shall conspicuously mark the same as "confidential," "not to be disclosed" or with other clear indication of its status. If the information which _____ (Company) Corp. is disclosing is not in written form, for example, a machine or device, _____ (Company) Corp. shall be required prior to or at the same time that the disclosure is made to provide written notice of the secrecy claimed by _____ (Company) Corp. _____ (Person Name) agrees upon reasonable notice to return the confidential tangible material provided by it by _____ (Company) Corp. upon reasonable request.

The obligation of non-disclosure shall terminate when if any of the following occurs:
(a) The confidential information becomes known to the public without the fault of _____ (Person Name), or;
(b) The information is disclosed publicly by _____ (Company) Corp., or
(c) a period of 12 months passes from the disclosure, or;
(d) the information loses its status as confidential through no fault of _____ (Person Name).

In any event, the obligation of non-disclosure shall not apply to information which was known to _____ (Person Name) prior to the execution of this agreement.

Dated: _____

_____
_____ (Company) Corp.
_____(Person Name)

# Business and Marketing Plan Instructions

1. If you purchased this Book via Amazon's Kindle or Print-on-Demand Systems, please send proof-of-purchase to Probusconsult2@Yahoo.com and we will email you the file.

2. Complete the Executive Summary section, as your final step, after you have completed the entire plan.

3. Feel free to edit the plan and make it more relevant to your strategic goals, objectives and business vision.

4. We have provided all of the formulas needed to prepare the financial plan. Just plug in the numbers that are based on your particular situation. Excel spreadsheets for the financials are available on the microsoft.com website and www.simplebizplanning.com/forms.htm http://office.microsoft.com/en-us/templates/

5. Throughout the plan, we have provided prompts or suggestions as to what values to enter into blank spaces, but use your best judgment and then delete the suggested values (?).

6. The plan also includes some separate worksheets for additional assistance in expanding some of the sections, if desired.

7. Additionally, some sections offer multiple choices and the word 'select' appears as a prompt to edit the contents of the plan.

8. Your feedback, referrals and business are always very much appreciated.

Thank you

Nat Chiaffarano, MBA
Progressive Business Consulting, Inc.
Pembroke Pines, FL 33027
ProBusConsult2@yahoo.com

# "Progressive Business Plan for a Mobile Food Truck"

## Copyright Notice

Copyright © 2017   Nat Chiaffarano, MBA
Progressive Business Consulting, Inc
All Rights Reserved.   **ISBN:** 9781973481492

This program is protected under Federal and International copyright laws. No portion of these materials may be reproduced, stored in a retrieval system or transmitted in any manner whatsoever, without the written consent of the publisher.

## Limits of Liability / Disclaimer of Warranty

The author and the publisher of "Progressive Business Plan for an Mobile Food Truck", and all accompanying materials have used their best efforts in preparing this program. The author and publisher make no representations and warranties with respect to the accuracy, applicability, fitness or completeness of the content of this program. The information contained in this program is subject to change without notice and should not be construed as a commitment by the author or publisher.

The authors and publisher shall in no event be held liable for any loss or damages, including but not limited to special, incidental, consequential, or other damages. The program makes no promises as to results or consequences of applying the material herein: your business results may vary in direct relation to your detailed planning, timing, availability of capital and human resources, and implementation skills.

This publication is not intended for use as a source of legal, accounting, or professional advice. As always, the advice of a competent legal, accounting, tax, financial or other professional should be sought. If you have any specific questions about your unique business situation, consider contacting a qualified business consultant. The fact that an organization or website is referred to as a 'resource' or potential source of information, does not mean that the publisher or authors endorse the resource. Websites listed may also have been changed since publication of the book.

# Mobile Food Truck Business Plan
_____ (date)

Business Name: _____
Plan Time Period:   2017 - 2019

Founding Directors:
Name: _____
Name: _____

Contact Information:
Owner: _____
Address: _____
City/State/Zip: _____
Phone: _____
Cell: _____
Fax: _____
Website: _____
Email: _____


Submitted to: _____
Date: _____
Contact Info: _____


This document contains confidential information. It is disclosed to you for informational purposes only. Its contents shall remain the property of _____ (business name) and shall be returned to _____ when requested. This is a business plan and does not imply an offering of securities.

# Mobile Food Truck Business Plan: Table of Contents

| Section | Description | Page |
|---|---|---|
| **1.0** | **Executive Summary** | ___ |
| 1.1.0 | Tactical Objectives | ___ |
| 1.1.1 | Strategic Objectives | ___ |
| 1.2 | Mission Statement | ___ |
| 1.2.1 | Core Values Statement | ___ |
| 1.3 | Vision Statement | ___ |
| 1.4 | Keys to Success | ___ |
| | | |
| **2.0** | **Company Summary** | ___ |
| 2.1 | Company Ownership | ___ |
| 2.2 | Company Licensing and Liability Protection | ___ |
| 2.3 | Start-up To-do Checklist | ___ |
| 2.4.0 | Company Location | ___ |
| 2.4.1 | Company Facilities | ___ |
| 2.5.0 | Start-up Summary | ___ |
| 2.5.1 | Inventory | ___ |
| 2.5.2 | Supply Sourcing | ___ |
| 2.6 | Start-up Requirements | ___ |
| 2.7 | SBA Loan Key Requirements | ___ |
| 2.7.1 | Other Financing Options | ___ |
| | | |
| **3.0** | **Products and Services** | ___ |
| 3.1 | Service Descriptions | ___ |
| 3.1.1 | Product Descriptions | ___ |
| 3.2 | Alternate Revenue Streams | ___ |
| 3.3 | Production of Products and Services | ___ |
| 3.4 | Competitive Comparison | ___ |
| 3.5 | Sale Literature | ___ |
| 3.6 | Fulfillment | ___ |
| 3.7 | Technology | ___ |
| 3.8 | Future Products and Services | ___ |
| | | |
| **4.0** | **Market Analysis Summary** | ___ |
| 4.1.0 | Secondary Market Research | ___ |
| 4.1.1 | Primary Market Research | ___ |
| 4.2 | Market Segmentation | ___ |
| 4.3 | Target Market Segment Strategy | ___ |
| 4.3.1 | Market Needs | ___ |
| 4.4 | Buying Patterns | ___ |
| 4.5 | Market Growth | ___ |

| Section | Description | Page |
|---|---|---|
| 4.6 | Service Business Analysis | |
| 4.7 | Barrier to Entry | |
| 4.8 | Competitive Analysis | |
| 4.9 | Market Revenue Projections | |
| **5.0** | **Industry Analysis** | |
| 5.1 | Industry Leaders | |
| 5.2 | Industry Statistics | |
| 5.3 | Industry Trends | |
| 5.4 | Industry Key Terms | |
| **6.0** | **Strategy and Implementation Summary** | |
| 6.1.0 | Promotion Strategy | |
| 6.1.1 | Grand Opening | |
| 6.1.2 | Value Proposition | |
| 6.1.3 | Positioning Statement | |
| 6.1.4 | Distribution Strategy | |
| 6.2 | Competitive Advantage | |
| 6.2.1 | Branding Strategy | |
| 6.3 | Business SWOT Analysis | |
| 6.4.0 | Marketing Strategy | |
| 6.4.1 | Strategic Alliances | |
| 6.4.2 | Monitoring Marketing Results | |
| 6.4.3 | Word-of-Mouth Marketing | |
| 6.5 | Sales Strategy | |
| 6.5.1 | Customer Retention Strategy | |
| 6.5.2 | Sales Forecast | |
| 6.5.3 | Sales Program | |
| 6.6 | Merchandising Strategy | |
| 6.7 | Pricing Strategy | |
| 6.8 | Differentiation Strategies | |
| 6.9 | Milestone Tracking | |
| **7.0** | **Website Plan Summary** | |
| 7.1 | Website Marketing Strategy | |
| 7.2 | Development Requirements | |
| 7.3 | Sample Frequently Asked Questions | |
| **8.0** | **Operations** | |
| 8.1 | Security Measures | |
| **9.0** | **Management Summary** | |
| 9.1 | Owner Personal History | |

| Section | Description | Page |
|---|---|---|
| 9.2 | Management Team Gaps | \_\_\_\_ |
| 9.2.1 | Management Matrix | \_\_\_\_ |
| 9.2.2 | Outsourcing Matrix | \_\_\_\_ |
| 9.3 | Employee Requirements | \_\_\_\_ |
| 9.4 | Job Descriptions | \_\_\_\_ |
| 9.4.1 | Job Description Format | \_\_\_\_ |
| 9.5 | Personnel Plan | \_\_\_\_ |
| 9.6 | Staffing Plan | \_\_\_\_ |
| | | |
| **10.0** | **Business Risk Factors** | \_\_\_\_ |
| 10.1 | Business Risk Reduction Strategies | \_\_\_\_ |
| 10.2 | Reduce Customer Perceived Risk Strategies | \_\_\_\_ |
| | | |
| **11.0** | **Financial Plan** | \_\_\_\_ |
| 11.1 | Important Assumptions | \_\_\_\_ |
| 11.2 | Break-even Analysis | \_\_\_\_ |
| 11.3 | Projected Profit and Loss | \_\_\_\_ |
| 11.4 | Projected Cash Flow | \_\_\_\_ |
| 11.5 | Projected Balance Sheet | \_\_\_\_ |
| 11.6 | Business Ratios | \_\_\_\_ |
| | | |
| **12.0** | **Business Plan Summary** | \_\_\_\_ |
| | | |
| **13.0** | **Potential Exit Strategies** | \_\_\_\_ |
| | | |
| | **Appendix** | \_\_\_\_ |
| | | |
| | **Helpful Resources** | \_\_\_\_ |
| | | |
| | **Marketing Worksheets** | \_\_\_\_ |

# 1.0 Executive Summary

## Industry Overview

A food truck, mobile kitchen, mobile canteen, or catering truck is a mobile venue that was originally created to sell local ethnic cuisine. Some sell prepackaged food; others are more like restaurants-on-wheels. Some may cater to specific meals, such as the breakfast truck, lunch truck or Mobile Food Truck, and snack truck, break truck or taco truck. Food trucks cater events (carnivals, construction sites, sporting events etc.) where potential customers gather, and places of regular work or study – college campuses, office complexes, industrial parks, auto repair shops, movie sets, military bases, etc. – where potential customers require regular meals or snacks.

The popularity of mobile food trucks has grown tremendously in the past few years. The industry is expected to grow from about $650 million during 2012 to more than $2 billion by 2018, according to a 2012 Intuit Inc. report. Mobile kitchens are the fastest growing trend in the food-service industry. The lower cost of entry has allowed chefs, barristers and restaurant industry insiders to experiment with gourmet-style street food and beverages, particularly since the recession severely limited accessible financing for small businesses.

The food truck has become an option for people to have a different level of satisfaction. Food trucks have become an increasingly popular alternative to the traditional restaurant visit. Sales in this 'mobile caterers segment', is projected to grow by nearly 4% this year, to $630 million, according to the National Restaurant Association, which rated food trucks and pop-up restaurants the top restaurant operational trend in 2014. In fact, this sub-sector is becoming so popular that the association is devoting an area at its annual trade show to mobile food service. The Food Truck Spot has been designed to educate attendees on everything they need to start a food truck, from vehicle purchase to kitchen equipment.

For restaurant entrepreneurs, food trucks provide opportunities to venture into the restaurant business or expand current concepts at relatively low cost. The startup cost for a truck is typically well below that of a bricks-and-mortar restaurant. Part of the appeal for customers is the affordable price points for quality meals and gourmet beverages, the convenience of them coming to the customer's location and the fun aspect of social media interaction.

Food trucks are also forming communities, including with competitors, in major cities to address local laws and regulations on mobile vending. As an example, several companies have formed the NYC Food Truck Association to work with a lobbyist to update some of the outdated New York City parking regulations and paperwork requirements, which can be daunting. New York City's Department of Health and Mental Hygiene oversees food truck vendor permits and licenses. A permit goes to the cart or truck itself, with one permit per cart or truck, which means mobile food vendors may have more than one license. They are comparable to a driver's license and means you can work at a permitted cart. The number of permits is usually capped under a city's administrative code, and may result in a long permit waiting list. Presently, according to the Southern California Mobile Food Vendors Association, Los Angeles is the "epicenter" of the food truck phenomenon because it does not have the same restrictions for mobile food vendors as New York. In fact, some of these mobile vendors use Twitter to alert customers where they would stop each day. Typical prime spots include parks and in front of museums, but roaming carts are constantly searching for significant revenue-generating areas, and maintain a flexible business model. It's also important to think about image, being approachable, and having an excellent differentiated product.

A Mobile Food Truck has many benefits as opposed to a fixed location due to the fact that the owner can transport the business to areas where demand is greatest for the product. The food truck business can be very lucrative as there are:
    No huge competitors dominating the market
    Low overhead
    Flexible hours (work as much or as little as you want)
    Low startup costs
    Customers experience a sense of urgency to buy.

**Market Statistics**
The industry is heavily concentrated in urban areas, particularly in the central parts of large cities. This industry is thriving in cities such as L.A, Portland, New York, Austin and San Francisco. Many of these cities now have several websites dedicated to tracking mobile food trucks. According the IBISWorld, the industry is most heavily concentrated in the Far West, the Great Lakes region, the Mid East (which includes New York), and the South East.

**Major Market Segments**
1. Street locations/corners 55.0%
2. Other locations/venues/events 18.0%
3. Industrial/construction work sites 15.0%
4. Shopping malls 12.0%

## Business Overview
_____ (company name) will be a start-up Mobile Food Truck located in _____ (leased/owned) space at _____ (address) in the _____ Plaza in \_\_\_\_ (city), \_\_\_\_ (state). The company was formed to offer a comprehensive assortment of healthy Mobile Food Truck products, and related products and services for consumers in the _____ (city), \_\_\_\_ (state) service area. A ninety-day option has been taken on this location, which will serve as our warehouse and vehicle garage. The estimated starting date is _____ (month) \_\_\_\_\_ (year).

Our truck will carry various types of \_\_\_\_ (premium) products, in addition to _____ (healthy sandwiches, soups, and salads). The truck will also sell traditional gourmet meals, and healthy beverages and snacks. Sales are anticipated to be $_____ in the first year and to increase at an average annual rate of \_\_\_\_% per year in the first five years of operation.

With creative branding and aggressive marketing, and a few different signboards and colored menus, we will make one food truck perform like three. A sandwich lunch menu, a breakfast menu, and an upscale dinner bistro menu will provide all the menu variables local customers want. Our ultimate food truck business model will mix street sales, catering, B2B service levels for corporate customers, and custom priced occasions for alternate profit streams.

We will search for companies full of employees in an unusually isolated area, or a curb location where employees with limited break time want better choices for lunch. Offering healthy choices, budget choices, high-energy choices and "treats" will bring customers to our Mobile Food Truck. Friday-only specials will tempt customers to sample our food truck selection.

**The Mobile Food Truck will compete on the following basis:**
1. Variety of all natural and organic ___ (gourmet) menu items.
2. A one-stop destination for healthy quick serve meals.
3. Superior level of cuisine knowledgeable and attentive customer service.
4. Convenient access at scheduled locations.
5. Overall value proposition.

Some of our products will be healthy alternatives to the items available at a conventional Mobile Food Truck. Located in the heart of the growing ___ community of __ (city) the truck will serve a community of ___ (#) residents. The creation of ___ (company name) is in direct response to the growing demand in the community for service convenience and more healthy alternatives to traditional fast food. We will be the all-natural and organic Mobile Food Truck. The area has a reputation of supporting people with healthy lifestyles. Our Mobile Food Truck will be a convenient place to experience the joys of eating gourmet style, nutritious meals at vale-driven prices. The closest competing Mobile Food Truck is in the _____ community, which is a ___ (#) minute drive.

## Concept Overview
Our healthy Mobile Food Truck will be a type of food truck that primarily sells healthy quick serve, causal restaurant quality meals. We will also offer meal items for people with special dietary needs, such as people with wheat germ allergies and who are lactose intolerant.

We believe that we can become the Mobile Food Truck of choice in the _____ area for the following reasons:
1. We will employ competent and well-trained staff that is dedicated to continuously improving their knowledge and skill sets to better serve our customers.
2. We will develop a questionnaire to survey changing customer needs and wants, and enable customers to express their level of satisfaction.
3. We will become a one-stop destination for customers in need of quick healthy convenient meals for a fast office or school break.
4. We will offer healthy replacement meal service at value-driven prices with

   convenient truck route touring and delivery scheduling.
5. We will offer a range of services, including the catering of parties for both kids and adults, and corporate events.

**In order to succeed, _____(company name) will have to do the following:**
1. Conduct extensive market research to demonstrate that there is a demand for a healthy Mobile Food Truck with our aforementioned differentiation strategy.
2. Make superior customer service our number one priority.
3. Stay abreast of developments in the health food and food truck industries.
4. Precisely assess and then exceed the expectations of all customers.
5. Form long-term, trust-based relationships with customers to secure profitable repeat business and referrals.
6. Develop process efficiencies to achieve and maintain profitability.
7. Market the uniqueness and convenience of our business model concept.

## Target Market

Our primary customers will be drawn from _____ trade area, which has a population of over \_\_\_\_\_ (#) people, and is projected to reach _____ (#) people by \_\_\_\_\_ (year). Customers shopping the area will purchase our healthy and tasty meals on an impulse basis during their shopping trip, or as a regular occurrence during a lunchtime or coffee break from work or school or after watching a movie at a local theater. _____ (company name) also anticipates that many patrons will make the shop their primary destination due to name recognition and uniqueness of our product quality and appeal, which are related to the health benefits from our low-fat, organic ingredients. Our target market is _____ residents of _____ (city), who have a preference for healthy organic foods and quick foodservice.

## Marketing Strategy

The foundation for this plan is a combination of primary and secondary research, upon which the marketing strategies are built. Discussions and interviews were held with a variety of individuals and other area small businesses to develop financial and proforma detail. We consulted census data, county business patterns, and other directories to develop the market potential and competitive situation. Our market strategy will be based on a cost-effective approach to reach our clearly defined target market. The basic approach to promote our products and services will be through establishing relationships with key influencers in the community and then through referral activities, once a significant client base has been established. _____ (company name) will focus on developing loyal client relationships by offering a full range of all natural and organic menu items. The certified organic products, reliable route scheduling, regular twitter tweets and Facebook posts, staff accessibility and value-based pricing will all serve to differentiate our company from the other Mobile Food Truck providers in our service area. With the help of an aggressive marketing plan, _____ (company name) expects to experience steady growth. _____ (company name) also plans to attract its customers through the use of local newspaper advertisements, sampling events, circulating flyers, a systematic series of direct mailings, press releases in local newspapers, a website, online directories, classified ads, educational seminars and limited Yellow Page ads. We will also become an active member of the local Chamber of Commerce and the Organic Trade Organization.

## Critical Risks

Management recognizes there are several internal and external risks inherent in our business concept. Quality, selection, value pricing and convenience will be key factors in the consumers' decision to utilize our mobile foodservices. Also, consumers must be willing to accept our convenient services and products on a regular basis in order for the food truck to meet its sales projections. Building a loyal and trusting relationship with our customers and referral partners is a key component to the success of _____ (company name).

## Customer Service

We will take every opportunity to help the customer, regardless of what the revenue might be. We will outshine our competition by doing something "extra" and offering added-value services and attentive support. We will take a long-term perspective and focus on the client's possible lifetime value to our business.

## Business Plan Objectives

The purpose of this business plan is to outline the parameters under which the principals will pursue the customization, development and operation of an Mobile Food Truck. This business plan serves to detail the direction, vision, and planning necessary to achieve our goal of establishing a superior Mobile Food Truck with a focus on providing healthy on-the-go meals. The purpose of this document is to provide a strategic business plan for our company and to support a request for a $ _____, five year bank loan to purchase a vehicle, cooking equipment and supplies, as part of the financing for a start-up Mobile Food Truck. The plan has been adjusted to reflect the particular strengths and weaknesses of _____ (company name). Actual financial performance will be closely tracked, and the business plan will be adjusted when necessary to ensure that full profit potential and loan repayment is realized on schedule. The plan will also help us to identify and quantify objectives, track and direct growth and create benchmarks for measuring success.

## The Company

The business _____ (will be/was) incorporated on _____ (date) in the state of _____ as a _____ (Corporation/LLC), and intends to register for Sub-chapter 'S' status for federal tax purposes. This will effectively shield the owner(s) from personal liability and double taxation.

## Business Goals

Our business goal is to continue to develop the _____ (company name) brand name. To do so, we plan to execute on the following:
1. Offer certified organic menu items, and a healthy quick foodservice.
2. Focus on quality controls and ongoing operational excellence.
3. Recruit and train the very best ethical employees.

4. Create a marketing campaign with a consistent branded look and message.

## Location

___ (company name) will have its commissary located in the ___ (complex name) on _____ (address) in __ (city), __ (state). The __ (purchased/leased) space is easily accessible and provides ample parking for __ (#) staff and ___ (#) food trucks. The service area is attractive due to the area demographics, which reflect our middle class family target customer profile.

## Mission Statement                                                                            (optional)

Our Mission is to address the following customer pain points or unmet needs and wants, which will define the opportunity for our business: _____
In order to satisfy these unmet needs and wants, we will propose the following unique solutions, which will create better value for our customers: _____

## Competitive Edge

_____ (company name) will be successful because it is based on solid market research demonstrating that there is a demand for a Mobile Food Truck selling premium organic and healthy meals. We will have the ability to transport our products to places where they are highly in demand, such as highly populated areas like mall fronts, parks, schools and the beach. We will also compete well in our market by offering competitive prices on an expanded line of certified organic ingredients and healthy foodservice items, and by using the latest in technological advances in convenient online ordering and route tracking. Furthermore, we will maintain an excellent reputation for trustworthiness and integrity with the community we serve.

## Marketing Plan Objective

Our marketing plan objective is to take advantage of the opportunity presented by the demand for health and wellness products. The approach is to market the entire food truck as a place where consumers can find wellness solutions. The ultimate goal is to effectively combine organic ingredients with healthy fast foods as a way of providing one-stop customer convenience.

## Differentiation Strategy

We will examine each touch point that engages our customers and challenge ourselves to brainstorm improvements to these touch points in ways that are original to our company and important to our customers. We will set up the mechanisms to constantly to listen to our customers, and create a better, faster, hassle-free customer experience. We will also pleasantly surprise our customers by throwing in something small and inexpensive to ramp up the customer experience. This may be as simple as a small container of our top selling sauce. We will also introduce a structured sampling program by gifting a free sample of a new menu item to try, and tweeting a picture of the customers' happy facial expression after trying it. Personalization and generosity will go a long way in fostering customer acquisition and retention.
Source:

http://mobile-cuisine.com/marketing/4-food-truck-differentiation-tactics-work/

## Services

By giving careful consideration to customer responsiveness, _____ (company name) goal will be to meet and exceed every service expectation. Quality service and quick responsiveness will be the philosophy guiding a customer-centric approach to our value-driven Mobile Food Truck business model.

## The Management Team

_____ (company name) will be led by _____ (owner name) and _____ (co-owner name). _____ (owner name) has a _____ degree from _____ (institution name) and a _____ background within the industry, having spent _____ (#) years with _____ (former employer name or type of business). During this tenure, _____ (he/she) helped grow the business from $_____ in yearly revenue to over $_____. _____ (co-owner name) has a _____ background, and while employed by _____ was able to increase operating profit by _____ percent. These acquired skills, work experiences and educational backgrounds will play a big role in the success of our Mobile Food Truck. Additionally, our president, _____ (name), has an extensive knowledge of the _____ area and has identified a niche market retail opportunity to make this venture highly successful, combining his _____ (#) years of work experience in a variety of businesses. _____ (owner name) will manage all aspects of the business and service development to ensure effective customer responsiveness while monitoring day-to-day operations.

**Past Successful Accomplishments**

_____ (company name) is uniquely qualified to succeed due to the following past successes:

1. **Entrepreneurial Track Record**: The owners and management team have helped to launch numerous successful ventures, including a _____.

2. **Key Milestones Achieved**: The founders have invested $_____ to-date to staff the company, build the core technology, acquire starting inventory, test market the _____ (product/service), realize sales of $_____ and launch the website.

## Start-up Funding

_____ (owner name) will financially back the new business venture with an initial investment of $_____, and will be the principal owner. Additional funding in the amount of $_____ will be sought from _____, a local commercial bank, with a SBA loan guarantee. This money will be needed to start the company. This loan will provide start-up capital, financing for a selected vehicle customization project, food supply purchases, pay for permits and licensing, staff training and certification, well-conceived marketing campaign, cooking equipment and working capital to cover expenses during the first year of operation.

Notes: The startup capital in food trucks ranges from $50,000 to $250,000. According to mobile-cuisine.com, if you buy a new food truck with all new high-end equipment and technology, you are looking at about $250,000 in operating capital and start-up costs. If you go the other route and get extremely frugal and able to do some of the build out work yourself, you can probably get away with $50,000 to $75,000. At Entrepreneur.com, Food Truck Franchise Group LLC states that a total investment of $99,000 to $150,000 will get you started with them.

## Financial Projections

We plan to open for business on ___(date). __ (company name) is forecasted to gross in excess of $___ in sales in its first year of operation, ending ___ (month/ year). Profit margins are forecasted to be at about __ percent. Second year operations will produce a net profit of $__. This will be generated from an investment of $__ in initial capital. It is expected that payback of our total invested capital will be realized in less than __ (#) months of operation. It is further forecasted that cash flow becomes positive from operations in year __ (one?). We project that our net profits will increase from $___ to over $ __ over the next three years.

## Financial Profile Summary

| Key Indicator | 2017 | 2018 | 2019 |
|---|---|---|---|
| Total Revenue | | | |
| Expenses | | | |
| Gross Margin | | | |
| Operating Income | | | |
| Net Income | | | |
| EBITDA | | | |

EBITDA = Revenue - Expenses (excluding tax, interest, depreciation and amortization)
    EBITDA is essentially net income with interest, taxes, depreciation, and amortization added back to it, and can be used to analyze and compare profitability between companies and industries because it eliminates the effects of financing and accounting decisions.
Gross Margin (%) = (Revenue - Cost of Goods Sold) / Revenue
Net Income = Total revenue - Cost of sales - Other expenses - Tax

## Growth Strategy

The Company plans continually expand its presence throughout _____ City by attending music concerts, trade shows, sporting events, and other venues that feature a large number of people. Additionally, over time, the business will generate a strong repeat customer base from the reliable servicing of the planned routes. In the ___ (#) year of operation, Mr. ____ (owner name) intends to acquire a ___ (#) food truck that will operate within selected sections of ____ City. It should also be noted, after the __ (#) year of operation, Management may acquire several additional mobile food service trucks in order to exponentially expand the revenues of the business.

## Exit Strategy

If the business is very successful, ____ (owner name) may seek to sell the business to a third party for a significant earnings multiple. Most likely, the Company will hire a qualified business broker to sell the business on behalf of _____ (company name). Based on historical numbers, the business could generate a sales premium of up to __(#) times earnings.

## Summary

Through a combination of a proven business model and a strong management team to guide the organization, _____ (company name) will be a long lasting, profitable business. We believe our ability to create future product and service opportunities and growth will only be limited by our imagination and our ability to attract talented people who understand the concept of branding.

# 1.1.0 Tactical Objectives (select 3)

The following short-term tactical objectives will specify quantifiable results and involve activities that can be easily tracked. They will also be realistic, tied to specific marketing strategies and serve as a good benchmark to evaluate our marketing plan success.
(Select Choices)

1. To provide our customers with the freshest, organically produced ice cream from our convenient scheduled truck locations.
2. Offer ice cream products without artificial colors, flavors, or additives.
3. Support organic farms that keep our earth and water pure.
4. Obtain necessary funding ($____ in investor/personal loans and $____ in small business administration loans).
5. Create a service-based company that exceeds customers' expectations.
6. Increase the number of repeat customers serviced by at least ____ (20?) % per year, through superior performance and word-of-mouth referrals.
7. Become an established community destination with a customer satisfaction rate of ____ (95?) % by the end of the first year.
8. Achieve cash flow self-sufficiency by the end of the ____ (first?) year.
9. Sales of $____ in the first year, with sales increasing to $____ in the second year and $____ in the third year.
10. Provide an income for the founders by the end of the second year with income growth possibilities.
11. Repay debt from original financing by the end of the ____ (fifth?) year.
12. To develop a cash flow that is capable of paying all salaries, as well as grow the business, by the end of the _____ (first?) year.
13. To be an active networking participant and productive member of the community by _____ (date).
14. Get a business website designed, built and operational by _____ (date), which will include an online shopping cart.
15. Realize gross margins higher than _____(15?) percent by _____ (date).
16. Achieve net income more than ____ percent of net sales by the ____ (#) year.

17. Reduce the cost of new customer acquisition by ___ % to $ ___ by _____ (date).
18. Turn in profits from the _____ (#) month of operations.
19. Provide employees with continuing training, benefits and incentives to reduce the employee turnover rate to _____%.
20. To reach cash break-even by the end of year ____ (one?).
22. Increase market share to ___ percent over the next ___ (#) months.
23. Become one of the top ___ (#) players in the emerging _____ category in __ (#) months.
24. Increase Operating Profit by ___ percent versus the previous year.
25. Achieve market share leadership in the ____ category by ____ (date).

## 1.1.1 Strategic Objectives

We will seek to work toward the accomplishment of the following strategic objectives, which relate back to our Mission and Vision Statements:
1. Improve the overall quality of our mobile foodservices.
2. Use mobile services to improve convenience for seniors.
3. Make the experience better, faster and more customer friendly.
4. Strengthen personal relationships with customers.
5. Enhance affordability and accessibility through mobile service offerings.
6. Foster a spirit of mobile innovation.
7. Open a second location by the end of Fiscal _____ (year).

## 1.2.0 Mission Statement

Our Mission Statement is a written statement that spells out our organization's overall goal, provides a sense of direction and acts as a guide to decision making for all levels of management. In developing the following mission statement we will encourage input from employees, volunteers, and other stakeholders, and publicize it broadly in our website and other marketing materials.

_____ (company name) is committed to providing the highest quality, fresh and natural foods that meet the nutritional standards of our customers. The mission of _____ (company name) is to provide ___ (city) residents and visitors with an upscale Mobile Food Truck experience that features fresh quick-serve packaged meals.

We are determined through our image, professionalism, and sound business practices to become the most respected and successful Mobile Food Truck in the _____ area. Our mission is to provide the ____ (city) metropolitan area with quality food served on a mobile basis.

We will organize our hours, products, staffing and route scheduling to create a positive and effective strategy in order to achieve our mission and to ensure the future growth of our Mobile Food Truck. Our mission is to realize 100% customer satisfaction, and generate long-term profits through referrals and repeat business.

## 1.2.1 Mantra

We will create a mantra for our organization that is three or four words long. Its purpose will be to help employees truly understand why the organization exists. Our mantra will serve as a framework through which to make decisions about product and business direction. It will boil the key drivers of our company down to a sentence that defines our most important areas of focus and resemble a statement of purpose or significance.
Our Mantra is _____

## 1.2.2 Core Values Statement

The following Core Values will help to define our organization, guide our behavior, underpin operational activity and shape the strategies we will pursue in the face of various challenges and opportunities. We will fulfill our mission through our commitment to:
- Selling the highest quality natural and organic products available.
- Satisfying and delighting our customers.
- Creating wealth through profits & growth.
- Caring about our communities & our environment
- Creating ongoing win-win partnerships with our suppliers.
- Being respectful and ethical.
- Seeking innovation in our industry.
- Practicing accountability to our colleagues and stakeholders.
- Pursuing continuous learning as individuals and as a business entity.

## 1.3 Vision Statement

The following Vision Statement will communicate both the purpose and values of our organization. For employees, it will give direction about how they are expected to behave and inspires them to give their best. Shared with customers, it will shape customers' understanding of why they should work with our organization.

_____ (company name) will strive to become one of the most respected and favored healthy Mobile Food Trucks in the _____ area. It is our desire to become a landmark business in ____ (city), ____ (state), and become known not only for the quality of our convenient healthy meals and quick services, but also for our community and charity involvement.

_____ (company name) is dedicated to operating with a constant enthusiasm for learning about the health food and Mobile Food Truck businesses, being receptive to implementing new ideas, and maintaining a willingness to adapt to changing customer needs and wants. To develop expansion plans for company owned and franchised Mobile Food Trucks in other cities in the state of _____.

## 1.4 Keys to Success

In broad terms, the success factors relate to providing what our customers want, and doing what is necessary to be better than our competitors. The following critical success factors are areas in which our organization must excel in order to operate successfully and achieve our objectives:

1. Provide consistency and reliability in both the product and service.
2. The service our truck provides will be a function of training, evaluation, and retraining in order to deliver it courteously and in a timely manner.
3. Build trust by adhering to our Code of Ethics and Service Guarantees.
4. Improve truck visibility with proper signage, music, bright vehicle paint color and exterior lighting.
5. Maintenance of a reputation for service excellence that encourages repeat business and word of mouth marketing.
6. Superior Customer Service executed by a knowledgeable and friendly staff.
7. Choose accessible truck stop locations for customer convenience, especially walk-by or foot-traffic from a steady volume of passersby.
8. Offer a variety of high quality, healthy foods sold at a fair price from a clean environment.
9. New product innovation is seen as the key to attracting and retaining customers.
10. Research several local dairies to source superior ice cream product.
11. Securing regular and ongoing customer feedback.
12. Offer lifestyle conveniences based on the scheduling needs of the target market.
13. Launch a website to showcase our services and customer testimonials, provide helpful information and facilitate online order placement.
14. Local community involvement and strategic business partnerships.
15. Conduct a targeted and cost-effective marketing campaign that seeks to differentiate our one-stop, convenient services from competitor offerings.
16. Institute a pay-for-performance component to the employee compensation plan.
17. Control costs and manage budgets at all times in accordance with company goals.
18. Institute management processes and controls to insure the consistent replication of operations.
19. Recruit screened employees with a passion for delivering exceptional service.
20. Institute an employee training to insure the best techniques are consistently practiced.
21. Competitive pricing in conjunction with a differentiated service business model.
22. Stay abreast of technological developments and new product/service offerings.
23. Build our brand awareness, which will drive customers to increase their usage of our services and make referrals.

24. Business planning with the flexibility to make changes based on gaining new insightful perspectives as we proceed.
25. Locate around business offices, college campuses and entertainment venues.
26. Use neon signage to improve the visibility of the truck and impulse sales.
27. Improve menu item presentation and profit margins with special dishes, sauces, garnishes and decorations.
28. Create special seasonal and holiday themed menu items.
29. In the menu, assign exotic names and mouthwatering detailed descriptions to innovative dessert creations.
30. Secure a board of health permit, sales tax collection license and other local permits that your city or county may require.
31. Create a product line that caters to the diet-conscious.
32. Feature menu items that reflect the cultural and taste preferences of the local residents.
33. Develop patented recipes that are unlike other products in the market to target a specific niche.
34. Locate the local commissary, which is a facility that provides food and beverages to catering trucks. (Buy hot foods, sandwiches and all items necessary for operation)
35. Use biodegradable cups and spoons to complement the earthy, healthy feel of the food truck.
36. Create route based on worker break times and logistics.
37. Specialize in a select number of location based food truck menu items.
38. Offer vegan-friendly menu items.
39. Feature special limited-run flavors for the holidays, such as pumpkin ice cream.
40. Feature sugar-free, such as sugar-free Italian ice, made by mixing ice and fresh fruit.
41. Keep the ice cream at a temperature that is ideal for scooping.
42. Regularly service the truck to prevent breakdowns and maintain cleanliness.
43. Scope out the best locations from which to operate a weekly route and adhere to a schedule so customers can expect you on a regular basis.
44. Consider selling gourmet coffees and pastries in the colder months.
45. Search for a custom-built truck that is specifically made for the mobile food business in the classified ads and on eBay.com.
46. Install on the truck a big sign with the business name on it and make sure that it is eye catching.
47. Use a stick-on message stating "Cross Behind Vehicle" or "Cross at Rear" to be placed near the front of the vehicle.
48. Must check with local Health Department for guidelines before even considering an food truck purchase.
49. Focus on business and museum crowds and post the truck's changing location via Twitter.
50. Create excitement with ever-changing specials.
51. The truck needs to always look clean, hygienic and presentable.
52. Food attendants must be happy, personable, accommodating, knowledgeable and approachable to build up the regular repeat customer base.

53. Design a sales brochure which can also double as a faxable advertising flyer.
54. The type of vehicle required will depend on menu selections, size of events catered, distance expected to travel, state government requirements and any on-site preparation needs.
55. Be prepared for periodic inspections by the health department.
56. Support events such as little league sports and other neighborhood activities.
57. Choose neighborhoods whose demographic corresponds to the type of product you have chosen.
58. Create signage for the truck or the cart that clearly states the types of ice cream or related products for sale.
59. Make sales quicker by including the tax in the price and keeping the total price easy to make change.
60. Incorporate music to announce the coming of the food truck.
61. Create an overall experience for customers with an awning and portable seating.
62. Chose a busy street corner that receives a constant flow of people such as one near a hospital or college campus.
63. Stick to a fixed route schedule to develop a sense of continuity and dependability.
64. Limit the menu to three items and do them well.
65. Befriend local city council representatives and establishment owners before choosing regular food truck parking spots.
66. In metropolitan areas, seek out neighborhood associations as helpful partners.
67. For special events or privately-owned areas, be ready to pay for a good location. (Perhaps a few thousand dollars a month for a prime tourist-heavy locale).
68. Stay away from competing brick-and-mortar establishments.
69. Form something of an outdoor food court with non-competing food trucks.
70. Must become familiar with and adhere to the local laws that govern the mobile food industry, as failure to do so could result in your mobile business failing inspection and potentially being shut down.
71. Be sure to know each city's and county's rules and obtain the proper licenses and permits.
72. Limit the menu and specialize in the food items that you prepare extremely well.
73. Print to-go menus so customers can see exactly what you have to offer while they are waiting in line and use the menu to promote your catering service.
74. List the possible emergency scenarios, like losing electric power, having a gas leak, running out of produce or water, or engine failure, and develop back-up procedures to remedy the situation.
    Source: http://smallbusinessbc.ca/article/9-tips-starting-a-food-truck/
75. Set up the procedures and systems to turn out a consistently quality product, because it is consistency that will be the key to establishing a regular customer base.
76. Reassess current supplier contracts om a regular basis to make sure we are getting the best deal possible.
77. Offer discounted combo meals or special themed menus on slow days.
    Source: https://mobile-cuisine.com/business/improving-food-truck-profitability/
78. Find a specific food truck niche that no other mobile business is occupying, and do the research to make certain there is a local demand for it.

79. Become familiar with and utilize the apps that help customers to locate mobile food trucks. Examples include TruckSpotting, TruxMap and Eat St. Directory: www.complex.com/pop-culture/2014/10/food-truck-locator-apps/
80. Take advantage of the profitable trend toward office catering, and explore the lunch box delivery business.
81. Promote your Food Truck Wedding Catering Service as a unique, much less-expensive dining alternative to reception or catering hall prices.

## 2.0 Company Summary

____ (company name) is a start-up _____ (Corporation/Limited Liability Company) consisting of __(#) principle officers with combined industry experience of __ (#) years.

The owner of the company will be investing $ ___ of ____ (his/her) own capital into the company and will also be seeking a loan of $ __ to cover start-up costs and future growth. _____ (company name) will be located in a _____ (purchased/rented) _____ (suite/complex) in the _____ on _____ (address) in _____ (city), _____ (state).

_____ (company name) is a new business located in _____ (downtown?) ____ (city), ___ (state) on _____ Street. The truck is an upscale healthy Mobile Food Truck, with a distinctive quick serve menu that includes authentic, all natural and organic ingredients. The vehicle will include an ice cream mix-in counter, refrigerated display cases, soft-serve ice cream machine, toppings display cases and canopied area.

The company plans to use its existing contacts and customer base to generate short-term revenues. Its long-term profitability will rely on focusing on referrals, networking within community organizations and a comprehensive marketing program that includes public relations activities and a structured referral program.

Sales are expected to reach $_____ within the first year and to grow at a conservative rate of ____ (20?) percent during the next two to five years.

### Vehicle Renovations

| The necessary renovations are itemized as follows: | Estimate |
|---|---|
| Build storage and sink areas. | _____ |
| Painting and other general cosmetic repairs | _____ |
| Install food preparation and refrigeration equipment. | _____ |
| Build counter and checkout station. | _____ |
| Other _____ | _____ |
| Total: | _____ |

### Operations

_____ (company name) will open for business on _____ (date) and will maintain the following office business hours:

| | | |
|---|---|---|
| Monday through Thursday: | _____ | (11 AM to 11 PM?) |
| Friday: | _____ | |
| Saturday: | _____ | |
| Sunday: | _____ | |

The company will invest in customer relationship management software (CRM) to track real-time sales data and collect customer information, including names, email addresses, key reminder dates and preferences. This information will be used with email, e-newsletter and direct mail campaigns to build personalized fulfillment programs, establish customer loyalty and drive revenue growth.

## 2.0.1 Traction (optional)

We will include this section because investors expect to see some traction, both before and after a funding event and investors tend to judge past results as a good indicator of future projections. It will also show that we can manage our operations and develop a business model capable of funding inventory purchases. Traction will be the best form of market research.

Period  _____
Product/Service Focus  _____
Our Sales to Date:  _____
Our Number of Users to Date:  _____
Number of Repeat Users  _____
Number of Pending Orders:  _____
Value of Pending Orders:  _____
Reorder Cycle:  _____
Key Reference Sites  _____
Mailing List Subscriptions  _____
Competitions/Awards Won  _____
Notable Product Reviews  _____
Actual Percent Gross Profit Margin  _____
Industry Average: GPM  _____
Actual B/(W) Industry Average  _____

Note: Percent Gross Profit Margin equals the sales receipts less the cost of goods sold divided by sales receipts multiplied by 100.

## 2.1 Company Ownership

_____ (company name) is a _____ (Sole-proprietorship /Corporation/Limited Liability Corporation (LLC)) and is registered to the principal owner, _____ (owner name). The company was formed in _____ (month) of ____ (year). It will be registered as a Subchapter S to avoid double taxation, with ownership allocated as follows: _____ (owner name) ____ % and _____ (owner name) ____ %.

The owner is a ____ (year) graduate of _____ (institution name), in _____ (city, ____ (state), with a _____ degree. He/she has ____ years of executive experience in the ____ (restaurant?) industry as a _____, performing the following roles: _____. His/her major accomplishments include: _____

**Ownership Breakdown:**

| Shareholder Name | Responsibilities | Number and Class of Shares | Percent Ownership |
|---|---|---|---|
| | | | |

The remainder of the issued and outstanding common shares are retained by the Company for _____ (future distribution / allocation under the Company's employee stock option plan).

**Shareholder Loans**

The Company currently has outstanding shareholder loans in the aggregate sum of $_____. The following table sets out the details of the shareholder loans.

| Shareholder Name | Loan Amount | Loan Date | Balance Outstanding |
|---|---|---|---|
| | | | |

**Directors**

The Company's Board of Directors, which is made up of highly qualified business and industry professionals, will be a valuable asset to the Company and be instrumental to its development. The following persons will make up the Board of Directors of the Company:

| Name of Person | Educational Background | Past Industry Experience | Other Companies Served |
|---|---|---|---|
| | | | |

## 2.2.0   Company Licensing & Liability Protection

The business will consider the need to acquire the following types of insurances. This will require extensive comparison shopping, through several insurance brokers, listed with our state's insurance department and discussions with our lawyers and insurance broker.

1. Workers' Compensation Insurance,
2. Business Policy:   Property & Liability Insurance
3. Health insurance.
4. Commercial Auto Insurance
5. State Unemployment Insurance
6. Business Interruption Insurance (Business Income Insurance)
7. Disability Insurance
8. Product Liability Insurance
9. Life Insurance

We will carry business liability and property insurance and any other insurance we deem necessary after receiving counsel from our lawyer and insurance agent. Health insurance and workers' compensation will be provided for our full-time employees as part of their benefit package. We feel that this is mandatory to ensure that they do not leave the business for one that does offer these benefits. Workers' Compensation covers employees in case of harm attributed to the workplace. The property and liability insurance protects the building from theft, fire, natural disasters, and being sued by a third party. Life and Disability Insurance may be required if a bank loan is sought.

The property that is insured under **inland marine coverage** is typically one of the following: actually in transit, held by a bailee, at a fixed location that is an instrument of transportation or a movable type of goods that is often at different locations.

**Liability Insurance** includes protection in the face of day-to-day accidents, unforeseen results of normal business activities, and allegations of abuse or molestation, food poisoning, or exposure to infectious disease.

**Property Insurance** - Property Insurance should take care of the repairs less whatever deductible you have chosen.

**Loss of Income Insurance** will replace our income during the time the business is shut-down. Generally, this coverage is written for a fixed amount of monthly income for a fixed number of months.

**Product Liability Insurance** covers injuries caused by products that are designed, sold or specified by the business.

**To help save on insurance cost and claims, management will do the following:**
1. Stress employee safety in our employee handbook.
2. Screen employees with interview questionnaires and will institute pre-employment drug tests and comprehensive background checks.
3. Videotape our equipment and inventory for insurance purposes.
4. Create an operations manual that shares safe techniques.
5. Limit the responsibilities that we choose to accept in our contracts.
6. Consider the financial impact of assuming the exposure ourselves.
7. Establish loss prevention programs to reduce the hazards that cause losses.
8. Consider taking higher deductibles on anything but that which involves liability insurance because of third-party involvement.
9. Stop offering services that require expensive insurance coverage or require signed releases from customers using those services.
10. Improve employee training and initiate training sessions for safety.
11. Require Certificate of Insurance from all subcontractors.
12. Make staff responsible for a portion of any damages they cause.
13. We will investigate the setting-up of a partial self-insurance plan.
14. Convince underwriters that our past low claims are the result of our ongoing safety programs and there is reason to expect our claims will be lower than industry averages in the future.
15. At each renewal, we will develop a service agreement with our broker and get their commitment to our goals, such as a specific reduction in the number of

incidents.
16. We will assemble a risk control team, with people from both sides of our business, and broker representatives will serve on the committee as well.
17. When an employee is involved in an accident, we will insist on getting to the root cause of the incident and do everything possible to prevent similar incidents from re-occurring.
18. At renewal, we will consult with our brokers to develop a cost-saving strategy and decide whether to bid out our coverage for competitive quotes or stick with our current carrier.
19. We will set-up a captive insurance program, as a risk management technique, where our business will form its own insurance company subsidiary to finance its retained losses in a formal structure.
20. Review named assets (autos and equipment), drivers and/or key employees identified on policies to make sure these assets and people are still with our company.
21. As a portion of our business changes, that is, closes, operations change, or outsourcing occurs, we will eliminate unnecessary coverage.
22. We will make sure our workforce is correctly classified by our workers' compensation insurer and liability insurer because our premiums are based on the type of workers used.
23. We will become active in Trade Organizations or Professional Associations, because as a benefit of membership, our business may receive substantial insurance discounts.
24. We will adopt health specific changes to our work place, such as adopting a no smoking policy at our company and allow yoga or weight loss classes to be held in our break room.
25. We will consider a partial reimbursement of health club membership as a benefit.
26. We will find out what employee training will reduce rates and get our employees involved in these programs.

The required business insurance package will be provided by _____ (insurance carrier name). The business will open with a _____ (#) million-dollar liability insurance policy, with an annual premium cost of $ _____.

Note: Lunch truck insurance shouldn't run you much more than regular vehicle insurance, but we will have to make clear to our underwriter any additional risks our truck might pose. For example, we will have to mention that we carry __ (#) propane tanks and have an open flame in our vehicle.
Resource:
http://insurance4foodtrucks.com/

## 2.2.1 Licenses

Note: Permit and license requirements vary widely from state to state and even city to city. It is highly recommended you contact your local chamber of commerce, and health and police departments to acquire specific information regarding licensing and permit requirements for your area.

**Food Truck Laws by City:** https://mobile-cuisine.com/food-truck-laws/

**There will be two types of permits/licenses we may have to deal with.**
1. A license from the local Health Department.
   This will basically authorize the selling of food in our area. It will require an inspection of our Trailer. Cost of this license will vary widely but will usually be about $100. These licenses will be either issued by our local town or by our state.
2. The other type of permit is related to the locations we choose to use to sell our product. In the case of Public property, Playgrounds, Beaches or City Streets, this may require a permit from our local police department. In the case of events such as Parades, Ball Games or Carnivals, a permit may be required. If we decide to sell on private property, usually only permission from the owner is required. The cost of these permits will vary widely.

Note: It will be our responsibility to determine our local health requirements and decide if our cart will pass "As Is". If any modifications or additions are required, the manufacturer should be contacted for support in satisfying our local requirements.

To set up shop on main roads, we may need to secure state, county and/or city business licenses for annual or monthly fees that vary significantly. Municipalities tend to issue vending cart licenses to a limited number of vendors, and in many cities, there are long waiting lists for open spots.
As an alternative, we may be able to park our truck inside a retail store, on a business's parking lot or other private property. Another option will be to work at festivals, sporting events, convention centers and other public venues, where the fees will also vary widely.

We will do the necessary research because the business may need to acquire the following special licenses, accreditations, certifications. tax IDs and permits:
1. A Sales Tax License is required through the State Department of Revenue.
2. Use Tax Registration Certificate
3. A County and/or City Occupational License.
4. Business and Professional License from State Licensing Agency
5. Permit from the State Health Department.
6. Building Code Inspections by the County Building Department.
7. Foodservice License from the Department of Agriculture
8. Food Safety Certificate
9. Zoning Approval
10. Mobile Food Vendor's Permit for the Park Authority
11. Solicitor's license
12. A federal tax ID
13. Certificate of Insurance
14. Certification from the County Fire Marshal

**Food Truck Inspections will revolve around the following:**
1. Preparation, handling, storage and display of any food products offered.
2. The health, cleanliness and hygiene of the personnel that work in the business.
3. All aspects of the equipment and utensils that are being used including what material they are manufactured of, the installation, and even how they are stored.
4. Every facet of the utilities and services, including the generators, propane and waste water, waste disposal methods, and the way pets are handled.
5. How the truck is constructed and whether it holds the proper features such as ventilation and lighting.

Note: Although necessary permits vary based on locality, in New York, a vendor needs a Mobile Food Vendor License and any vending vehicle needs to be equipped with a Mobile Food Vending Unit Permit. Securing a truck permit can be tough; certain cities, including New York, have a cap on the number of permits in existence at one time. Some cities' departments of health also require that vending vehicles be stored in approved commissary locations when not on duty, owners must expect to pay for this parking, including electricity and refrigeration costs.

**Resources:**
Workers Compensation Regulations
    http://www.dol.gov/owcp/dfec/regs/compliance/wc.htm#IL
New Hire Registration and Reporting
    www.homeworksolutions.com/new-hire-reporting-information/
State Tax Obligations
    www.sba.gov/content/learn-about-your-state-and-local-tax-obligations
Resource:
www/sba.gov/content/what-state-licenses-and-permits-does-your-business-need

Note: In most states, you are legally required to obtain a business license, and a dba certificate. A business license is usually a flat tax assessment and a percentage of your gross income. A dba stands for Doing Business As, and it is the registration of your trade name if you have one. You will be required to register your trade name within 30 days of starting your business. Instead of registering a dba, you can simply form an LLC or Corporation and it will have the same effect, namely register your business name.

Note: Check with your local County Clerk and state offices or Chamber of Commerce to make sure you follow all legal protocols for setting up and running your business. Visit your town hall and ask about the laws regarding ice cream vending for your town. You can also search online at your state government's website and search business licensing to discover the requirements. Check the Department of Motor Vehicles in our state for specific vehicle codes and operating permits. Other certifications may include a business license, food handler's certificate, health permit, insurance and ice cream vendor's permit.

Note; Some city ordinances prohibit cooking aboard trucks.
    The truck should adhere to state and local NSF (National Sanitation Foundation) food safety regulations.

Note: In most states a person must display their vendor's license on either their clothing or around their neck. In order to be issued a vendor's license, a complete criminal history check and finger printing session must be completed. The person must also fill out an application form and individual history form. If the person is driving an food truck, it must be inspected by the Environmental Health Department and have a motor vehicle record. The application and license fees are usually in the $300.00 range.

Note: In most states, must have some kind of store or commissary available to meet Health Dept. regulations. Such commissaries are required to have facilities to wash the trucks and access to hot water, among other things.

Note: Some cities have rules to keep trucks away from schools during the school day. Rules also limit how late a truck can operate, how long it can stop and how often it can drive on a street. Residents and city officials are trying to prevent grungy trucks in disrepair, overly persistent vendors, those who have added unapproved items to the menu or outright illegal operators.

Resources:
Block Insurance                www.blockinsurance.com
Insurance Information Institute        www.iii.org/individuals/business/
Independent Insurance Agents & Brokers of America    www.iiaa.org
Find Law    http://smallbusiness.findlaw.com/starting-business/starting-business-licenses-permits/starting-business-licenses-permits-guide.html
Business Licenses            www.iabusnet.org/business-licenses
Legal Zoom                www.legalzoom.com

## 2.3    Start-up To-Do Checklist

1. Describe your business concept and model, with special emphasis on planned multiple revenue streams and services to be offered.
2. Create Business Plan and Opening Menu of Products and Services.
3. Determine startup costs of Mobile Food Truck business, and operating capital and capital budget needs.
4. Seek and evaluate alternative financing options, including SBA guaranteed loan, equipment leasing, social networking loan (www.prosper.com) and/or a family loan (www.virginmoney.com).
5. Do a name search: Check with County Clerk Office or Department of Revenue and Secretary of State to see if the proposed name of business is available.
6. Decide on a legal structure for business.
Common legal structure options include Sole Proprietorship, Partnership, Corporation or Limited Liability Corporation (LLC).
7. Make sure you contact your State Department of Revenue, Secretary of State, and the Internal Revenue Service to secure EIN Number and file appropriate paperwork. Also consider filing for Sub-Chapter S status with the Federal

government to avoid the double taxation of business profits.
8. Protect name and logo with trademarks, if plan is to go national.
9. Find a suitable location with proper zoning.
10. Research necessary permits and requirements your local government imposes on your type of business. (Refer to: www.business.gov)
11. Call for initial inspections to determine what must be done to satisfy Fire Marshall, and Building Inspector requirements.
12. Adjust our budget based on build-out requirements.
13. Negotiate lease or property purchase contract.
14. Obtain a building permit.
15. Obtain Federal Employee Identification Number (FEIN).
16. Obtain State Sales Tax ID/Exempt Certificate.
17. Open a Business Checking Account.
18. Obtain Merchant Credit Card /PayPal Account.
19. Obtain City and County Business Licenses
20. Create a prioritized list for equipment, furniture and décor items.
21. Comparison shop and arrange for appropriate insurance coverage with product liability insurance, public liability insurance, commercial property insurance and worker's compensation insurance.
22. Locate and purchase all necessary equipment and furniture prior to final inspections.
23. Get contractor quotes for required alterations.
24 Manage the alterations process.
25. Obtain information and price quotes from possible supply distributors.
26. Set a tentative opening date.
27. Install 'Coming Soon' sign in front of building and begin word-of-mouth advertising campaign.
28. Document the preparation, project and payment process flows.
29. Create your accounting, purchasing, payroll, marketing, loss prevention, employee screening and other management systems.
30. Start the employee interview process based on established job descriptions and interview criteria.
31. Contact and interview the following service providers: uniform service, security service, trash service, utilities, telephone, credit card processing, bookkeeping, cleaning services, etc.
32. Schedule final inspections for premises.
33. Correct inspection problems and schedule another inspection.
34. Set a Grand Opening date after a month of regular operations to get the bugs out of the processes.
35. Make arrangements for website design.
36. Train staff.
37. Schedule a couple of practice lessons for friends and interested prospects.
38. Be accessible for direct customer feedback.
39. Distribute comment cards and surveys to solicit more constructive feedback.
40. Remain ready and willing to change your business concept and offerings to suit the needs of your actual customer base.

## 2.3.1  EMPLOYER RESPONSIBILITIES CHECKLIST

1. Apply for your SS-4 Federal Employer Identification Number (EIN) from the Internal Revenue Service. An EIN can be obtained via telephone, mail or online.
2. Register with the State's Department of Labor (DOL) as a new employer. State Employer Registration for Unemployment Insurance, Withholding, and Wage Reporting should be completed and sent to the address that appears on the form. This registration is required of all employers for the purpose of determining whether the applicants are subject to state unemployment insurance taxes.
3. Obtain Workers Compensation and Disability Insurance from an insurer. The insurance company will provide the required certificates that should be displayed.
4. Order Federal Tax Deposit Coupons – Form 8109 – if you didn't order these when you received your EIN. To order, call the IRS at 1-800-829-1040; you will need to give your EIN. You may want to order some blanks sent for immediate use until the pre-printed ones are complete. Also ask for the current Federal Withholding Tax Tables (Circular A) – this will explain how to withhold and remit payroll taxes, and file reports.
5. Order State Withholding Tax Payment Coupons. Also ask for the current Withholding Tax Tables.
6. Have new employees complete an I-9 Employment Eligibility Verification form. You should have all employees complete this form prior to beginning work. Do not send it to Immigration and Naturalization Service – just keep it with other employee records in your files.
7. Have employees complete a W-4 Employees Withholding Allowance Certificate.


## 2.4.0  Company Location

_____ (company name) will be located in the _____ (complex name) in _____ (city), \_\_\_ (state). It is situated on a _____ (turnpike/street/avenue) just minutes from _____ (benchmark location), in the neighborhood of _____. It borders a large parking lot which is shared by all the businesses therein. Important considerations relative to practice location are accessibility, community growth trends, demographics, and drive by traffic patterns.

**The location has the following advantages:**                                (Select Choices)
1. It is easy to locate and accessible to a number of major roadways.
2. Easy access from public transportation.
3. Ground level access.
4. Plentiful parking for employees.
5. Proximity to _____ and _____ income growth areas.
6. Reasonable rent.
7. Proximity to the growing residential community of _____.

8. Good police and fire protection.
9. Favorable location survey test results.
10. Near commissary and/or supply stores.
11. Avoidance of major fast-food chain competitors.
12. Right alignment with traffic patterns.

Many of the best locations are on private property, and not public property. In the case of private property locations, it is usually a matter of confirming that the city's zoning rules allow for it and approaching the owner or property manager to seek permission to set up shop. We may have to negotiate a monthly rent amount, if they ask for it. It may be best to agree to a fixed amount of rent as opposed to a percentage of our total sales.

**Possible lunch truck locations will include the following (must get appropriate permit and/or property owner permission):**

| | | | |
|---|---|---|---|
| 1. | Tourist Stops | 2. | University Campus |
| 3. | Theme Park | 4. | Railway or Subway Station Entrance |
| 5. | Superstore Parking Lot | 6. | Hospital Parking Lot |
| 7. | Mall Entrance/Corridor | 8. | Convention Center |
| 9. | Home Renovation Stores | 10. | Automotive Chain Stores |
| 11. | Large Grocery Stores | 12. | Big Box Stores (Costco) |
| 13. | Strip Malls / Plazas | 14. | Shopping Centers |
| 15. | Industrial Parks | 16. | Business Parks |
| 17. | Large Factories | 18. | Office Complexes |
| 19. | Large Office Buildings | 20. | Government Complexes |
| 21. | Court Houses | 22. | Hospitals |
| 23. | Call Centers | 24. | Colleges, Universities, High Schools |
| 25. | Military Bases | 26. | Golf Courses |
| 27. | Busy Downtown Streets | 28. | Parks |
| 29. | Beaches | 30. | Parking Lots |
| 31. | Transportation Hubs | 32. | Freeway Off Ramps |
| 33. | Service Stations | 34. | Truck Stops |
| 35. | Car Washes | 36. | Amusement Parks, Zoos |

Note: Most malls require that vendors pay them a percentage of their sales (anywhere from 4%-8%), and most require that the cart be leased directly from the mall in order to ensure a consistent look among vendors. Most will also want to approve the layout of the cart and how merchandise is displayed.

**Other Special Events and Temporary Locations include:**

| | | | |
|---|---|---|---|
| 1. | Amateur Sporting Events | 2. | Sales Events / Grand Openings |
| 3. | Large Construction Sites | 4. | Charity Events |
| 5. | School / Church / Club functions | 6. | Business anniversaries |
| 7. | Open Houses | 8. | Golf tournaments |
| 9. | Boat shows | 10. | Air Shows and Fly Ins |
| 11. | Car Shows/Rallies | 12. | Conventions |
| 13. | Music Festivals | 14. | Carnivals |

15. County Fairs
16. Antique Shows
17. Farm Shows
18. Craft Shows
19. Cultural Events
20. Flea Markets/Swap Meets
21. Home Shows
22. Industrial Shows
23. Parades
24. Auctions
25. Estate Sales
26. Tourist Attractions
27. Parks

## 2.4.1   Company Facilities

_____ (company name) signed a _____ (#) year lease for _____ (#) square foot of space. The cost is very reasonable at $____/sq. foot. We also have the option of expanding into an additional _____ sq. ft. of space. Cost of Living (CPI) will be capped at _____ (5.00?)%. Two five-year options will be included in the lease agreement.

A leasehold improvement allowance of $___ /sq. ft. would be given. Consolidated area maintenance fees would be $___/month initially. _____ (company name) has obtained a _____ (three) month option on this ___ (warehouse/garage) space effective _____ (date), the submission date of this business plan, and has deposited refundable first and last lease payments, plus a $ _____ security deposit with the leasing agent.

**The facilities will incorporate the following space parameters into the layout:**

|   |   | Percentage | Square Footage |
|---|---|---|---|
| 1. | Freezer Storage | _____ | _____ |
| 2. | Refrigeration Storage | _____ | _____ |
| 3. | Supplies Storage | _____ | _____ |
| 4. | Product Inventory Storage | _____ | _____ |
| 5. | Admin Offices | _____ | _____ |
| 6. | Vehicle Garage Area | _____ | _____ |
| 7. | Restroom | _____ | _____ |
| 8. | Reception Area | _____ | _____ |
| 9. | Food Prep Area | _____ | _____ |
| Totals: | | _____ | _____ |

## 2.4.2   Food Truck Design Layout

We will thoroughly research the most-compact, best-performing kitchen equipment and experiment a lot with the setup to get the most efficient workflow possible. We plan to utilize a mix of electric- and propane-powered equipment, which can be run by a much smaller and quieter generator. After deciding upon a menu, we will design the kitchen layout with some flexibility because it will be expensive to swap equipment out of a truck if our sales mix changes. A refrigerated sandwich table will be particularly handy for storing the ingredients and garnishes used in the cuisine. To conserve on space, we will install under-counter refrigerated drawers and under-counter warmers.

Because all custom truck manufacturers should be familiar with the building codes required for a food truck to operate, we will have our builder guarantee that the truck will pass code in the location where we are going to be operating, or we will get our money back.

To make the truck stand out, we will consider the following enhancements:
1. A speaker system to broadcast music that is linked to our food theme.
2. An exterior truck wall mounted flatscreen TV to show news and sportscasts.
3. A full truck graphics wrap.
4. Cuisine themed costumes for the staff.
5. Foldable tables and chairs with logo imprinted umbrellas.

Resources:
http://www.customconcessions.com/sample-floorplans.php
http://www.foodrepublic.com/2017/01/18/how-to-build-your-own-food-truck/

Examples:
http://foodtruckfiesta.com/mobile-kitchen-build-outs-east-coast-custom-coaches/
http://www.800buycart.com/lunch_trucks.htm

## 2.5.0  Start-up Summary

The start-up costs for the Mobile Food Truck will be financed through a combination of an owner investment of $ _____ and a short-term bank loan of $ _____.
The total start-up costs for this business are approximately $ _____ and can be broken down in the following major categories:

1. Land, Building and Improvements                $ _____
2. Equipment and Installation Expenses            $ _____
3. Refrigerated Display Cases                     $ _____
4. Office Furniture and Equipment                 $ _____
5. Initial Product Inventory                      $ _____
6. Working Capital (6 months)                     $ _____
   For day-to-day operations, including payroll, etc.
7. Customize Vehicle                              $ _____
8. Marketing/Advertising Expenses                 $ _____
   Includes sales brochures, direct mail, opening expenses.
8. Utility Deposits                               $ _____
9. Licenses and Permits                           $ _____
10. Contingency Fund                              $ _____
11. Other ( Includes training, legal expenses, etc.)  $ _____

The company will require $_____ in initial cash reserves and additional $_____ in assets. The start-up costs are to be financed by the equity contributions of the owner in the amount of $ _____ , as well as by a ____ (#) year commercial loan in the amount of $ _____ . The funds will be repaid through earnings.

Note: Forbes estimates that most food truck ventures can get started for between $50,000 and $80,000, while a restaurant will typically cost at least $100,000 to $300,000 to get up and running.

### 2.5.1 Inventory

| Inventory: | Supplier | Qty | Unit Cost | Total |
|---|---|---|---|---|
| Packaging Supplies | | | | |
| Soda/Juice | | | | |
| Packaged Snacks | | | | |
| Bread | | | | |
| Meat | | | | |
| Cheeses | | | | |
| Veggies/Fruits | | | | |
| Dairy | | | | |
| Coffee/Tea | | | | |
| Seasonings | | | | |
| Cooking Oils | | | | |
| Rice/Pasta | | | | |
| Condiments | | | | |
| Ice Cream Novelties | | | | |
| Disposable Spoons/Containers | | | | |
| Flatware & Napkins | | | | |
| Potato/Nacho Chips | | | | |
| Energy Bars | | | | |
| Bottled Drinks/Water | | | | |
| Foodservice Supplies | | | | |
| Cleaning Supplies | | | | |
| Office Supplies | | | | |
| Computer Supplies | | | | |
| Marketing Materials | | | | |
| Printed Menus | | | | |
| Misc. Product Inventory | | | | |
| Spare Truck Parts | | | | |
| Misc. Supplies | | | | |
| **Totals:** | | | | |

### 2.5.2 Supply Sourcing

Initially, _____ (company name) will purchase all of its foodservice equipment from _____ and supplies from _____, the _____ (second/third?) largest supplier in _____ (state), because of the discount given for bulk purchases.

However, we will also maintain back-up relationships with two smaller suppliers, namely _____ and _____. These two suppliers have competitive prices on certain products.

**Resources:**
Food Truck Builders
    http://eastcoastlaunchpad.com/
    www.turnkeytruck.com/new_page_30.htm
    www.cateringtruckking.com/1954233.html
    www.californiacartbuilder.com/
    www.customconcessions.com/

Directory of Food Truck Builders:
    https://mobile-cuisine.com/food-truck-builders/

Custom Concessions builds and customizes mobile food trucks for companies including Disney/ESPN, Domino's Pizza, Texas Roadhouse and others. The headquarters has moved from Richmond, Va., to Pittsburgh but manufacturing of the food trucks is in Middlebury, Ind.

To lower food truck business start-up costs even further, we will take the following approaches:
1. Buy used mobile food truck
2. Lease or rent portable food trucks
3. Purchase business supplies in bulk

## 2.5.3 Supplier Assessments

We will use the following form to compare and evaluate suppliers, because they will play a major role in our procurement strategies and significantly contribute to our profitability.

|  | Supplier #1 | Supplier #2 | Compare |
|---|---|---|---|
| Supplier Name | | | |
| Website | | | |
| Address | | | |
| Contacts | | | |
| Annual Sales | | | |
| Distribution Channels | | | |
| Memberships/Certifications | | | |
| Quality System | | | |
| Positioning | | | |
| Pricing Strategy | | | |
| Payment Terms | | | |
| Discounts | | | |

Delivery Lead-time   _____
Return Policy        _____
Rebate Program       _____
Technical Support    _____
Core Competencies    _____
Primary Product      _____
Primary Service      _____
New Products/Services _____
Innovative Applications/Uses _____
Competitive Advantage _____
Capital Intensity    _____
State of Technology  _____
Capacity Utilization _____
Price Volatility     _____
Vertical Integration _____
References           _____
Overall Rating       _____

## 2.5.4 Equipment Leasing

Equipment Leasing will be the smarter solution allowing our business to upgrade our equipment needs at the end of the term rather than being overly invested in outdated equipment through traditional bank financing and equipment purchase. We also intend to explore the following benefits of leasing some of the required equipment:

1. Frees Up Capital for other uses.  2. Tax Benefits
3. Improves Balance Sheet           4. Easy to add-on or trade-up
5. Improves Cash Flow               6. Preserves Credit Lines
7. Protects against obsolescence    8. Application Process Simpler

Our leasing strategy will also be shaped by the following factors:
1. Estimated useful life of the equipment.
2. How long our business plans to use the equipment.
3. What our business intends to do with the equipment at the end of the lease.
4. The tax situation of our business.
5. The cash flow of our business.
6. Our company's specific needs for future growth.

**List Any Leases:**

| Leasing Company | Equipment Description | Monthly Payment | Lease Period | Final Disposition |
|---|---|---|---|---|
| | | | | |
| | | | | |

**Resource:**

LeaseQ                                 www.leaseq.com
An online market place that connects businesses, equipment dealers, and leasing companies to make selling and financing equipment fast and easy. The LeaseQ Platform is a free, cloud based SaaS solution with a suite of on-demand software and data solutions for the equipment leasing industry. Utilizes the Internet to provide business process optimization (BPO) and information services that streamline the purchase and financing of business equipment across a broad array of vertical industry segments.

Innovative Lease Services          http://www.ilslease.com/equipment-leasing/
This company was founded in 1986 and is headquartered in Carlsbad, California. It is accredited by the Better Business Bureau, a long-standing member of the National Equipment Finance Association and the National Association of Equipment Leasing Brokers and is the official equipment financing partner of Biocom.
Resources:   Road Stoves leases turnkey mobile restaurants.

## 2.5.5      Funding Source Matrix

| Funds Source | Amount | Interest Rate | Repayment Terms | Use |
|---|---|---|---|---|
| | | | | |

## 2.5.6      Distribution or Licensing Agreements   (if any)
Note:   These are some of the key factors that investors will use to determine if we have a competitive advantage that is not easily copied.

| Licensor | License Rights | License Term | Fee or Royalty |
|---|---|---|---|
| | | | |

## 2.5.7      Trademarks, Patents and Copyrights (if any)

Our trademark will be virtually our branding for life. Our choice of a name for our business is very important. Not only will we brand our business and services forever, but what may be worthless today will become our most valuable asset in the years to come. A trademark search by our Lawyer will be a must, because to be told down the road that we must give up our name because we did not bother to conduct a trademark search would be a devastating blow to our business. It is also essential that the name that we choose suit the expanding product or service offerings that will be coming down the pike.

To maintain our competitive advantage, we will copyright our recipes and insist that each of our employees sign non-disclosure (at minimum) and non-compete agreements. We will also share recipes with only those employees that have a "need to know" and break the preparation of the recipe into different job functions.

Source: http://mobile-cuisine.com/culinary-lessons/are-your-food-truck-recipes-really-your-own/

Note: These are some of the key factors that investors will use to determine if we have a competitive advantage that is not easily copied.

---

Resources:
Patents/Trademarks         www.uspto.gov
Copyright                  www.copyright.gov


## 2.5.8  Innovation Strategy                          (optional)

\_\_\_\_ (company name) will create an innovation strategy that is aligned with not only our firm's core mission and values, but also with our future technology, supplier, and food preparation strategies. The objective of our innovation strategy will be to create a sustainable competitive advantage. Our education and training systems will be designed to equip our staff with the foundations to learn and develop the broad range of skills needed for innovation in all its forms, and with the flexibility to upgrade skills and adapt to changing market conditions. To foster an innovative workplace, we will ensure that employment policies facilitate efficient organizational change and encourage the expression of creativity, engage in mutually beneficial strategic alliances and allocate adequate funds for research and development. Our radical innovation strategies include _____ to achieve first mover status. Our incremental innovation strategies will include modifying the following _____ (products/services/processes) to give our customers added value for their money.

Resource: https://hbr.org/2015/04/the-5-requirements-of-a-truly-innovative-company


## 2.5.9  Summary of Sources and Use of Funds

**Sources:**
Owner's Equity Investment           $ _____
Requested Bank Loans                $ _____
Total:                              $ _____

**Uses:**
Capital Equipment                   $ _____
Beginning Inventory                 $ _____
Start-up Costs                      $ _____
Working Capital                     $ _____
Total:                              $ _____

## 2.5.9.1 Funding to Date (optional)

To date, _____'s (company name) founders have invested $_____ in _____ (company name), with which we have accomplished the following:
1. _____ (Designed/Built) the company's website
2. Developed content, in the form of ___ (#) articles, for the website.
3. Hired and trained our core staff of __(#) full-time people and ___ (#) part-time people.
4. Generated brand awareness by driving ___ (#) visitors to our website in a ___ (#) month period.
5. Successfully _____ (Developed/Test Marketed) ___ (#) new _____ (products/services), which compete on the basis of _____.
6. _____ (Purchased/Developed) and installed the software needed to _____ (manage _____ operations?)
7. Purchased $ _____ worth of _____ (supplies)
8. Purchased $ _____ worth of _____ equipment.

## 2.6 Start-up Requirements

| Start-up Expenses: | | Estimates |
|---|---|---:|
| Legal | _____ | 400 |
| Accountant | _____ | 300 |
| Accounting Software Package | _____ | 300 |
| State Licenses & Permits | _____ | 4000 |
| Vehicle Set-up | _____ | 10000 |
| Unforeseen Contingency | _____ | 3000 |
| Market Research Survey | _____ | 300 |
| Office Supplies | _____ | 300 |
| Sales Brochures | _____ | 300 |
| Direct Mailing | _____ | 500 |
| Other Marketing Materials | _____ | 2000 |
| Logo Design | _____ | 500 |
| Advertising (2 months) | _____ | 2000 |
| Consultants | _____ | 1000 |
| Insurance | _____ | 1200 |
| Rent (2 months security) | _____ | 3000 |
| Rent Deposit | _____ | 1500 |
| Utility Deposit | _____ | 600 |
| DSL Installation/Activation | _____ | 100 |
| Telephone System Installation | _____ | 200 |
| Telephone Deposit | _____ | 200 |
| Expensed Equipment | _____ | 1000 |

| | | |
|---|---|---|
| Website Design/Hosting | _____ | 2000 |
| Computer/Printer | _____ | |
| Used Office Equipment/Furniture | _____ | 2000 |
| Organization Memberships | _____ | 300 |
| Cleaning Supplies | _____ | 200 |
| Training Materials | _____ | |
| Promotional Signs | _____ | 7000 |
| Other | _____ | |
| **Total Start-up Expenses** | _____ (A) | |

Start-up Assets:

| | | |
|---|---|---|
| Cash Balance Required | _____ (T) | 15000 |
| Start-up Equipment | _____ | See schedule |
| Start-up Inventory | _____ | See schedule |
| Other Current Assets | _____ | |
| Long-term Assets | _____ | |
| **Total Assets** | _____ (B) | |
| Total Requirements | _____ (A+B) | |

# Start-up Funding

| | |
|---|---|
| Start-up Expenses to Fund | _____ (A) |
| Start-ups Assets to Fund | _____ (B) |
| **Total Funding Required:** | _____ (A+B) |

Assets

| | |
|---|---|
| Non-cash Assets from Start-up | _____ |
| Cash Requirements from Start-up | _____ (T) |
| Additional Cash Raised | _____ (S) |
| Cash Balance on Starting Date | _____ (T+S=U) |
| **Total Assets:** | _____ (B) |

# Liabilities and Capital

**Short-term Liabilities:**

| | |
|---|---|
| Current Borrowing | _____ |
| Unpaid Expenses | _____ |
| Accounts Payable | _____ |
| Interest-free Short-term Loans | _____ |
| Other Short-term Loans | _____ |
| **Total Short-term Liabilities** | _____ (Z) |

**Long-term Liabilities:**

| | |
|---|---|
| Commercial Bank Loan | _____ |
| Other Long-term Liabilities | _____ |
| **Total Long-term Liabilities** | _____ (Y) |
| **Total Liabilities** | _____ (Z+Y = C) |

## Capital
### Planned Investment
Owner Personal Funds          _____
Family                        _____
Other                         _____
Additional Investment Requirement  _____
**Total Planned Investment**  _____  (F)

**Loss at Start-up (Start-up Expenses)**  (-)_____  (A)
**Total Capital**             (=)_____  (F+A=D)
**Total Capital and Liabilities**  _____  (C+D)
Total Funding                 _____  (C+F)

## One-Year Schedule of Funds Sources and Uses
### Sources of Cash:
Personal Funds                _____
Loan Proceeds                 _____
Cash Receipts from Business (Net)  _____
**Total Sources:**                                    _____  (A)

### Uses of Cash:
Equipment/Supplies            _____
Fixtures                      _____
Security Deposits             _____
Signs                         _____
Utilities                     _____
Rent                          _____
Insurance Premiums            _____
Leasehold Improvements        _____
Costs of Goods Sold           _____
License and Permit Fees       _____
Advertising                   _____
Payroll Wages                 _____
Payroll Taxes and Benefits    _____
Loan Payments                 _____
Misc. Expenses                _____
Owner's Draw                  _____
**Total Uses:**                                       _____  (B)
**Net Cash Flow for the Year**                        _____  (A - B)


2.6.1     Capital Equipment List                             (select)

Note: The type of kitchen on the food truck will depend on the type of food served and how much of it needs to be prepared on the truck itself.

| Equipment Type | Model No. | New/ Used | Lifespan | Quantity | Unit Cost | Total |
|---|---|---|---|---|---|---|
| Built-in oven | | | | | | |
| Microwave | | | | | | |
| Prep Tables | | | | | | |
| Propane Grill | | | | | | |
| Fryer | | | | | | |
| Propane Generator | | | | | | |
| Exhaust Hood | | | | | | |
| Freezer | | | | | | |
| Freezer Display Case | | | | | | |
| Refrigerated Display Case | | | | | | |
| Pastry Display Case | | | | | | |
| Fountainette Cabinet | | | | | | |
| Single Door Reach-in Freezer | | | | | | |
| Refrigerator | | | | | | |
| Soft-serve Machine w/Faucet | | | | | | |
| Frozen Yogurt Machine | | | | | | |
| Dispensing Topping Units | | | | | | |
| Milk Shake Machine | | | | | | |
| Blender | | | | | | |
| 5-quart Mixer/Blender | | | | | | |
| Spoon Dispenser | | | | | | |
| Pot and pan washing sink | | | | | | |
| Vegetable washing sink | | | | | | |
| 2-Compartment Sink | | | | | | |
| Hand Sink | | | | | | |
| Beverage Dispensing Equipment | | | | | | |
| Custom Vehicle Windows | | | | | | |
| Vehicle/Truck | | | | | | |
| Music Box | | | | | | |
| Subtotal: | | | | | | |

**Beverage Equipment:**

| | | | | | | |
|---|---|---|---|---|---|---|
| Auto Coffee Brewer | (500) | | | | | |
| Iced Tea Brewer | (500) | | | | | |
| Ice Machine | | | | | | |
| **Total Major Equipment** | | | | | | |

**Truck Safety Equipment**

Stop/Warning Swing Arm
Alternating front/rear lights

Reflective Warning Signs  _____
Convex Mirrors  _____
Flashing beacon/Strobe light  _____
Bells  _____
Bumper Stickers  _____

**Other Equipment**
Computer System  _____
Fax Machine  _____
Copy Machine  _____
Answering Machine  _____
TV and DVD Player  _____
Office Furniture  _____
Accounting Software  _____
Scale  _____
Shelving Units            (150)  _____
Mobile Carts  _____
Canopy  _____
Water Storage Tank  _____
Walter Filtration System  (500)  _____
Waste Containers          (100)  _____
Hand Truck                (100)  _____
Hand Sink  _____
Decorative Signs  _____
Hot Water Heater  _____
Safe  _____
Work Table  _____
Tackboard  _____
Filing & Storage Cabinets  _____
Credit Card Machine  _____
Cash Register  _____
Cup/Lid Dispensers  _____
Storage Equipment Units  _____
Freezer Storage Shelving Set  _____
Storage Shelf Unit  _____
Electric Can Opener  _____
Display Equipment  _____
Menu Board  _____
Quality Statement Panel  _____
Fire Extinguishers  _____
Bowls with covers  _____
S/S Insert Pan  _____
GPS System  _____
First Aid Kit  _____
**Total Other Equipment**  _____

Total Capital Equipment  _____

**Note: Equipment costs dependent on whether purchased new or used or leased.**
All items that are assets to be used for more than one year will be considered a long-term asset and will be depreciated using the straight-line method.

Resources:
www.zesco.com/
www.webstaurantstore.com/restaurant-equipment.html

**New Types of Equipment: The Greaseless Fryer**

QNC, Inc.(QNC) is a Dallas, Texas based company that manufactures and markets a line of innovative commercial cooking appliances called the Quik n' Crispy Greaseless Fryer. The Quik n' Crispy is a patented compact, counter top "hot air" unit used for quickly reconstituting, by convection and radiant heat, frozen, fully cooked or oven ready "fried" type foods. Products such as french fries, chicken nuggets and strips, fried chicken, egg rolls, battered vegetables and finger foods are prepared to the consistency of deep fat fried foods, without grease. The Quik n' Crispy can also grill other frozen foods such as pre-cooked hamburgers, grilled chicken breast fillets and hot dogs. Also, it can bake pizzas, pretzels, hot sandwiches and other menu items to a high quality with a flaky and "freshly baked" finish.

Source:    http://q-n-c.com

## 2.7.0    Key Catering Contract Elements

We plan to work with our lawyer to develop a standard catering contract that includes the following elements:
1. Date and day of catering event.
2. Location of catering job.
3. Minimum guaranteed guest count for menu pricing.
4. Date of notification for final guest count.
5. Exact time catering job starts and ends.
6. Fire safety floor plan and seating arrangements.
7. Final menu selection and price per person.
8. Description of service and labor quotation.
9. Staff schedule.
10. Appropriate additional costs/subcontractors.
11. Deposit money and payment schedule for balance.
12. Cancellation policy and refund of deposit terms.
13. Dispute resolution options.
14. Anticipated total cost.
15. Authorized Signatures.
16. Names, addresses and telephone numbers of parties involved (buyer and seller);
17. Room set-up, decorations, tablecloths, etc., to be used;
18. Entertainment
19. Pricing arrangements and potential price increases;

20. Discount (if any) for full payment at the time contract is signed;
21. Applicable taxes

## 2.7.1 Event Budgeting

We will use the following worksheet to calculate the net profit potential from an individual event.

|  |  | Forecast | Actual | Act B/(W) Fcst |
|---|---|---|---|---|
| Revenues: |  |  |  |  |
| Gross Income | (A) | _____ |  |  |
| Expenses: |  |  |  |  |
| Food |  | _____ |  |  |
| Beverage |  | _____ |  |  |
| Kitchen Labor |  | _____ |  |  |
| Set-up/Site Labor |  | _____ |  |  |
| Rentals |  | _____ |  |  |
| Décor |  | _____ |  |  |
| Facility Rental |  | _____ |  |  |
| Transportation |  | _____ |  |  |
| Disposables |  | _____ |  |  |
| Additional Labor |  | _____ |  |  |
| Unpacking |  | _____ |  |  |
| Cleanup Labor |  | _____ |  |  |
| Total Estimated Costs: | (B) | _____ |  |  |
| Gross Profit | A - B = C | _____ |  |  |
| Overhead (15 percent) | (D) | _____ |  |  |
| **Net Profit** | **C - D = E** | _____ |  |  |

## 2.8.0 SBA Loan Key Requirements

In order to be considered for an SBA loan, we must meet the basic requirements:
1. Must have been turned down for a loan by a bank or other lender to qualify for most SBA Business Loan Programs. 2. Required to submit a guaranty, both personal and business, to qualify for the loans. 3. Must operate for profit; be engaged in, or propose to do business in, the United States or its possessions; 4. Have reasonable owner equity to invest; 5. Use alternative financial resources first including personal assets.

All businesses must meet eligibility criteria to be considered for financing under the SBA's 7(a) Loan Program, including: size; type of business; operating in the U.S. or its possessions; use of available of funds from other sources; use of proceeds; and repayment. The repayment term of an SBA loan is between five and 25 years, depending on the lift of the assets being financed and the cash needs of the business. Working capital loans (accounts receivable and inventory) should be repaid in five to 10 years. The SBA also has short-term loan guarantee programs with shorter repayment terms.

## A Business Owner Cannot Use an SBA Loan:

To purchase real estate where the participant has issued a forward commitment to the developer or where the real estate will be held primarily for investment purposes. To finance floor plan needs. To make payments to owners or to pay delinquent withholding taxes. To pay existing debt, unless it can be shown that the refinancing will benefit the small business and that the need to refinance is not indicative of poor management.

## SBA Loan Programs:
**Low Doc**:   www.sba.gov/financing/lendinvest/lowdoc.html
**SBA Express**   www.sba,gov/financing/lendinvest/sbaexpress.html
**Basic 7(a) Loan Guarantee Program**
> For businesses unable to obtain loans through standard loan programs. Funds can be used for general business purposes, including working capital, leasehold improvements and debt refinancing.
> www.sba.gov/financing/sbaloan/7a.html

**Certified Development Company 504 Loan Program**
> Used for fixed asset financing such as purchase of real estate or machinery.
> www. Sba.gov/gopher/Local-Information/Certified-Development-Companies/

**MicroLoan 7(m) Loan Program**
> Provides short-term loans up to $35,000.00 for working capital or purchase of fixtures.
> www.sba.gov/financing/sbaloan/microloans.html

# 2.8.1   Other Financing Options

1. Grants:
   Health care grants, along with education grants, represent the largest percentage of grant giving in the United States. The federal government, state, county and city governments, as well as private and corporate foundations all award grants. The largest percentage of grants are awarded to non-profit organizations, health care agencies, colleges and universities, local government agencies, tribal institutions, and schools. For profit organizations are generally not eligible for grants unless they are conducting research or creating jobs.

   A. Contact your state licensing office.
   B. Foundation Grants to Individuals:         www.fdncenter.org

|   |   |   |   |
|---|---|---|---|
| | C. | US Grants | www.grants.gov |
| | D. | Foundation Center | www.foundationcemter.org |
| | E. | The Grantsmanship Center | www.tgci.com |
| | F. | Contact local Chamber of Commerce | |
| | G. | The Catalog of Federal Domestic Assistance is a major provider of business grant money. | |
| | H. | The Federal Register is a good source to keep current with the continually changing federal grants offered. | |
| | I. | FedBizOpps is a resource, as all federal agencies must use FedBizOpps to notify the public about contract opportunities worth over $25,000. | |
| | J. | Fundsnet Services | http://www.fundsnetservices.com/ |
| | K. | SBA Women Business Center www.sba.gov/content/womens-business-center-grant-opportunities | |
| | L. | http://usgovinfo.about.com/od/smallbusiness/a/stategrants.htm | |
| 2. | Friends and Family Lending | | www.virginmoney.com |
| 3. | National Business Incubator Association | | www.nbia.org/ |
| 4. | Women's Business Associations | | www.nawbo.org/ |
| 5. | Minority Business Development Agency | | www.mbda.gov/ |
| 6. | Social Networking Loans | | www.prosper.com |
| 7. | Peer-to-Peer Programs | | www.lendingclub.com |
| 8. | Extended Credit Terms from Suppliers | | 30/60/90 days. |
| 9. | Community Bank w/ Established Relationship | | |
| 10. | Leasing Companies | | www.businessfinance.com |
| 11. | Prepayments from Customers | | |
| 12. | Seller Financing: when purchasing an existing Lunch Truck business. | | |
| 13. | Business Funding Directory | | www.businessfinance.com |
| 14. | FinanceNet | | www.financenet.gov |
| 15. | SBA Financing | | www.sbaonline.sba.gov |
| 16. | Private Investor | | |
| 17. | Use retirement funds to open a business without taxes or penalty. First, establish a C-corporation for the new business. Next, the C-corporation establishes a new retirement plan. Then, the owner's current retirement funds are rolled over into the C-corporation's new plan. And last, the new retirement plan invests in stock of the C-corporation. Warning: Check with your accountant or financial planner. Resource: http://www.benetrends.com/ | | |
| 18. | Business Plan Competition Prizes www.nytimes.com/interactive/2009/11/11/business/smallbusiness/Competitions-table.html?ref=smallbusiness | | |
| 19. | Unsecured Business Cash Advance based on future credit card transactions. | | |
| 20. | Micro-Loans | | www.accionusa.org/ |
| 21. | Commercial Loan Applications | | www.c-loans.com/onlineapp/ |
| 22. | Sharing assets and resources with other non-competing businesses. | | |
| 23. | Angel Investors | | www.angelcapitaleducation.org |
| 24. | The Receivables Exchange | | http://receivablesxchange.com/ |
| 25. | Bootstrap Methods: Personal Savings/Credit Card/Second Mortgages | | |

26. Community-based Crowd-funding   www.profounder.com
27. On Deck Capital   http://www.ondeckcapital.com/
Created the Short-term Business Loan (up to $100,000.00) for small businesses to get quick access to capital that fits their cash flow, with convenient daily payments.
28. Royalty Lending   www.launch-capital.com/
With royalty lending, financing is granted in return for future revenue or company performance, and payback can prove exceedingly expensive if a company flourishes.
29. Stock Loans   Southern Lending Solutions, Atlanta. GA.
Custom Commercial Finance, Bartlesville, OK
A stock loan is based on the quality of stocks, Treasuries and other kinds of investments in a businessperson's personal portfolio. Possession of the company's stock is transferred to the lender's custodial bank during the loan period.
30. Lender Compatibility Searcher   www.BoeFly.com
29. Community-based Crowd-funding   www.profounder.com
These platforms include Kickstarter, IndieGogo, RocketHub and PeerBackers. A funding option designed to link small businesses and entrepreneurs with pools of prospective investors. Crowdfunding lenders are often repaid with goods.
30. On Deck Capital   www.ondeckcapital.com/
Created the Short-term Business Loan (up to $100,000.00) for small businesses to get quick access to capital that fits their cash flow, with convenient daily payments.
31. Royalty Lending   www.launch-capital.com/
With royalty lending, financing is granted in return for future revenue or company performance, and payback can prove exceedingly expensive if a company flourishes.
32. Stock Loans   Southern Lending Solutions, Atlanta. GA.
Custom Commercial Finance, Bartlesville, OK
A stock loan is based on the quality of stocks, Treasuries and other kinds of investments in a businessperson's personal portfolio. Possession of the company's stock is transferred to the lender's custodial bank during the loan period.
33. Lender Compatibility Searcher   www.BoeFly.com
34. Strategic Investors
Strategic investing is more for a large company that identifies promising technologies, and for whatever reason, that company may not want to build up the research and development department in-house to produce that product, so they buy a percentage of the company with the existing technology.
35. Bartering
36. Small Business Investment Companies   www.sba.gov/INV
37. Cash-Value Life Insurance
38. Employee Stock Option Plans   www.nceo.org
39. Venture Capitalists   www.nvca.org
40. Initial Public Offering (IPO)
41. Meet investors through online sites, including LinkedIn (group discussions), Facebook (BranchOut sorts Facebook connections by profession), and CapLinked

(enables search for investment-related professionals by industry and role).
42. SBA Community Advantage Approved Lenders
www.sba.gov/content/community-advantage-approved-lenders
43. Small Business Lending Specialists
https://www.wellsfargo.com/biz/loans_lines/compare_lines
http://www.bankofamerica.com/small_business/business_financing/
https://online.citibank.com/US/JRS/pands/detail.do?ID=CitiBizOverview
https://www.chase.com/ccp/index.jsp?pg_name=ccpmapp/smallbusiness/home/page/bb_business_bBanking_programs
44. Startup America Partnership    www.s.co/about
Based on a simple premise: young companies that grow create jobs. Once startups apply and become a Startup America Firm, they can access and manage many types of resources through a personalized dashboard.
45. United States Economic Development Administration    www.eda.gov/
46. Small Business Loans    http://www.iabusnet.org/small-business-loans
47. Tax Increment Financing (TIF)
A public financing method that is used for subsidizing redevelopment, infrastructure, and other community-improvement projects. TIF is a method to use future gains in taxes to subsidize current improvements, which are projected to create the conditions for said gains. The completion of a public project often results in an increase in the value of surrounding real estate, which generates additional tax revenue. Tax Increment Financing dedicates tax increments within a certain defined district to finance the debt that is issued to pay for the project. TIF is often designed to channel funding toward improvements in distressed, underdeveloped, or underutilized parts of a jurisdiction where development might otherwise not occur. TIF creates funding for public or private projects by borrowing against the future increase in these property-tax revenues.
48. Gust    https://gust.com/entrepreneurs
Provides the global platform for the sourcing and management of early-stage investments. Gust enables skilled entrepreneurs to collaborate with the smartest investors by virtually supporting all aspects of the investment relationship, from initial pitch to successful exit.
49. Goldman Sachs 10,000 Small Businesses    http://sites.hccs.edu/10ksb/
50. Earnest Loans    www.meetearnest.com
51. Biz2Credit    www.biz2credit.com
52. Funding Circle    www.fundingcircle.com
A peer-to-peer lending service which allows savers to lend money directly to small and medium sized businesses
53. Lending Club    www.lendingclub.com
54. Equity-based Crowdfunding    www.Indiegogo.com    www.StartEngine.com
www.SeedInvest.com
55. National Funding    www.nationalfunding.com
Their customers can to get working capital, merchant cash advances, credit card processing, and, equipment leasing.
56. Quick Bridge Funding    www.quickbridgefunding.com
Offers a flexible and timely financing program to help assist small and medium

sized businesses achieve their goals.
57. Kabbage                www.kabbage.com
The industry leader in providing working capital online.
58. Opportunity Fund Loan    http://opportunityfundloan.org
Invests in small businesses that have been shut out of the financial mainstream. California's largest non-profit lender to small businesses, including food trucks.

**Resources:** www.sba.gov/category/navigation-structure/starting-managing-business/starting-business/local-resources

http://usgovinfo.about.com/od/moneymatters/a/Finding-Business-Loans-Grants-Incentives-And-Financing.htm

## 3.0 Products and Services (Select)

In this section, we will not only list all of our planned products and services, but also describe how our proposed products and services will be differentiated from those of our competitors and solve a real problem or fill an unmet need in the marketplace.

_____ (company name) will specialize in the offering of ____ (organic/all natural) products, in addition to traditional favorites. The products are:
1. Free of artificial preservatives.
2. Free of artificial colors.
3. Free of chemical additives.
4. Organically grown.
5. Least processed version available.
6. Non-irradiated.
7. Cruelty free.

Our quality standards will ensure that customers purchase no foods with artificial anything, and no trans fats. All our products will be in its purest state, unadulterated by artificial additives, sweeteners, colorings, and preservatives. We will only carry natural and organic products because we believe that food in its purest state is the best tasting and most nutritious food available.

Our business goal is to sell the highest quality products we can find at the most competitive prices possible. We will evaluate quality in terms of nutrition, freshness, appearance, and taste. Our search for quality products will be a never-ending process and will require the following activities:
1. Careful evaluation of each and every menu item we sell.
2. Feature foods that are free of artificial preservatives, colors, flavors, sweeteners, and hydrogenated fats.
3. A commitment to foods that are fresh, wholesome and safe to eat.
4. Promotion of organically grown foods.
5. Provide food and nutritional products that support health and well-being.
6. Seek out the freshest, most healthful, minimally processed products available.

**Menu Design Logic**
We will adhere to the following menu design guidelines for our food truck:
1. We will build our menu around a limited number of core protein-based products such as chicken, seafood, beef, and pork.
2. We will manage down core protein food product availability, portion size, and food costs.
3. We will focus on higher margin protein product carriers like French fries or mashed potatoes, rice or noodles because they are lower cost, have longer service hold times, and can be prepared or seasoned to create a point of differentiation.
4. We will limit initially the number of 'accent sauces' to three sauces, because of their high food cost per ounce.
5. We will limit the number of add-ons used to build check average. Examples include biscuits, fresh vegetable sides, breads, jalapeno peppers, etc.
6. We will limit the dessert menu and resulting food waste cost exposure.
7. We will focus on the taste preferences of the local ethnic community.

8. We will create a menu with a narrow focus on two or three core items plus a dessert option and drinks.
9. We will create a menu that is oriented towards regional specialty foods and artisanal offerings.
9. We will strive to be known for a particular signature menu item.
10. We will cross-utilize foods in a few different menu items for maximum efficiency and inventory turnover.

Sources:
www.foodbevbiz.com/2012/08/common-food-truck-menu-execution-mistakes/
http://openforbusiness.opentable.com/tips/how-much-does-a-food-truck-cost/

## Products

We will sell a range of products that accommodate the following diet requirements:

1. Dairy-free
2. Gluten-free
3. Low Fat
4. Low Sodium
5. Soy-based
6. Sugar-free
7. Vegetarian
8. Wheat-free
9. Fat free
10. High fiber

**Mini-Delicatessen**

The rotating menu will feature healthy freshly made sandwiches, sliders, burritos, hot dogs, tacos, burgers, soups, salads, energy drinks, bottled water, and low-fat desserts. All menu items will be prepared fresh each morning and displayed for easy and quick pick-up. The breakfast menu will include items such as gourmet coffee and bagels, and the lunch/dinner menu will consist of healthy sandwiches, salads, packaged soups, and daily frozen treat specials. We will serve high quality organic coffee, tea, smoothies and fresh squeezed all-natural juice.

### Other Sample Menu Items                              (select)

**Beverages**

- Organic Ricemilk Vanilla
- Organic Coffees and Teas
- Organic Spiced Apple Cider
- Organic Chocolate Soy Milk
- Low-fat Milkshakes
- Fresh Fruit Smoothies
- Organic Juices
- Reduced Calorie Root Beer Floats
- Organic Lemonade
- Bottle Water
- Vitamin Water
- Sugar-free Hot Chocolate
- Sugar-free Cappuccino
- All-natural Soft Drinks
- Sorbet Smoothies
- Frozen/Iced Coffee Drinks
- Ice Cream Soda Floats
- Nacho/Potato Chips

**Healthy Snacks**

- Energy Power Bars
- Organic Chips

**Ice Cream Treats (freshly prepared)**

- Single Scoop Waffle Cones
- Sundaes
- Double Scoop Waffle Cones
- Premium Sundaes

Banana Split                    Ice Cream Sandwiches

**Other Frozen Treats**
Low-fat Gelato                  Sorbet
Low-fat Yogurt                  Italian Lemon Ice
Regular Yogurt                  Frozen Custard

**Warm Desserts**
Low-fat Brownies w/ice cream    Apple Pie a La Mode
Custards

**Cookie Ice Cream Sandwiches**
Custom ice cream sandwiches, using a variety of homemade cookies for the outside, and an ice cream flavor of choice for the middle.

**Homemade Baked Goods**
Brownies                        Butter Cookies

**Coffee and Espresso Bar**


Services
1. On-site Event Catering Services    2. Custom Cakes and Pies
3. Custom Blending/Mixing             4. Custom Gift Baskets
5. Shipping Service                   6. Mobile Food Services
7. Educational Seminars               8. Consulting Services

Merchandise
_____ (company name) will offer the following merchandise for sale.
- Logo Imprinted T-Shirts       - Logo Imprinted Hats
- Party Supplies                - Gourmet Organic Coffee
- Gourmet Organic Tea           - Logo Imprinted Mugs

Party Supplies
- Balloons                      - Table Cloths
- Napkins                       - Paper Plates
- Candy Bags                    - Party Hats
- Party Games

Party Packs
Include various combinations of ice cream, food and drink items, will be offered to help make party planning a snap.

## 3.0.1     Sample Menu

**BREAKFAST**
Breakfast plates served with your choice of toast with jelly or hash browns
Breakfast plate: Two eggs any style-w/choice of bacon, ham, or sausage
Mini Plate: One egg any style- w/choice of bacon, ham, or sausage
$2.25 French toast with Bacon or Sausage $2.75 Ham & Cheese Omelet $2.95 Denver Omelet $ 2.95 Mushroom & Cheese Omelet $3.00 Sandwich on Toast or Muffin $2.50 Breakfast Croissant $3.00 Polish Sausage and Egg Sandwich $2.75 Hot Link Sausage and Egg Sandwich $2.75 Linguisa and Egg Sandwich $3.00 Steak and Egg Sandwich $3.50

**SANDWICHES**
Served with lettuce, mayonnaise and tomato
Vegetarian $ BLT $2.75 Roast Beef and Cheese $2.75 Ham and Cheese $2.75 Turkey Breast and Cheese $2.50 Tuna Salad $2.50 Egg Salad $2.00 Chicken Salad $2.75 Club Triple Decker Sandwich $3.00

# 3.1 Service Descriptions

In creating our service descriptions, we will provide answers to the following types of questions:
1. What does the service do or help the customer to accomplish?
2. Why will people decide to buy it?
3. What makes it unique or a superior value?
4. How expensive or difficult is it to make or copy by a competitor?
5. How much will the service be sold for?

## On-site Event Catering
We will offer catering as a value-added service. We will make certain to always prepare a catering proposal, which is the quote given by the caterer to the client. It will outline the services, food and beverages that will be provided for an event as well as the cost of each service and menu item. The proposal will also double as a contract. If the client is happy with it and wants to contract our services as their caterer, they will sign it at the bottom and give their payment information. For the most professional-looking proposal, we will use our catering company's letterhead. To create a catering proposal, we will have to outline everything we will provide to our client, with a price attached to each piece, as well as a grand total price quote for the entire event.

We will provide on-site catering at the client's event for ___ (#) or more people. Event catering includes the following:
1. Full Service: Set-up, service and clean-up
2. Self-service Option.
3. Optional party supplies, such as balloons, streamers, games, etc.

**The Cover Letter will include all the following general information for the event:**
1. Type of event. Whether it is a fancy event or a casual, or full-service or buffet.

2. Date of the event. Will impact the final cost if scheduled on or near a holiday.
3. Time of the event. The required amount of the caterer's time will impact cost.
4. Venue location. Distance will add additional fees for delivery and gas costs.
5. Minimum guaranteed guest count. Pricing is based on that guest count.

Resource: http://mobile-cuisine.com/business/developing-a-food-truck-catering-proposal-and-quote/

**Typical events will be comprised of the following types:**

| | |
|---|---|
| Picnics | BBQ's |
| Outings | Family Days |
| Car shows | Corporate Events |
| Grand Openings | Employee / Customer Appreciations |
| Promotional Events | Birthday Parties |
| Sporting events | Weddings |
| Graduations | Reunions |
| Fairs | Carnivals |
| Concerts | Bar mitzvahs |
| School functions | Outdoor fairs. |

## Shipping Service

We will offer a shipping service that lets our customers ship our premium menu items anywhere in the continental United States. This service will popular for former customers who have moved away, or current customers who want to enjoy our products far away at their family reunion. These packages will also be excellent for a truly differentiated corporate gift. The service fee will include dry ice and packaging. Shipping costs will vary based on geography, but can be estimated at the FedEx web site by using _____ (#) as "ship from" zip code.

## Leased Mobile Services

We plan to lease out ___ (#) licensed food carts to vendors that commit to using our products. These carts will serve as another sales distribution channel and will also improve our name recognition because of their signage.

## Mobile Wi-Fi Hotspot

We will turn our Food Truck into a Mobile Wi-Fi Hotspot, because buried inside many of the latest smartphones is a feature called tethering, which lets a phone go beyond talk, email and Web surfing to act as a mobile hotspot that can supply Web access to nearby computers, tablets and other devices.

Resource: http://mobile-cuisine.com/technology/turn-your-food-truck-into-a-mobile-wifi-hotspot/

## 3.2     Types of Catering Services:             (Select)

1. **Full Service Catering**
    Includes everything from glassware to napkins, flowers, music, decorations, the

theme and even the party site.

2. **No Service or Drop-off Catering**
   We provide and deliver only the food in disposable trays, either delivered to the client's door, or picked up at our location, and nothing else.

3. **Express Catering**
   The client picks up the order at our _____ location.

4. **Partial Service Catering**
   In Partial Service Catering, we prepare the meal at our location or at the party site, and arrange it as a self-serve buffet.

5. **Social Catering**
   This can include special events such as weddings, anniversaries, bat and bar mitzvahs, sweet-sixteen parties, anniversaries, Christenings, Communions, Confirmations, class reunions, golf outings, birthday parties, etc. We are also called upon to prepare breakfast, lunch and dinner.

6. **Corporate Catering**
   We prepare an event production plan that can include extra services such as valet parking, themed decorations, bar service, clean-up, venue selection, logistical plans, and equipment rentals, etc. Possible events include breakfast meetings, gourmet lunch boxes, management training seminars, holiday parties, executive promotions, board meetings, theme parties, company picnics, grand openings, conventions, and promotional events. ____ (company name) will offer our clients easy ordering, fresh and tasty food presented in a professional manner and consistent service every day.
   Resource:
   www.foodtruckinvasion.com/top-11-trends-corporate-catering/

7. **School Programs**
   School districts using our mobile catering services will consistently experience greater student participation in school lunch programs, improved quality and service, boost student satisfaction and achieve cost reductions.

8. **Community Affairs**
   Includes the catering of fundraisers, charity auctions, etc.

9. **On-Premise Catering**
   Food is prepared, cooked and served at the same venue.

10. **Off-Premise Catering**

Food is prepared and cooked in a workstation prepared by the caterer but served somewhere else, such as a wedding reception.

11. Mobile Chef Services
    A personal chef service that caters to the small event, that is, events that entertain 25 persons or less. Includes in-home meal preparation services. After a free consultation where we determine customer food likes and dislikes, a menu will be prepared for approval, then on the date agreed upon, our chef shops for the groceries, then arrives at customer's home to prepare meals then packages them. We then leave with easy to follow heating instructions and a clean kitchen.

12. Boxed Lunch Catering Service
    A box lunch is a lunch consisting of a sandwich, chips, fruit and a dessert. A box lunch will typically be dropped off to a location for a client's dining needs. Box lunches are used primarily in the corporate arena for working lunches when they do not have time to take a break from their meeting yet still need to eat. A box lunch order will be placed a couple of days before the delivery date and is a cheaper way to go instead of a full sit-down lunch. The box lunch option will strictly be a drop off service and will not involve any type of wait staff or cleanup. In some cases, the caterer can setup the food, which means placing the individual cartons on a table or another area that is easily accessible to the clients. A box lunch will be prepared for each person, so that they have all their food in one container. Dinks such as sodas, waters and juices will also be dropped off by the caterer in individual containers but may or may not be included in the box lunch itself. The boxes or bags will be visibly marked with the type of sandwich included for easy identification.

13. Home Delivery Services
    We will use the following types of independent restaurant delivery services to deliver our meals, and expand our business reach.
    Examples:
    www.grubhub.com
    www.doordash.com

Resources:
www.foodtruckinvasion.com/15-tips-to-insure-your-food-truck-catering-event-is-a-success/

# 3.2.1 Mobile Food Truck Benefits

1. Allows owners to experiment with menu dishes and test different market locations across the region before opening a fixed location.

2. The vehicle signage acts as a moveable billboard for the fixed location.

3. Generates a secondary revenue stream at special events.

4. Facilitates the catering side of the business.

5. Improves the customer convenience factor.

## 3.3 Alternative Revenue Streams

1. Classified Ads in our Newsletter
2. Vending Machine Sales
3. Product sales and rentals.
4. Website Banner Ads
5. Content Area Sponsorship Fees
6. Online Survey Report Fees
7. Subcontracting Commissions
8. Facility Rentals
9. Consulting Services

## 3.4 Production of Products and Services

We will use the following methods to locate the best suppliers for our business:
- Attend trade shows and seminars to spot upcoming trends, realize networking opportunities and compare prices.

- Subscribe to appropriate trade magazines, journals, newsletters and blogs.

**Mobile Cuisine Magazine**   http://mobile-cuisine.com/
Mobile Cuisine started in 2010 as a simple one-man blog. Today, it's the mobile food industry's go to online trade magazine with nearly 1 million unique visitors — and it was all done with useful content any mobile food vendor can use.
Ex:   http://mobile-cuisine.com/off-the-wire/hot-b2b-food-truck-small-biz-options/

**Mobile Food News**   www.MobileFoodNews.com
A leading site for news, resources, information, opinions and insight about the mobile food industry, equipment, food product and the people who own and work in the mobile food industry.

**Small Food Business**   www.smallfoodbiz.com
**Food Business News**   www.foodbusinesnesw.net

**FoodTruckr**   www.foodtruckr.com
A one-stop destination for all the inspired instruction and resources needed to grow a food truck business.

- Join our trade association to make valuable contacts, get listed in any online directories, and secure training and marketing materials.

Convenience Caterers & Food Manufacturers Association
http://www.mobilecaterers.com/index.html

National Association of Concessionaires          http://www.naconline.org/
National Restaurant Association                  http://www.restaurant.org/
National Association for the Self Employed       http://www.nase.org/Home.aspx
National Association of Specialty Food Trade     www.specialtyfood.com/do/Home
Southern California Mobile Food Vendors          http://site.socalmfva.com/Home.html
Resource:      http://www.mobilefoodnews.com/vending-associations/

## 3.5 Competitive Comparison

There are only ___ (#) other Mobile Food Trucks in the neighborhood. _____ (company name) will differentiate itself from its local competitors by filling the following roles:
1.   Food truck/Mobile Food Truck
2.   Mobile Smoothie and Juice Bar
3.   Quick Service Restaurant
     (Multigrain Sandwiches, Low-salt Soups and Organic Salads)
4.   Mobile Gourmet Coffee Shop. (organic coffee beans)

 The competition facing _____ (company name) includes all the grocery stores, coffee shops, and some of the eating establishments in the _____ area. ____ (city) has ___ (#) chain grocery stores that carry a limited selection of healthy food choices, and ___ (none?) in the ethnic food category. There are ___ (#) fast food businesses that we consider to be indirect competitors due to the vast differences between us in quality of product and combination of healthy foodservices. Our direct competitors have a component similar to what _____ (company name) is proposing, but do not offer the same combination of services with a comprehensive healthy nutrition focus.

We believe that our mix of certified organic products and high-quality healthy foodservices, combined with our location convenience and quick service, will help us compete with the existing small businesses.

Additionally, _____ (company name) does not have to pay for under-utilized staff. Our flexible employee scheduling procedures and use of part-timers ensure that the truck is never overstaffed during slow times. We will also adopt a pay-for-performance compensation plan, and use referral incentives to generate new business.

We will reinvest major dollars every year in professional and educational materials. We will participate in online webinars to bring customers the finest selection of ice cream products and services, and health food industry trend information.

Our prices will be competitive with other retail businesses that offer far less in the way of  health benefits, innovative novelties, convenience and organic flavor and toppings selection.

## 3.6 Sales Literature

_____ (company name) has developed sales literature that illustrates a professional organization with vision. _____ (company name) plans to constantly refine its marketing mix through a number of different literature packets. These include the following:
- direct mail with introduction letter and product price sheet.
- product information brochures
- press releases
- new product/service information literature
- email marketing campaigns
- website content
- corporate brochures

A copy of our informational brochure is attached in the appendix of this document. This brochure will be available to provide referral sources, leave at seminars, and use for direct mail purposes.

## 3.7 Fulfillment

The key fulfillment and delivery of services will be provided by our director/owner, and certified sales associates. The real core value is the industry expertise of the founder, and staff experience and company training programs.

## 3.8 Technology

_____ (company name) will employ and maintain the latest technology to enhance its office management, inventory management, payment processing, customer profiling and record keeping systems. Each item that gets sold will be deducted from our inventory list. Additionally, tracking items in our mobile units will easily be managed with handheld inventory devices that integrate with the Cash Register system.

Our point of sale system will include a small form factor computer, cash drawer, receipt printer and laser bar code scanner or tabletop scanner. An optional pole display will be easily added, which will inform our customers how much they are paying so they are likely to have the cash out quickly. A laser bar code scanner will aggressively scan bar codes that might be on bags or around bottles and quickly add the item to the invoice. All these devices help to reduce the time it takes to process a customer.
Resource:   https://mobile-cuisine.com/technology/consider-point-of-sale-systems/

Resources:
**POS for Food Trucks**               https://www.redfynn.com/food-truck

**LevelUp**                               https://www.thelevelup.com/how-it-works

The company has created an app that allows mobile food truck operators to accept credit and debit card payments. The service is marketed to consumers as a way to securely store payment cards in order to pay for their food truck purchases using unique QR Codes that display on the screens of their mobile devices. This technology allows consumers to connect with LevelUp mobile food truck businesses for the purpose of earning rewards for repeat business loyalty. Customers who download the LevelUp mobile app are encouraged to link up a debit or credit card so that they can pay for their mobile food truck purchases with their smartphones. Registered users receive notifications about nearby trucks that are offering discounts to people with LevelUp, which are automatically applied to customers' purchases when they pay with the mobile app.

**NCR Corporation**                       www.ncrsilver.com

The global leader in consumer transaction technologies, turning everyday interactions with businesses into exceptional experiences. With its software, hardware, and portfolio of services, NCR enables more than 485 million transactions daily across retail, financial, travel, hospitality, telecom and technology, and small business. NCR Silver is an advanced tablet point-of-sale (POS) system for small businesses. More than just a mobile POS, NCR Silver offers back-office technology to run an entire food truck business – from integrating customer loyalty to automating different tax rates.

**Mobile Phone Credit Card Reader**       https://squareup.com/

Square, Inc. is a financial services, merchant services aggregator and mobile payments company based in San Francisco, California. The company markets several software and hardware products and services, including Square Register and Square Order. Square Register allows individuals and merchants in the United States, Canada, and Japan to accept offline debit and credit cards on their iOS or Android smartphone or tablet computer. The app supports manually entering the card details or swiping the card through the Square Reader, a small plastic device which plugs into the audio jack of a supported smartphone or tablet and reads the magnetic stripe. On the iPad version of the Square Register app, the interface resembles a traditional cash register.

**Google Wallet**                         https://www.google.com/wallet/

A mobile payment system developed by Google that allows its users to store debit cards, credit cards, loyalty cards, and gift cards among other things, as well as redeeming sales promotions on their mobile phone. Google Wallet can be used NFC to make secure payments fast and convenient by simply tapping the phone on any PayPass-enabled terminal at checkout.

**Apple Pay**                             http://www.apple.com/apple-pay/

A mobile payment and digital wallet service by Apple Inc. that lets users make payments using the iPhone 6, iPhone 6 Plus, Apple Watch-compatible devices (iPhone 5and later models), iPad Air 2, and iPad Mini 3. Apple Pay does not require Apple-specific contactless payment terminals and will work with Visa's PayWave, MasterCard's PayPass, and American Express's ExpressPay terminals. The service has begun initially only for use in the US, with international roll-out planned for the future.

Resource: www.wired.com/2017/01/shadow-apple-pay-google-wallet-expands-online-reach/

**WePay**　　　　　　　　　　https://www.wepay.com/
An online payment service provider in the United States. WePay's payment API focuses exclusively on platform businesses such as crowdfunding sites, marketplaces andsmall business software. Through this API, WePay allows these platforms to access its payments capabilities and process credit cards for the platform's users.

**Wireless Credit Card Machine**　　　http://www.merchantanywhere.com/

**Chirpify**
Connects a user's PayPal account with their Twitter account in order to enable payments through tweeting.

**Articles:**
www.prnewswire.com/news-releases/tips-to-leverage-mobile-payments-in-your-marketing-strategy-300155855.html

http://mobile-cuisine.com/technology/food-truck-owners-can-accept-credit-cards-with-phone-swipe/

# 3.9  Future Products and Services

_____ (company name) will continually expand our offering of services based on industry trends and changing client needs. We will not only solicit feedback via surveys and comments cards from customers on what they need in the future, but will also work to develop strong relationships with all of our customers and vendors. We also plan to open ____ (#) additional locations in the _____ area starting in _____ (year).

_____ (company name) will introduce new menu items as time and profitability permit. We will also monitor where our profits are coming from and enhance those areas of the business quarterly.

**We plan to expand our offering of services to include the following:**
1. Programmed and Pre-ordering of desserts via our website and fax transmissions.
2. Fresh Food Lunchboxes by day of the week.
3. Mobile Foodservice to fulfill office organic coffee and dessert programs.
4. A catering program for company sales meetings, staff promotion celebrations, company parties, birthdays and luncheons.
5. Expanded Healthy Foods Selections: Low Cal/Low Salt/Low Carb/Organic
6. All-natural Gift Baskets for special events and holiday celebrations.

An additional marketing strategy of the business will be sales generated from freezer carts bearing the company logo. There are many fairs, festivals and parties within the geographic service area (including the _____ County Fair, and Renaissance Days) where significant additional sales may be generated on ice cream novelties. Most importantly, these outside sales and an eventual central storefront location will give the business name recognition.

**To generate more morning business, we plan to do the following:**
1.  Sell gourmet coffee, bagels and donuts.
2.  Offer smoothies and other breakfast related treats

Our plan is to book more events, because like catering, they are a reliable source of income. Online sales will be another promising arena for less-perishable food products, as well as t-shirts, and other novelty products. Distribution to coffee shops, grocery stores, and other vendors will be another option to create our wholesale business. The truck will be a moving, 20-foot-long billboard for us, that will increase our visibility.

## Food Truck-based Marketing Programs for Restaurants

We will use our food truck to set up a temporary marketing program for existing brick-and-mortar restaurants. We will use signage to temporarily brand the truck in the image of the restaurant that we are marketing. We will get trained in offering a simplified version of the menu offered at the client restaurant. Our marketing food truck will help the client restaurant to test market new menu items and possible locations for a second restaurant site. Our mobile food truck will also serve as a moveable billboard for the client restaurant, and provide a way to widely distribute samples of menu items and collect the email addresses of potential new customers. We will develop a fixed daily rate for this marketing service, with the restaurant client supplying all of the menu ingredients. We will also rent out the food truck to clients who want to handle all of the aspects of their own marketing plan. Our mobile food truck will basically serve the same function as a temporary pop-up store, but with the added benefit of a moveable storefront sign.

# 4.0 Market Analysis Summary

**Our Market Analysis will serve to accomplish the following goals:**
1. Define the characteristics, and needs and wants of the target market.
2. Serve as a basis for developing sales, marketing and promotional strategies.
3. Influence the e-commerce website design.

_____ (city) is a very desirable place to live and work, and offers a wealth of opportunities for its _____ (#) residents. In addition, within a 5-mile radius there are _____ (#) residents and within a 10-mile radius there are _____ (#) people and _____ (#) industrial parks and construction sites.

The most prominent age group is from _____ to _____, which is a prime age range for first and second marriages and other types of special events. The average income within a 5 mile radius is $_____ per household. There are also ___ (#) little league ball fields, ___ (#) flea markets, ___ (#) stadiums, ___ (#) colleges and universities and
____ (#) _____.

The marketing of 'healthy' and 'premium' menu items will provide two purchase options for our customers.

The purchase of menu items and related products is basically an impulse-type purchase by a consumer relating to one of the following stimuli:
    Passing by the truck on the way to another destination,
    Visual contact with the truck's signs,
    Observing someone else consuming one of the truck's products,
    The final course (dessert) after a meal has been consumed elsewhere.

In the past ten years, the _____ section of _____ (city) has grown tremendously. The growing student community combined with the new families in the area are a perfect customer support base for our healthy Mobile Food Truck.

**Our main target markets are:**
The biggest buyers of foods from mobile vendors are young adults and parents with children at home. Those aged 25 to 34 are the largest consumers of snacks from mobile vendors, spending an average of $ 44 a month.

    People who live and work in _____ (city), who are looking for menu items with quality organic ingredients.
    Surrounding businesses looking for a tasty and healthy quick lunch for their customers and staff.
    International and domestic travelers visiting _____ (city).
    Families looking for quality, affordable and healthy indulgences for their kids to combat the teen obesity epidemic.
    People looking for a convenient way in which to enjoy a cup of organic coffee with

their sandwich made with organic ingredients.
People looking for high quality, unique, natural and organic food items.

Our target market includes events held by individuals (birthdays, anniversaries, showers, weddings, special occasions), corporate parties (holiday party, birthday, promotion celebration, "Friday treats", etc.), and other events. Individuals who purchase our food will likely be making impulse buying decisions, thus allowing our company to charge a premium for our product.

Each market segment consists of people who either live, work, or vacation in the ___ (city), ___ (state) area. Each market will be seeking an outlet that will meet their desire for authentic, healthy frozen treats, quality service, and convenient access.

Forces and trends in the market environment will affect _____ (company name), like all businesses. These include economic, competitive, legal/political, technology, and recordkeeping issues.

> **Economic Environment**—Positive forces include the generally prosperous local economy that is currently in place, steady employment, stable wages and low inflation, leading more people and businesses to be willing to purchase healthy quick service meals from our Mobile Food Truck.
> **Legal/Political Environment**—Town of _____ supports the opening of this needed business venture and has issued and approved vehicle permits and licenses to support the use of our Mobile Food Truck.
> **Technology and Recordkeeping Environment**—Use of computerized scales and cash registers will capture and generate accounting/inventory detail. Computer programs greatly simplify the financial recordkeeping and tax preparation with which all businesses must comply. We will outsource the accounting tax functions, but will maintain the daily financial records in-house.

_____ (company name) has a defined target market of middle class consumers that will be the basis of this business. Effective marketing combined with an optimal product and service offering mix is critical to our success. The owner possesses solid information about the health food markets and knows a great deal about the common attributes of those that are expected to be loyal customers. This information will be leveraged to better understand who we will serve, their specific needs, and how to better communicate with them.

In summary, the general market analysis shows that both 'healthy' and 'premium' food sales are on the increase and will continue to increase. Further, the target market for these products is middle and upper income families. The market analysis also reveals that it is highly desirable to serve a limited assortment of healthy pre-prepared sandwiches, soups and salads, and to become a one-stop, quick service mobile food truck destination.

## 4.1 Secondary Market Research

**We will research demographic information for the following reasons:**
1. To determine which segments of the population, such as Hispanics and the elderly, have been growing and may now be underserved.
2. To determine if there is a sufficient population base in the designated service area to realize the company's business objectives.
3. To consider what products and services to add in the future, given the changing demographic profile and needs of our service area.

**We will pay special attention to the following general demographic trends:**
1. Population growth has reached a plateau and market share will most likely be increased through innovation and excellent customer service.
2. Because incomes are not growing, and unemployment is high, process efficiencies and sourcing advantages must be developed to keep prices competitive.
3. The rise of non-traditional households, such as single working mothers, means developing more innovative and personalized programs.
4. As the population shifts toward more young to middle aged adults, ages 30 to 44, and the elderly, aged 65 and older, there will be a greater need for child-rearing and geriatric mobile support services.
5. Because of the aging population, increasing pollution levels and high unemployment, new 'green' ways of dealing with the resulting challenges will need to be developed.

**We will collect the demographic statistics for the following zip code(s):**

_____

We will use the following sources: www.census.gov, www.zipskinny.com, www.city-data.com, www.demographicsnow.com, www.freedemographics.com, www.ffiec.gov/geocode, www.esri.com/data/esri_data/tapestry and www.claritas.com/claritas/demographics.jsp. This information will be used to decide upon which targeted programs to offer and to make business growth projections.
**Resource:** www.sbdcnet.org/index.php/demographics.html

**Snapshots of consumer data by zip code are also available online:**
http://factfinder.census.gov/home/saff/main.html?_lang=en
http://www.esri.com/data/esri_data/tapestry.html
http://www.claritas.com/MyBestSegments/Default.jsp?ID=20

1. **Total Population**         _____
2. **Number of Households**     _____
3. **Population by Race:**      White ____% Black ____%
                                Asian Pacific Islander ____% Other ____%
4. **Population by Gender**     Male ____% Female ____%
5. **Income Figures:**          Median Household Income $_____
                                Household Income Under $50K ____%
                                Household Income $50K-$100K ____%
                                Household Income Over $100K ____%

6. **Housing Figures**  Average Home Value - $_____
   Average Rent  $_____
7. **Homeownership**: Homeowners  % _____
   Renters  % _____
8. **Education Achievement**  High School Diploma  % _____
   College Degree  % _____
   Graduate Degree  % _____
9. **Stability/Newcomers**  Longer than 5 years  % _____
10. **Marital Status**  ___% Married   ___% Divorced   ___% Single
    __% Never Married  __% Widowed  __% Separated
11. **Occupations**  ___%Service   ___% Sales ___% Management
    ___% Construction ___% Production
    ___% Unemployed ___% Below Poverty Level
12. **Age Distribution**  ___%Under 5 years  ___%5-9 yrs  ___%10-12 yrs
    ___% 13-17 yrs  ___%18-years
    ___% 20-29  ___% 30-39  ___% 40-49  ___% 50-59
    ___% 60-69  ___% 70-79  ___% 80+ years
13. **Average Age**  ___ years.
14. **Prior Growth Rate**  _____ % from _____ (year)
15. **Projected Population Growth Rate**  _____ %
16. **Employment Trend**  _____
17. **Unemployment Rate**  _____

**Secondary Market Research Conclusions:**
This area will be demographically favorable for our business for the following reasons:
Ex: The number of families with kids in the middle and high-income categories in ____ (city) are both increasing at a significant ____ rate.
_____
_____
_____

**Resources:**
www.allbusiness.com/marketing/segmentation-targeting/848-1.html
http://www.sbdcnet.org/industry-links/demographics-links
http://factfinder2.census.gov/faces/nav/jsf/pages/index.xhtml

## 4.1.1  Primary Market Research

We plan to develop a survey for primary research purposes and mail it to a list of local food magazine subscribers, purchased from the publishers by zip code. We will also post a copy of the survey on our website and encourage visitors to take the survey. We will use the following survey questions to develop an Ideal Customer Profile of our potential client base, so that we can better target our marketing communications. To improve the response rate, we will include an attention-grabbing _____ (discount coupon/ dollar?) as a thank you for taking the time to return the questionnaire.

1. What is your zip-code?
2. Are you single, divorced, separated, widowed or married?
3. Are you male or female?
4. What is your age?
5. What is your approximate household income?
6. What is your educational level?
7. What is your profession?
8. Are you a dual income household?
9. Do you have children? If Yes, what are their ages?
10. What are your favorite magazines?
11. What is your favorite local newspaper?
12. What is your favorite radio station?
13. What are your favorite television programs?
14. What organizations are you a member of?
15. How frequently do you use the services of a caterer?
16. On what occasions do you use a catering service?
17. Please prioritize the importance of the following factors when choosing a mobile catering service.     Scale: 1 to 12
    - ___ Price
    - ___ Menu Selection
    - ___ Overall Value
    - ___ Wraparound Services
    - ___ References
    - ___ Organic Items
    - ___ Food Quality
    - ___ Service Quality
    - ___ Cleanliness
    - ___ Signature Items
    - ___ Convenience
    - ___ Other _____
18. What is your favorite local restaurant? Why?
19. What items would you like to see on a lunch truck menu?
20. What average price per person are you interested in spending?
21. Who presently handles your catering business?
22. What are their strengths and weaknesses?
23. Would you consider buying from a food truck for breakfast or lunch?
24. What is your favorite breakfast item? _____ Price: _____
25. What is your favorite lunch item? _____ Price: _____
26. Would you be interested in the delivery of freshly cooked home replacement meals?
27. What will it take for you to switch your patronage to our mobile lunch truck?
28. What can we do to improve/differentiate our mobile service offerings?
29. What is the best way for us to market our mobile catering services?
30. Would you like to be a free subscriber to our newsletter?     Yes / No
31. Does our community have an adequate number of Mobile Food Trucks?
32. Does your family currently patronize a local Mobile Food Truck? Yes / No
33. Are you satisfied with your current Mobile Food Truck?
34. How many times on average per month do you buy from a Food Truck?
35. What menu items do you typically purchase?
36. On average, how much do you spend on Mobile Food Truck purchases per

month?
37. What is the name of your currently patronized Mobile Food Truck?
38. What are their strengths as service providers?
39. What are their weaknesses or shortcomings?
40. What would it take for us to earn your Mobile Food Truck business?
41. What is the best way for us to market our Mobile Food Truck?
42. Describe your experience with other Mobile Food Trucks.
43. Please rank (1 to 17) the importance of the following factors when choosing an Mobile Food Truck:

    ___ Quality of service     ___ Professional competence
    ___ Reputation     ___ Staff Personality/Attitude
    ___ Waiting time before service     ___ Custom blending
    ___ Availability of catering services     ___ Organic product selection
    ___ Convenient location scheduling     ___ Scheduling Convenience
    ___ Value Proposition     ___ Referral/References
    ___ Complaint Handling     ___ Security Measures
    ___ Vehicle Cleanliness     ___ In-stock availability
    ___ Other Foodservice Options     ___ Other _____

44. What information would you like to see in our Mobile Food Truck newsletter?
45. Which online social groups have you joined? Choose the ones you access.

    ___ Facebook     ___ MySpace
    ___ Twitter     ___ LinkedIn
    ___ Ryze     ___ Ning

46. What types of Mobile Food Truck services would most interest you?
47. What is your general need for an Mobile Food Truck?
Circle Months: J F M A M J J A S O N D (All)
Circle Days:     S M T W T F S (All)
Indicate Hours: _____ or (24 hours)
48. What are your suggestions for realizing a better Mobile Food Truck experience?
49. Are you on our mailing list? Yes/No     If No, can we add you?     Yes / No
50. Would you be interested in attending a free seminar on the health benefits of organic food?

Please note any comments or concerns about Mobile Food Trucks in general.
We very much appreciate your participation in this survey. If you provide your name, address and email address, we will sign you up for our e-newsletter, inform you of our survey results, advise you of any Mobile Food Truck opening in your community, and enter you into our monthly drawing for a free _____.
Name     Address
Email     Phone

## 4.1.2 Voice of the Customer

To develop a better understanding of the needs and wants of our Mobile Food Truck customers, we will institute the following ongoing listening practices:

1. Focus Groups
   Small groups of customers (6 to 8) will be invited to meet with a facilitator to answer open-ended questions about priority of needs and wants, and our company, its products or other given issues. These focus groups will provide useful insight into the decisions and the decision-making process of target consumers.
2. Individual Interviews
   We will conduct face-to-face personal interviews to understand customer thought processes and taste preferences.
3. Customer Panels
   A small number of customers will be invited to answer open-ended questions on a regular basis.
4. Customer Tours
   We will invite customers to visit our facilities to discuss how our processes can better serve them.
5. Visit Customers
   We will observe customers as they actually use our products to uncover the pains and problems they are experiencing during product consumption.
6. Trade Show Meetings
   Our trade show booth will be used to hear the concerns of our customers.
7. Toll-free Numbers
   We will attach our phone number to all products and sales literature to encourage the customer to call with problems or positive feedback.
8. Customer Surveys
   We will use surveys to obtain opinions on closed-ended questions, testimonials, constructive feedback, and improvement suggestions.
9. Mystery Shoppers
   We will use mystery shoppers to report on how our employees treat our customers.
10. Salesperson Debriefing
    We will ask our salespeople to report on their customer experiences to obtain insights into what the customer faces, what they want and why they failed to make a catering sale.
11. Customer Contact Logs
    We will ask our sales personnel to record interesting customer revelations.
12. Customer Serviceperson's Hotline
    We will use this dedicated phone line for service people to report problems.
13. Discussions with competitors.
14. Installation of suggestion boxes to encourage constructive feedback. The suggestion card will have several statements customers are asked to rate in terms of a given scale. There are also several open-ended questions that allow the customer to freely offer constructive criticism or praise. We will work hard to implement reasonable suggestions to improve our service offerings as well as show our commitment to the customer that their suggestions are valued.

## 4.2 Market Segmentation

Market segmentation is a technique that recognizes that the potential universe of users may be divided into definable sub-groups with different characteristics. Segmentation enables organizations to target messages to the needs and concerns of these subgroups. We will segment the market based on the needs and wants of select customer groups. We will develop a composite customer profile and a value proposition for each of these segments. The purpose for segmenting the market is to allow our marketing/sales program to focus on the subset of prospects that are "most likely" to purchase our mobile food truck products and services. If done properly this will help to insure the highest return for our marketing/sales expenditures.

Many truck operators are experimenting with new flavors and cuisines not typical of street vendors in order to reach a new clientele. Traditionally, taco trucks were very working class, janitors, secretaries, people on public transit, but now they've been adopted by the middle class as a legitimate way to buy and sell food

The end-user of our healthy food truck menu items can be categorized as follows; they are professionals between the ages of 25 and 55, living in the greater _____ area with a salary of greater than $__ (35,000?) per year. They are health conscious and enjoy eating more adventurous, good-tasting healthy foods and prefer to shop on specialty food trucks for convenience and time savings.

The _____ (city) retail market for gourmet healthy foods is estimated to be $___ million and sales have grown at an average annual rate of ____ (7?) per cent over the last ____ (5?) years. This translates into more than ____ (#) units of product being sold per year in the greater _____ (city) area.

_____ (company name) will focus on the following significant customer groups:

1. **Working Families with Children**:
   Working couples have the surplus incomes to try out places which are trendy and healthy at the same time. Many of the young families moving into the _____ area, are doing so because of its unique community environment. Its close proximity to the university also attracts young families where one or both parents are students or employees of the university. These families are a strong customer base for _____ (company name). Additionally, dual income families rely on catering and meal replacement support because of their time-deprived schedules.
2. **Students**:
   A significant number of students prefer to shop at an organic or all-natural food store. Our truck will be within walking distance for most area residents. Our location will make our truck a convenient place to shop on the way home from classes for healthy snacks and treats.
3. **Seniors:**
   Seniors will welcome the opportunity to purchase healthy foods that support their doctor ordered special diets.

4. **Professionals**
   This group is very educated and health conscious, and wants to look and feel healthier to better deal with the stress of normal life, and live a longer and healthy lifestyle.
5. **Dieters**
   This group is particularly interested in healthy foods that are both very delicious and very low in fats and sugars.
6. **Medical Providers**
   We will make medical providers aware of the health benefits of our organic meals so they can recommend us to their customers.

The total potential market in units is shown in the following table and chart.
   There are approximately ____ (#) business in ____ (city) that could potentially be our customers. We used ____ (20?) % market share as a starting point with ____ (10?)% growth per year.
   There are ____ (#) residents in ____ (city), according to the 2000 U.S. Census, with ____ (3?) % projected growth over the next ten years.
   Visitors were estimated using _____ Visitation Report. From ____ to ____ (years), an average of _____ (#) people visited the city attractions annually. We did not include projected growth, because we used an average number, and believe that visitation will remain similar over the next five years.

Even though the commuter population appears to be the largest market segment, it is probable that much of our sales will come from local business people at lunch time looking for a quick light dessert and a spirit lifting, but healthy frozen treat indulgence. The local population is important, because they can carry us through the slow visitation months, and will determine whether we become an established community attraction. The profile of the _____ (company name) client consists of the following geographic, demographic, psychographic and behavior factors:

**Geographics**
   - The geographic market is the _____ (middle class/ affluent) sector within the ____ (city), with a population of _____ people.
   - The total target market population is estimated to be _____ (#) people.

**Demographics**
   The biggest buyers of foods from mobile vendors are young adults and parents with children at home. Those aged 25 to 34 are the largest consumers of snacks from mobile vendors, spending an average of $ 44 a month

**Psychographics**
   - Reads lifestyle magazines, including Home, Country Home and Vegan.
   - Maintains an active and healthy lifestyle.

**Behaviors**
   - Takes pride in personal appearance.
   - Have limited time for lunch or to prepare family meals.

# Composite Ideal Customer Profile:

By assembling this composite customer profile, we will know what customer needs and wants our company needs to focus on and how best to reach our target market. We will use the information gathered from our customer research surveys to assemble the following composite customer profile:

**Ideal Customer Profile**

Who are they?
- age _____
- gender _____
- occupation _____
- location: zip codes _____
- income level _____
- marital status _____
- ethnic group _____
- education level _____
- family life cycle _____
- number of household members _____
- household income _____
- homeowner or renter _____
- association memberships _____
- leisure activities _____
- hobbies/interests _____
- core beliefs _____

Where are they located (zip codes)? _____
Most popular product/service purchased? _____
Lifestyle Preferences? Trendsetter/Trend follower/Other _____
How often do they buy? _____
What are most important purchase factors? Price/Brand Name/Quality/Financing/Sales Convenience/Packaging/Other_____

What is their key buying motivator? _____
How do they buy it? Cash/Credit/Terms/Other_____
Where do they buy it from (locations)? _____
What problem do they want to solve? _____
What are the key frustrations/pains that these customers have when buying? _____
What search methods do they use? _____
What is preferred problem solution? _____

**Table: Market Analysis**

| | | Number of Potential Customers | | |
|---|---|---|---|---|
| **Potential Customers** | **Growth** | **2017** | **2018** | **2019** |
| Working Families | 10% | _____ | | |
| Local Businesses | 10% | _____ | | |
| Students | 10% | _____ | | |

76

| | | |
|---|---|---|
| Commuters | 10% | _____ |
| Seniors | 10% | _____ |
| Professionals | 10% | _____ |
| Dieters | 10% | _____ |
| Totals: | 10% | _____ |

## 4.3  Target Market Segment Strategy

Our target marketing strategy will involve identifying a group of customers to which to direct our mobile food truck products and services. Our strategy will be the result of intently listening to and understanding customer needs, representing customers' needs to those responsible for product production and service delivery, and giving them what they want. In developing our targeted customer messages, we will strive to understand things like: where they work, worship, party and play, where they food shop and go to school, how they spend their leisure time, and where they volunteer their time. We will use research, surveys and observation to uncover this wealth of information to get our product details and brand name in front of our customers when they are most receptive to receiving our messaging.

Target Market Worksheet                                              (optional)

**Product Benefits:** Actual factor (cost effectiveness, design, performance, etc.) or perceived factor (image, popularity, reputation, etc.) that satisfies what a customer needs or wants. An advantage or value that the product will offer its buyer.

**Products Features:** One of the distinguishing characteristics of a product or service that helps boost its appeal to potential buyers. A characteristic of a product that describes its appearance, its components, and its capabilities. Typical features include size and color.

| Product or Service | Product/ Service Benefits | Product/ Service Features | Potential Target Markets |
|---|---|---|---|
| | | | |

The last ten years have seen an increase in American's explorations of health, ethnic and gourmet foods. Whether this can be attributed to celebrity chefs, travel to foreign countries, new health diets, or the increasing accessibility of once-obscure ingredients, it seems that gourmet and adventurous palates seeking healthier alternatives are here to stay.

Many residents are now just as sophisticated in their food tastes as our tourists. In ___ (city), residents often use travel to larger cities as occasions to stock up on health food and gourmet items not available locally. However, they prefer to shop locally whenever possible, and would welcome a healthy ice cream and mobile service that offers this combination of features.

____ (city) is growing at ___ (3?) % a year, allowing for increased business opportunities. Our natural attractions are in no danger of becoming polluted or otherwise less accessible, and so we expect continued market growth for the foreseeable future. Our marketing programs towards different target market segments will utilize different publications and media, but all will emphasize our good value, high quality, unique and varied healthy selections, convenience and great fast service. Our marketing strategy will create awareness, interest and demand from our target markets for our healthy menu items.

Restaurant industry consulting group Technomic's October, 2010 ConcepTrac focused on food trucks. The report said that while the mobile units offer cost savings and agility, their customers are more likely to be value seekers and those interested in trying something new.

## Target Marketing

| Business | Event | Marketing Tactic |
| --- | --- | --- |
| Law Offices | Entertain customers<br>Welcome New Associates | Direct Mail |
| General Contractor | Completed Renovation<br>Ground Breaking | Flyers |
| Real Estate Agents | Property Closing<br>Housewarming | Business Cards<br>Sales Brochures |
| Church Groups | Religious Occasions | Church Bulletin/Donation |

**Target Local Corporations**

Many large companies choose to use both mobile catering and vending as food service options for their employees. Instead of fighting this fact, we will embrace it, find a reliable partner, and use it as a competitive advantage. By introducing a lunch truck to the account, the removal of an underutilized fresh food vending machine will seem much less painful. The cost of maintaining refrigerated food machines combined with the decrease in waste and service frequency will make using a mobile catering partner a smart decision for local corporations. We will also bring in catering trucks, at no charge to the customer, to replace costly, subsidized cafeterias.

To market to businesses, we will visit businesses in the areas we plan to work in and ask to speak with the manager. We will leave a sales packet for future reference. Our sales packet will include a business card, sales letter, brochure, a list of clients and companies we have worked for in the past, and a price sheet so they will have an idea of what it will cost to hire our mobile catering services. We will also help the business to perform a cost-benefit analysis to compare alternative foodservice arrangements.

Businesses will expect us to fill the role of party planner and handle every aspect of the event, including the knowing of client requirements and preferences. We plan to create a list of all the possible reasons why a business might need the services of a mobile caterer, and incorporate that list into your sales literature and presentation.

Examples: Trade shows, seminars, conferences, employee appreciation/recognition events, executive promotions and retirement parties, Christmas Party, semi-annual field day, project milestone accomplishments, business meeting luncheons, etc.

**Target Vending Companies**
As a mobile caterer we will operate our own commissary. Vending companies large and small can always use new frozen treat and sandwich sources. We plan to provide frozen novelties and sandwiches for vending operators. Based on volume, daily deliveries, private labeling, and even special orders will be accommodated to vending companies.
Resources:
National Automated Merchandising Association		www.namanow.org/

**Target Mobile Food Fairs and Festivals**
Mobile Food Festivals and Fairs are always looking for unique vendors to enhance their overall attendance. Diversity in frozen desserts will be one way for our company to stand out amongst other food vendors. We will also have to cater to the tastes of our local customers and the needs of the festivals and fairs that we attend. By attending local fairs and festivals, we will be maximizing our visibility and positioning our food truck where crowds of hungry diners will be congregated.
Resources:
http://www.sacfoodtrucks.net/2011/12/tips-for-mobile-food-festivals.html
http://www.foodreference.com/html/upcomingfoodevents.html
http://www.festivals-and-shows.com/festivals.html
http://festivalnet.com/

**Target Retail Sponsored Special Events**
We will target businesses, such as car dealerships, that have special day or weekend events and supply food. We will visit the car and motorcycle dealerships and leave behind a flyer or business card. We will contact the local radio stations because they will provide a D.J. for special events and actually host the show from the event, and will be aware of those events weeks in advance and may be willing to pass leads on or create a package which includes a D.J. and food. We will send flyers out in the mail to local businesses. We will also approach strip plazas, because many have merchant groups who are looking for promotions and other methods to draw customers to their stores. Local charitable events, such as walk-a-thons and bicycling events, draw large crowds and we will offer the organizers a piece of the gross proceeds towards their charity, if we can set-up at the event.

Example:
Off-the-Grid			http://offthegrid.com
Began in June 2010 with the idea of grouping Street Food vendors together to create an experience that allows neighbors to connect with friends, and families to reconnect with each other. Since then, their events have become a Bay Area icon and quintessential San

Franciscan activity, known for its unique food and cultural experiences. They currently operate 50+ weekly public events throughout the San Francisco Bay Area.

### Target Factories, Industrial Complexes, and Office Buildings
We will target the workers at these facilities because they have the potential to generate steady repeat business on a daily basis.

### Target Groups Holding Private Events
The new market for vending cart operators is private events; everything from birthday and anniversary parties, company picnics, little league sports events, to boys' and girls' club outings. The group or individual holding the event contracts with the vending cart operator to supply ice cream services at their event. We will market this service through our Yellow Page Ads and Website.

### Target Vineyards and Wineries
We will target these businesses because they often like to introduce food to their wine tasting events.
Example:
https://mobile-cuisine.com/events/food-truck-friday-at-sebastiani-vineyards-and-winery/
Resources:
Directories of Wineries
www.winesandvines.com/template.cfm?section=subscribe&product=directory

### Target Farmer's Markets
At Farmers Market locations we will offer locally-sourced ingredients, such as home-grown meat and picked-that-day produce. We will thoroughly test this market as this type of location can supply a recurring, ample supply of foot traffic.
Source:
http://restaurantengine.com/food-trucks-choose-best-locations/
Resources:
National Farmer's Market Directory
www.ams.usda.gov/local-food-directories/farmersmarkets

### Target Event Planners
We will advise event and corporate promotion planners of our mobile catering capabilities.

### Target Event and Facility Managers
We will visit with these managers and make them aware of our mobile foodservice capabilities. We will also attend their trade shows and networking events.

Resources:
### Directory of Event Planning Associations:
- ILEA: International Live Events Association
- NACE: National Association for Catering and Events
- ESPA: Event Services Professional Association

- MPI: Meetings Professionals International
- ICCA: International Congress and Convention Association
- GMIC: Green Meetings Industry Council
- CEMA: Corporate Event Marketing Association
- IAVM: International Association of Venue Managers
- NCBMP: National Coalition for Black Meeting Planners
- Eventovation: A Community for Anyone in The Events Industry
- PCMA: Professional Convention Management Association
- SGMP: Society of Government Meeting Professionals

Source:
https://blog.bizzabo.com/event-planning-associations

## Target Local Concert and Festival Promoters

We will approach concert and festival promoters about the possibility of servicing their attendees at scheduled events.
Resources:
North American Concert Promoters Association
    www.guidestar.org/profile/54-1490468
    https://greatnonprofits.org/org/north-american-concert-promoters-association

## Target City's Park District

We will target local park district's because they are creating event series in their parks, that also serve to welcome food trucks to enhance the experience and build the attendance factor.
Examples:
https://mobile-cuisine.com/events/food-trucks-in-chicagos-grant-park-new-event-series/

## Target College Administrators

We will ask about the possibility of providing our mobile food truck services on-campus and at major school events, such as graduation ceremonies, guest lectures, and sports tournaments.

## Target Construction Sites

We will target construction sites and contract our services with the foreman.

## Target Big Box Retailers

We will seek to operate in the parking lots of high traffic big box retailers, providing we have obtained the necessary permission. We will ask to allow our cart or truck on their property in return for a share of the profits.

## Target Little League Parks

We will target Little League Parks to perfect our operating procedures and menu.
Resources:
Find a Local League
    www.littleleague.org/learn/Start_Find_a_League/LLB_League_Finder.htm

**Target Local Schools**
We will contact local schools and colleges to support their sports team celebrations. We will also seek to service college students during the slower summer months when many of their local foodservice businesses temporarily close for the vacation period.

**Target Fitness Clubs**
Contact local fitness clubs and get permission to set-up a temporary booth to give free menu tastings of our healthy ice cream products to their members.
Resources:
Find Gyms by Location          www.gymsandfitnessclubs.com/gyms-by-location/

**Target Daycare Centers**
We will give daycare providers what they need for easy and delicious desserts that kids love. By enrolling in our Home Service Daycare Program licensed daycares will be eligible to receive one free* product with a $___ purchase. Child care providers will need to provide their state issued licensed, registered or certified daycare number. The USDA operates a federal program that allows daycares to be reimbursed for serving nutritious desserts and snacks that meet United States Department of Agriculture (USDA) requirements. For providers participating in the Child and Adult Care Food Program (CACFP), ____ (company name) offers Child Nutrition (CN) labeled products and also provides specific product analysis sheets on several other products.
Resources:
www.gsa.gov/resources-for/citizens-consumers/child-care/child-care-services/find-a-child-care-center-near-you

**Target Families with Children**
Studies indicate that children influence parents as to which shop to patronize, and mothers make the final decision. Therefore, we will keep our truck mounted flat screen TV tuned to programs for our target kid audience.

**Target Mothers**
Our sweet spot will be free-spending women 18 to 34. They will buy more of our made-fresh home replacement meals. But half of them will show up with kids. For mothers, convenience means convenient access, flexible times and offerings, and value-driven pricing. Working mothers are also concerned about purchasing healthy meals for their children.

**Target Professional Women**
This segment is comprised of women in the age range of 25 to 50. They are married, have a household income >$80,000, own at least one home, and are socially active. They are members of at least one club or organization. They have the discretionary income to be adventurous with respect to uncovering new health-focused foodservice providers.

**Target Professional Young People**
This group is comprised of couples between the ages of 25 and 35, and are in the process of setting up their first adult household. They both work, earn in excess of $75,000

annually, and now want to invest in themselves. They seek to communicate a successful image to their friends and may have an interest in convenient, good-tasting, healthy food products and services.

**Target Millenials (ages 21 to 34)**
Millenials represent a quarter of the U.S. population, more than $200 billion in annual buying power and $500 billion in indirect spending, which considers their impact on other generations. They account for 21 to 25 percent of consumer discretionary purchases, and that is going to increase has they acquire more earning power. Millennials are reaching out to social networks and observing behaviors of their friends to look for new, novel, authentic experiences. Millennials don't look exclusively to their friends for information. They also process information from lots of sources, because they do want an accurate, authoritative portrayal of an experience they are hoping to enjoy. As marketers, we will provide useful information to potential clients via social networking sites. In fact, JWT data from March 2014 suggests that millennial travelers are more likely to grab their smartphones to access their social networks, Yelp reviews or foursquare users to garner real-time suggestions and find local information while on the go. We will provide these types of "concierge-like" services to reach millennials. And to gain the initial trust of these customers, we will join conversations, participate in forums and comment on blogs, already in progress, rather than interrupt them to start and control conversations of our own. We will also practice nostalgia marketing to connect with millenials and use content that reminds them how they have changed from their common, shared experiences in the 90s.

**Target Aging Baby Boomers**
Since people age 50 and older have more discretionary money and are more prone to ailments, they are more likely to take advantage of new health food products and processes. As the baby boomers hit this age, we will see an even bigger trend toward healthy food consumption. This is also a group with an appreciation for delicious desserts and a need for comfort and relaxation. Our Mobile Food Truck will be a haven for the busy and successful who want to treat themselves to something good and tasty. These people will value the high-quality product presented without pretension. Our customers will also appreciate the fun, good value and fast service, whether celebrating a birthday or indulging before or after a concert.

**Target Gourmets**
Gourmets watch the Food Network and easily spend money exploring new taste sensations. They are adventuresome consumers and can become valuable influencers.

**Target Seniors**
Seniors with mobility problems will appreciate the convenience of our drive-up services. We will offer them discounts on healthy food products and services, and promote this program through the National Association of Area Agencies on Aging. We also plan to visit local nursing homes, assisted living facilities and independent living centers to learn how we can better accommodate the needs and taste preferences of local seniors. We will meet with senior physicians to learn more about senior dietary guidelines, and incorporate that knowledge into our product line. We will provide healthy eating classes

to local adult community centers.

**Target Teenagers**
This group increasingly suffers from obesity and diabetes, and needs to be educated on how to make healthier food choices. We will develop educational programs on healthy eating that we will introduce to local schools.

**Target Colleges and Universities**
We will market to local colleges and universities. Many colleges and universities set up short classes for individuals, and when they arrange these classes, they usually offer some kind of refreshments, lunch or dinner. We will market to colleges and universities through the college or university's newspaper, newsletter or magazine. In addition, we will run advertisements in magazines that are targeted at colleges student events.

Example:
Daymar College will be hosting a unique event Friday featuring food trucks and live bands with the intent of creating a block party experience for students and the community at large.
Source:  www.theleafchronicle.com/story/entertainment/events/2017/07/14/daymar-
college-hosts-food-truck-roundup-friday/86990046/

**Target Fund-Raisers**
We will contact schools, churches, non-profit organizations, and businesses that plan annual fund-raiser events. We will also contact the place hosting the fund-raiser and market our mobile catering business to them. The best person to contact is usually the fund-raiser's organizer.
Resources:
Association of Fundraising Professionals        www.afpnet.org/

**Target Bridal Centers and Wedding Consultants**
We will pursue bridal centers and wedding planners, because the catering of weddings on location can be very profitable because purchases are driven by emotions rather than logic. We will provide our food samples to a few wedding and event planners, and church members, and maintain good relations with them for future referrals. We will also place classified ads in church bulletins, and exhibit at wedding expos. We will develop several catering package options for wedding receptions to be held in park locations.
Resources:
American Association of Certified Wedding Planners    http://aacwp.org/
Association of Bridal Consultants        www.bridalassn.com/

**Target Local Ethnic Groups**
Ongoing demographic trends suggest that, in the coming decades, early childhood programs will be serving a population of children which is increasingly diverse in economic resources, racial and ethnic background, food preferences and family structure. Our plan is to reach out to consumers of various ethnic backgrounds, especially Hispanics, who comprise nearly 13 percent of the country's total population. In addition

to embarking on an aggressive media campaign of advertising with ethnic newspapers and radio stations, we will set up programs to actively recruit bilingual employees and make our truck more accessible via signage printed in various languages based on the truck's community. We will accurately translate our marketing materials into other languages. We will enlist the support of our bilingual employees to assist in reaching the ethnic people in our surrounding area through a referral program. We will join the nearest _____ (predominate ethnic group) Chamber of Commerce and partner with _____ (Hispanic/Chinese/Other?) Advocacy Agencies. We will also develop organic dessert-based programs that reflect ethnic ingredient and brand preferences.

**Helpful Resources:**
U.S. census Bureau Statistics                www.census.gov
U.S. Dept. of Labor/Bureau of Labor Statistics      www.bls.gov/data/home.htm
National Hispanic Medical Association

# 4.3.1     Market Needs

_____ (city) is in need of a quality ethnic foods that are currently only available in large cities or over the internet. Many residents tell stories of traveling to large cities with empty luggage so that they can fill their suitcase with specialty healthy foods they cannot find locally. The residents of \_\_\_ (city) are dedicated to protecting its "small town" feel and make a point to shop locally whenever possible. However, the residents of \_\_\_\_ (city) and its surrounding communities would be thrilled to be able to experience the healthy specialty meals and nutritious snacks they want near home.

Local and visiting customers desire high quality, healthy food that will appeal to their aesthetics. In addition, they desire a pleasant shopping experience that allows them to learn about and purchase the specialty items they want in a convenient, friendly, hassle-free environment. The market will respond to our distinct logo and slogan, reputation for fast service and the making of healthy meals with only the freshest ingredients.

The targeted market segment needs can be broken down into the following categories:
 1. High quality, healthy fast food products and catering services.
 2. Convenience
 3. High customer service.
 4. Good value.

# 4.4  Buying Patterns

A Buying Pattern is the typical manner in which /buyers consumers purchase goods or services or firms place their purchase orders in terms of amount, frequency, timing, etc. In determining buying patterns, we will need to understand the following:
   - Why consumers make the purchases that they make?
   - What factors influence consumer purchases?
   - The changing factors in our society.

In most cases, customers make the purchase decision on the basis of the following criteria:
1. Referrals and relationship with other customers.
2. Personality and expected relationship with the truck personnel.
3. Information gathering.

____ (company name) will gear its offerings, marketing, and pricing policies to establish a loyal client base. Our value-based pricing, convenient access, healthy foodservice programs, and basic quality organic products will be welcomed in _____ (city) and contribute to our success.

The health food industry, was founded on the fact that American consumers increasingly regarded health as a primary concern when buying food. The average food bill per individual at that time was more than four thousand dollars per year, of which almost half was spent on food away from home. As people became more concerned about healthful food in the 1980s and 1990s, consumption of organic foods increased. Because they are cultivated without synthetic additives, fertilizers, or pesticides, organic foods are better for consumers because many pesticides are systemic, meaning that the food absorbs so that they cannot be washed off. Organic coffee began gaining popularity as an alternative to conventional coffee sprayed with synthetic chemicals. From the late 1970s, increasing numbers of U.S. consumers turned to bottled water as an alternative to alcohol and chlorinated tap water as part of a health regimen.

Beside natural foods, food supplements such as vitamins and herbal products made up a large part of the health food industry. These supplements constituted a form of alternative medicine for people disenchanted with over-the-counter drugs and concerned about side effects of pharmaceuticals. Despite Food and Drug Administration regulations prohibiting the manufacturers of food supplements from making specific medical claims, sales of herbal supplements have risen at a double-digit rate for the past 10 years. We also plan to research the possibility of adding nutritional supplements to our organic smoothies.

Upscale Frozen Desserts Consumers are also taking a liking of upscale frozen desserts. Ice cream, gelato, frozen yogurt and even shaved ice concoctions are keeping customers cool as the industry heats up. Iced coffee has become very popular. Among iced coffee's biggest fans: women and teenage girls. Teens thrive on the hit from the caffeine while many women gravitate to iced coffee's aura of being lower in calories. In fact, teen girls are 84% more likely to have iced coffee than the average American, and women 18 to 34 are 68% more likely.

## 4.5     Market Growth

**We will assess the following general factors that affect market growth:**
Current Assessment

1. Interest Rates                      _____
2. Government Regulations              _____
3. Perceived Environment Impact        _____
4. Consumer Confidence Level           _____
5. Population Growth Rate              _____
6. Unemployment Rate                   _____
7. Political Stability                 _____
8. Currency Exchange Rate              _____
9. Innovation Rate                     _____
10. Home Sales                         _____
11. Gasoline Prices                    _____
12. Trend Linkage                      _____
13. Overall Economic Health            _____

Demographics, consumer tastes, and personal income drive demand. The profitability of individual companies can vary: while QSRs rely on efficient operations and high-volume sales, FSRs rely on high-margin items and effective marketing. Large companies have advantages in purchasing, finance, and marketing. Small companies can offer superior food or service. The industry is labor-intensive: annual revenue per worker is less than $50,000. Mobile Food Trucks compete with companies that serve desserts or prepared foods, including grocery stores, warehouse clubs, delis, and convenience stores.

We believe there is a market for our products and services in ___ (city) and that the market has potential for growth. _____ County's population in the year 2000 was ____ (#) and is expected to grow at a rate of ___ (3?) % over the next ten years.

It is expected that our business will grow as customers become familiar with the health need for our certified organic, freshly made meals.

American Demographics projects the number of U.S. households will grow by 15% to 115 million by the year 2014. These busy households will require a greater range of health store products and meals-on-the-go services.

One important factor is that married couples in the 35 to 65 age range represent a growth segment and enjoy larger incomes than other family structures. They welcome the choice to spend their disposable income on home replacement meals. Overall, the environment appears very positive for the ____ (company name). The forces driving market demand, mainly economic, are strong, with industry growth healthy and new residents moving into the area resulting in a greater demand for a nutritious fast-serve foodservice.

The general industry analysis shows that _____ (city) is expected to experience substantial population, housing and commercial business growth. This suggests that as more families continue to move into the _____ area, there will be an increasing demand for quality foodservices, and this makes it a prime location for a mobile healthy food truck service.

The health trend is also playing a significant role. With growing waistlines and little time for exercise, consumers are increasingly looking for short-cuts to improved health. While convenience and indulgence are the top priorities, diet-oriented consumers are growing in prominence. Common themes in their desired products include lower calories, lower fat, dairy-free, organic, low-carbohydrates, sugar-free and portion control. The third major growth stream is likely to be the development of exotic flavors and ingredients that cater to the tastes of particular ethnic groups and adventurous eaters.

Finally, people have less disposable income and are sticking around and not going on vacation. For these people, a break from the usual home foods is a much needed, inexpensive self-indulgence or form of escapism.

## 4.5.1 Other Buying Patterns

**Customer buying patterns typically revolve around the following factors:**
1. Speed of service compared with the time to assemble and prepare a home cooked affair.
3. Level of food and service quality compared to the many different options available in the marketplace.
4. The value proposition compared to the cost of buying all the ingredients and factoring in the opportunity time costs and energy to cook the meals from scratch.
5. The buying habits of the high end of the market revolve around the depth of the menu offerings, the branded reputation of the caterer, the attention to service and the uniqueness of the food presentation style and matching theme.
6. The middle end of the market is price sensitive and often selects the partial or no service options, with the best quality of food.
7. The availability of surplus income to pay for extra food services.
8. A lack of time for food preparation.
9. A population growth in the 18 to 60 age group.
10. The availability of funds for community development, charitable as well as industry-oriented, and increased marketing efforts.
11. A strong presence of charitable organizations that sponsor fundraising functions.
12. A strong interest from outside sources in holding meetings and conferences within the community.

Food Trucks are popular for their source of quality and value priced food. Mobile restaurants are naturally drawn to spaces of temporary density where outdoor activities benefit from the value-driven food and convenience of a curbside restaurant.

## 4.6.0 Service Business Analysis

Our success will depend on knowing our clientele, and what they want. Our challenges are to keep enough popular items in stock for repeat customers, while introducing new and seasonal items and specials frequently enough to keep buyers interested. Many gourmet food trucks offer desserts or individual dishes prepared in the truck. In addition to our frozen treats, _____ (company name) will have a deli, open for breakfast, lunch and dinner, and a canopy seating area. This part of our business competes with local restaurants and supermarkets. Our mini-deli must offer healthy foods that are familiar enough not to intimidate customers, but interesting, with new combinations of unique organic ingredients, to provide them with a sense of adventure and indulgence.

The demand for Mobile Food Trucks with expanded menus is increasing for the following reasons:
1. Dual income families need more healthy home replacement dessert options.
2. Busy professionals require more efficient shopping experiences and less wasted search time.
3. Consumers appreciate the one-stop convenience of healthy ice cream products, and nutritious fast food, delivered in a friendly and clean vehicle.
4. The number of older Americans is increasing almost three times as fast as the rest of the population, and subsequently adds to the demand for drive-thru services that offer healthy options for people on special diets.

Although _____ (company name) is striving to create a new niche in the food service industry, we do share similarities, and therefore compete with several kinds of quick-service dessert businesses:
1. Restaurants: any restaurant offering take-out food.
2. National Ice Cream Shops: Baskin & Robbins, Ben & Jerry's, etc.
3. Donut and Coffee Shops offering breakfast items.
4. Supermarkets selling replacement meals.
5. Bakeries selling exotic breads, bagels and sandwiches.

Food trucks encourage innovation and diversification by allowing passionate people to specialize in just a few menu items. Because of the low overhead for truck and street vendors, they can offer what is sometimes a superior food product for a price cheaper than a brick-and-mortar restaurant. And since most items are made fresh daily — some within hours, or even minutes of being ordered, the trucks represent a desirable alternative to chain restaurants. Food truck owners have created a community of like-minded business owners who benefit from a shared mission.

Overall this mature industry is expected to continue to consolidate, with some operators ceasing to trade. Meanwhile others may see the opportunity to expand their operations further into the foyers of shopping malls, offices, railway and bus stations, and other public areas. Employment in this industry is forecast to decline marginally over the next few years.

## 4.7 Barriers to Entry

_____ (company name) will benefit from the following combination of barriers to entry, which cumulatively present a moderate degree of entry difficulty or obstacles in the path of other Mobile Food Truck businesses wanting to enter our market.

1. Business Experience.
2. Community Networking
3. Referral Program
4. People Skills
5. Marketing Skills
6. Supplier Relationships
7. Operations Management
8. Cash Flow Management
9. Website Design
10. Capital Investment
11. Health Food Knowledge
12. Vehicle Customization
13. Innovative Recipe Design

## 4.7.1 Porter's Five Forces Analysis

We will use Porter's five forces analysis as a framework for the industry analysis and business strategy development. It will be used to derive the five forces which determine the competitive intensity and therefore attractiveness of our market. Attractiveness in this context refers to the overall industry profitability.

**Competitors**   The degree of rivalry is high in this segment, but less when compared to the overall category. There are _____ (#) major competitors in the _____ area and they include: _____

**Threat of Substitutes**
Substitutes are high for this industry. These include other mobile food trucks, restaurants, food carts, diners, burger stands, etc.

**Bargaining Power of Buyers**
Buyer power is moderate in the business. Buyers are sensitive to quality, convenience and pricing as the segment attempts to capitalize on the pricing, convenience and food quality advantage.

**Bargaining Power of Suppliers**
Supplier power is moderate in the industry. Supplies can be obtained from a number of wholesale food distributors. A high level of operational efficiency for managing supplies can be achieved.

**Threat of New Entrants**
Relatively high in this segment. The business model can be easily copied.

**Conclusions:** _____ (company name) is in a competitive field and has to move fast to retain its competitive advantage. The key success factors are to develop operational efficiencies, innovative programs, cost-effective marketing and customer service excellence.

## 4.8 Competitive Analysis

**Competitor analysis** in marketing and strategic management is an assessment of the strengths and weaknesses of current and potential competitors. This analysis will provide both an offensive and defensive strategic context through which to identify our business opportunities and threats. We will carry out continual competitive analysis to ensure our market is not being eroded by developments in other firms. This analysis will be matched with the target segment needs to ensure that our products and services continue to provide better value than the competitors. The competitive analysis will show very clearly why our products and services are preferred in some market segments to other offerings and to be able to offer reasonable proof of that assertion.

| Competitor | What We Can Do and They Can't | What They Can Do and We Can't |
|---|---|---|
| | | |
| | | |

In the Mobile Food Truck/health food industry, businesses must distinguish themselves from competitors (grocery stores, restaurants, cafes) by offering unique, hard-to-find organic products, and/or interesting, difficult-to-make healthy prepared foods. They must convince customers that the special nutritional quality of their products and service is worth the price they pay.

In ____ (city), customers shop for food products based on convenience, selection, and price. _____ (company name) does not intend to compete with regular grocery stores on standard items. Instead, we will exploit a previously unoccupied niche: the combination of gourmet meals and Mobile Food Truck convenience, offering items otherwise unobtainable locally. ____ (city) residents looking for gourmet foods are also looking for convenience, healthy food selection and price, and our competitors for their business (stores in larger towns, online, etc.) are less convenient (farther away or longer waits for delivery), although they offer similar selections and prices.

Food trucks are starting to find some stiff competition to attract the same customers. We will do some reconnaissance work to see what our competition is charging for similar menu items. We will also check out the prices of fast casual restaurants in our area to find how they are pricing their menus. We will attempt to make up for some pricing differences by offering better or faster customer service and/or higher quality ingredients.

We will conduct good market intelligence for the following reasons:
1. To forecast competitors' strategies.
2. To predict competitor likely reactions to our own strategies.
3. To consider how competitors' behavior can be influenced in our own favor.
Overall competition in the area is _____ (weak/moderate/strong).

Competitive analysis conducted by the company owners has shown that there are _____ (# or no other?) Mobile Food Trucks currently offering the same combination of products and services in the _____ (city) area. However, the existing competitors offer only a limited range of traditional food products and services. In fact, of these _____ (#) competitors only _____ (#) offered a range of organic products and healthy gourmet meals comparable with what _____ (company name) plans to offer to its customers.

## Self-assessment

**Competitive Rating Assessment:**  1 = Weak ........................5 = Strong

|  | Our Company | Prime Competitor | Compare |
|---|---|---|---|
| Our Location | _____ | _____ | _____ |
| Our Facilities | _____ | _____ | _____ |
| Our Services and Amenities | _____ | _____ | _____ |
| Our Management Skills | _____ | _____ | _____ |
| Our Training Programs | _____ | _____ | _____ |
| Our Research & Development | _____ | _____ | _____ |
| Our Company Culture | _____ | _____ | _____ |
| Our Business Model | _____ | _____ | _____ |
| Overall Rating | _____ | _____ | _____ |

Rationale: _____

**The following businesses are considered direct competitors in _____ (city):**

| Competitor | Address | Market Share | Primary Focus | Secondary Prod/Svcs | Strengths | Weaknesses |
|---|---|---|---|---|---|---|
| | | | | | | |

_____
_____

**Indirect Competitors include the following:**
_____
_____

## Alternative Competitive Matrix

| Competitor Name: | <u>Us</u> | _____ | _____ | _____ |
|---|---|---|---|---|
| Location: | | _____ | _____ | _____ |
| Location Distance (miles) | | _____ | _____ | _____ |

**Comparison Items:**

| | |
|---|---|
| Sales Revenue | _____ |
| Buying Power | _____ |
| Product Focus | _____ |
| Membership Programs | _____ |
| Franchise Y/N | _____ |
| National Chain Y/N | _____ |
| Breakfast Menu Y/N | _____ |
| Lunch Menu Y/N | _____ |
| No. of Flavors | _____ |
| Ice Cream Grade | _____ |
| Yogurt Y/N | _____ |
| Services | _____ |
| Custom Blending Y/N | _____ |
| Catering Y/N | _____ |
| Profitability | _____ |
| Market Share | _____ |
| Brand Name | _____ |

Specialty  _____
Services  _____
Capitalization  _____
Target Markets  _____
Service Area  _____
Open Days  _____
Operating Hours  _____
Operating Policies  _____
Payment Options  _____
Other Financing  _____
Pricing Strategy  _____
Price Level  L/M/H  _____
Discounts  _____
Yrs in Business  _____
Reputation  _____
Reliability  _____
Quality  _____
Marketing Strategy  _____
Methods of Promotion  _____
Alliances  _____
Brochure/Catalog  _____
Website  _____
Sales Revenues  _____
No. of Staff  _____
Competitive Advantage  _____
Manufacturers Used  _____
Comments  _____

## Competitor Profile Matrix

|  | Our | Competitor 1 | | Competitor 2 | | Competitor 3 | |
|---|---|---|---|---|---|---|---|
| Critical Success Factors | Score | Rating | Score | Rating | Score | Rating | Score |
| Advertising | | | | | | | |
| Product Quality | | | | | | | |
| Service Quality | | | | | | | |
| Price Competition | | | | | | | |
| Management | | | | | | | |
| Financial Position | | | | | | | |
| Customer Loyalty | | | | | | | |
| Brand Identity | | | | | | | |
| Market Share | | | | | | | |
| Total | | | | | | | |

**We will use the following sources of information to conduct our competition analysis:**

1. Competitor company websites.

2. Mystery shopper visits.
3. Annual Reports (www.annual reports.com)
4. Thomas Net (www.thomasnet.com)
5. Trade Journals
6. Trade Associations
7. Sales representative interviews
8. Research & Development may come across new patents.
9. Market research can give feedback on the customer's perspective
10. Monitoring services will track a company or industry you select for news. Resources: www.portfolionews.com www.Office.com
11. Hoover's www.hoovers.com
12. www.zapdata.com (Dun and Bradstreet) You can buy one-off lists here.
13. www.infousa.com (The largest, and they resell to many other vendors)
14. www.onesource.com (By subscription, they pull information from many sources)
15. www.capitaliq.com (Standard and Poors).
16. Obtain industry specific information from First Research (www.firstresearch.com) or IBISWorld, although both are by subscription only, although you may be able to buy just one report.
17. Get industry financial ratios and industry norms from RMA (www.rmahq.com) or by using ProfitCents.com software.
18. Company newsletters
19. Industry Consultants
20. Suppliers and Distributors
21. Customer interviews regarding competitors.
22. Analyze competitors' ads for their target audience, market position, product features, benefits, prices, etc.
23. Attend speeches or presentations made by representatives of your competitors.
24. View competitor's trade show display from a potential customer's point of view.
25. Search computer databases (available at many public libraries).
26. Competitor Yellow Book Ads.

## 4.9 Market Revenue Projection

For each of our chosen target markets, we will estimate our market share in number of customers, and based on consumer behavior, how often do they buy per year? What is the average dollar amount of each purchase? We will then multiply these three numbers to project sales volume for each target market.

| Target Market | Number of Customers | No. of Purchases per Year | Average Dollar Amount per Purchase | Total Sales Volume |
|---|---|---|---|---|
| | A x | B x | C = | D |

Using the target market number identified in this section, and the local demographics, we have made the following assessments regarding market opportunity and revenue potential in our area:

**Potential Revenue Opportunity** =

|     |        |                                        |
|-----|--------|----------------------------------------|
|     | _____ | Local No. of Households (>40K Income)  |
| (x) | _____ | Expected ___% Market Share             |
| (=) | _____ | Number of likely local customers       |
| (x) | $_____ | Average annual fee dollar amount      |
| (=) | $_____ | Annual Revenue Opportunity.           |

Or

|                     | No. of customers Per Day | (x) Avg. Sale | (=) Daily Income |
|---------------------|--------------------------|---------------|------------------|
| Gourmet Meals       | _____               | _____    | _____       |
| Healthy Beverages   | _____               | _____    | _____       |
| Healthy Desserts    | _____               | _____    | _____       |
| Replacement Meals   | _____               | _____    | _____       |
| Other               | _____               | _____    | _____       |
| Total:              |                          |               | _____       |
| Annualized:         |                          | (x)           | 300              |
| Annual Revenue Potential: |                    |               | _____       |

Recap

| Month | Jan Feb Mar Apr May Jun Jul Aug Sep Oct Nov Dec   Total |
|-------|---------------------------------------------------------|
| Products | _____ |
|          | _____ |
| Services | _____ |
|          | _____ |
| Gross Sales: | _____ |
| (-) Returns | _____ |
| Net Sales | _____ |

**Revenue Assumptions:**
1. The sources of information for our revenue projection are:
   _____
2. If the total market demand for our product/service = 100%, our projected sales volume represents ____% of this total market.
3. The following factors might lower our revenue projections:
   _____

# 5.0 Industry Analysis

SIC Code 596316, **Coffee & Food Svc-Mobile**
NAICS Code 722330, **Mobile Food Svcs**

This industry comprises establishments primarily engaged in preparing and serving meals and snacks for immediate consumption from motorized vehicles or non-motorized carts. The establishment is the main location from which the caterer route is serviced, not each cart or vehicle. Included in this industry are establishments primarily engaged in providing food services from vehicles, such as hot dog carts and food trucks.

Lunch trucks additionally called as food trucks are mobile food courts that sell food things at totally different locations. They reap more benefits than the restaurants that are stationary and have a restricted customer base which provides limited quantity of revenue. They are conjointly referred to as restaurants on wheels. There are completely different lunch trucks accessible within the markets that are specifically targeted to cater to the needs of various varieties of food items. From the daily breakfast to the fast lunch, consumers have a wide selection of menu items to choose from. Festival periods, carnival times, college campuses, industrial areas, IT parks, and office complexes are thought of to be the best places to find completely different folks approaching these lunch trucks as they serve quality food at an affordable price. Additionally, many lunch trucks have created an account on Twitter to update their daily menu for loyal following customers.

The food truck offers a low start-up cost opportunity to go out and be entrepreneurial and make a living. In fact, the food truck business has become one of the few bright spots in this current recession. Minimal start-up costs (less than $5,000 in some regions), a quick return on investment (most pay off in a matter of months) and location flexibility also make mobile food trucks an attractive start-up venture.

Food trucks, a truck converted into a mobile kitchen, are gaining wide-spread popularity for the ease in which a variety of appliance can be installed to prepare an unrestrained assortment of food. Everyday new food trucks hit the streets offering something new and unique. Some trucks represent restaurant owners trying to make up for lost wages in recent years.

The industry has a variety of mobile operators, though over 91% of revenue for street vendors come from the sale of take-away food and drink for immediate consumption. A traditional street vendor cart may have 2-3 wheels and is used to sell one or two items. Drive through stands, such as a drive through espresso stand, are often located in parking lots and shopping centers and offer a wider variety of goods.

**The following factors are driving the growth in food trucks:**
1. Increased production/labor capacity
2. Menu updates/upgrades
3. Looking off-premise
4. More marketing & promos

5. Lower corporate profits and consumer incomes.
6. Increases in two-income families requiring convenience and time management.
7. Working mothers
8. The aging of the overall population.
9. Increased retail food costs relative to the price for prepared food items.
10. Social networking technologies to track mobile food unit location paths.
11. The need to reduce service tipping costs.

The profitability of individual companies depends on cost controls and effective marketing. Large company competitive advantages include the offering of expanded services such as rentals and economies of scale. Small companies compete by serving small groups with more personalized services and fresher ingredients.

## 5.1 Key Industry Companies

We plan to study the best practices of industry leaders and adapt certain selected practices to our business model concept. Best practices are those methods or techniques resulting in increased customer satisfaction when incorporated into the operation.

**Korilla BBQ** www.korillabbq.com/
A New York City based lunch/dinner truck owned by Eddie Song that specializes in Korean-theme burritos, also known as ssams. They also serve Korean-style tacos. They have been positively reviewed by Antenna Magazine, were listed in the Village Voice's Top 10 Vegetarian Street Foods listing, and mentioned first in Zagat's overview of the Korean Taco trend. The name "Korilla" is a "a portmanteau of 'Korean' and 'Grill'.

**Kogi Korean BBQ-To-Go** http://kogibbq.com/
The Kogi truck is a traveling Los Angeles landmark that serves up Korean Mexican tacos, day and night. Spicy Pork Tacos, Kimchi Quesadillas and Short Rib Sliders satiate the hungry mouths of Angelenos who crave excellent food on a budget. Quality Korean barbecue meets traditional, homemade tortillas and fresh veggies to create a taste that carries the rhythms of LA street culture and exudes the warmth of all that California sun. Under the direction of Chef Roy Choi, Kogi has developed a menu that delivers high-end food at street level prices. Currently Kogi operates 5 trucks and out of 1 bar. Most recently the Kogi family has opened up its first sit-down restaurant, Chego, in Palms. More food trucks have followed Kogi's example, using Twitter, cell phone alerts, and Facebook to alert customers on their whereabouts.

**Spencer on the Go!** San Francisco www.spenceronthego.com
Four years ago, noted chef Laurent Katgely, who has cooked at renowned restaurants on both coasts (Lespinasse in New York, Boulevard in San Francisco), got a vision: French food on the street. Chez Spencer, a satellite operation, serves sautéed skate cheeks with caper emulsion and green beans in a butter-lettuce bowl; sweetbreads with smoked bacon and truffle sauce; and a substantial lobster salad with sliced citrus. You can snack vigorously for less than ten bucks or enjoy a three-course meal for about $25.

**Mmmpanadas            Austin, Texas                          www.mmmpanadas.com**
Having lived in Costa Rica, Cody Fields recognized that no food is better suited for the street than the empanada. So back in Austin, he found a truck on eBay, plunked down twenty grand, and worked out a recipe—having never made an empanada in his life. He started small by cooking his empanadas at home and selling a few dozen at a time to local bars and coffee shops. Now Mmmpanadas serves fifteen varieties of encased mains and desserts whose perfectly seasoned fillings range from green-chili chicken to ground beef, egg, and olive; from barbecued brisket to mango-ginger. Since the truck serves a breakfast option (egg and chorizo inside its signature crispy, buttery shell), here exists a rare opportunity in street food: three meals a day.

**Cravings            New York City            www.nyccravings.com**
Thomas Yang, 22, learned his on food trucks. He made tacos and dumplings for a couple of prominent New York City mobile operations before opening his own this summer. From their refitted Italian-bread truck, they serve the finest fried-chicken lunch in town for the bargain price of $6. Done Taiwanese-style, the chicken is not battered but rather deep-marinated in Chinese five-spice powder and soy sauce, then plunged into boiling soybean oil and served over rice with "secret pork sauce." The crispy, juicy thigh-and-leg combo makes a case for the supremacy of Taiwanese-style frying.

**Fojol Bros. of Merlindia        Washington, D.C.    www.fojol.com**
Fojol's food actually comes from a reliable D.C.-area Indian restaurant whose identity the "brothers" won't disclose. But you're not supposed to believe you're eating Indian food, anyway: Everything off the carnivalesque truck—tender meat and vegetable curries, brilliant mango-lassi Popsicles, Fojol-brand sweet-and-savory bagged snacks—expressly comes from the fictional utopia of Merlindia. Pick among chicken masala, pumpkin stew, potatoes and cauliflower, and Punjabi-style spinach and cheese—all delicious. Listen to blaring big-top tunes. Watch your hosts roller-skate around the truck. It's part stylized Wes Anderson set piece, part mock–Baz Luhrmann musical, all eco-friendly (sustainable plates and sporks!). And it's more fun than anyone's had on the streets of Washington, D.C., perhaps ever.

**Marination            Seattle                    www.marinationmobile.com**
Based in part on Hawaii's thriving lunch-truck culture, this SWAT-team-blue Seattle venture brings a taste of the pan-Pacific to the streets of the Pacific Northwest. That means kimchi quesadillas, Korean Kalbi-style short-rib tacos with a special vegetable slaw, kalua pork sliders, and more than a few opportunities to get down with Spam. The menu takes cues from Korean and Mexican street food as well as from the traditional luau: That succulent kalua pork tastes like it was cooked in a beachside hole-in-the-earth imu oven. Some tricks, however, are unique to Marination, like on-site customer hula-hooping and a classified spicy, creamy sauce for the sliders called "nunya," as in "nunya business."

**Fresh Local    Portsmouth, New Hampshire            www.freshlocaltruck.com**
Josh Lanahan, a Culinary Institute of America–trained chef, conceives and cooks the comfort-food menu. His fiancée, Michelle Lozuaway, plays ultimate curbside host. And a

butcher named Popper mans the grill. The burger meat is freshly ground and tastiest on the rare side with diced tomato and white American. The pulled pork is really porchetta, the saliva-inducing slow-roasted pork of Italy. That alone is worth the hour's drive up from Boston, as are the tart local blueberry soda and Josh's riff on the banh mi.

**Border Grill          Los Angeles                    www.bordergrill.com**
It takes real balls to challenge the grand Los Angeles taco-truck tradition head-on. But it helps, of course, to have the pedigree of Border Grill, the Santa Monica restaurant that helped elevate south-of-the-border grub to gourmet status. Here tacos contain slow-roasted pork, pickled onion, and orange salsa, or fried avocado and wild mushrooms. You can even get ginger-spiked mahimahi ceviche in a corn-tortilla cone.

**Streetza            Milwaukee              www.streetza.com**
Streetza, the new Milwaukee-area, 650-degree oven on wheels, is putting an end to all that. Their pies aren't exactly modeled on D.O.C regulations. Delicious populism: Customers suggesting pizza recipes on Twitter, introducing the hungry Cheesehead public to ultra-local slices like The Brew Crew Sausage Race. That's five kinds of hometown Klement's sausages on one pie, including hot dog, plus six kinds of cheese. It's artisanal and balanced in every way, right down to the hand-stretched, cornmeal-dusted crust.

**The Green Truck**
Sells sustainably harvested fish tacos, roams the streets of Los Angeles in vehicles fueled by vegetable oil.

**The Dessert Truck**
A New York based operation, is owned by a former Le Cirque pastry sous chef who donates proceeds from desserts such as a pavlova with red fruit gel to charity.

**The RoliRoti**
A San Francisco Bay area operation, their rotisserie truck serves free-range chicken, heritage pork and local lamb, prepared by owner Thomas Odermatt, a Swiss former organic farming student whose business card reads Rotisseur.

**On the Fly**
In Washington D.C., sells organic, vegetarian or local ingredient-based versions of classic lunch-truck tacos and burgers. Michel Heitstuman, On the Fly s chief executive officer, started the company in late 2007. Today, On the Fly operates eight carts, five cafes and a catering company, and is working on a franchising agreement to expand to other cities.

## 5.2     Key Industry Statistics

1.    The conventional food industry is producing a 2 to 3 percent annual growth rate, while the organic industry has enjoyed several years of 17 to 20 percent

growth.
2. U.S. sales of organic food and beverages have grown from $1 billion in 1990 to an estimated $20 billion in 2007, and are projected to reach nearly $25 billion in 2014.
3. Organic food sales are anticipated to increase an average of 18 percent each year from 2007 to 2014. Source: 2007 OTA Manufacturer Survey
4. Representing approximately 2.8 percent of overall food and beverage sales in 2006, this continues to be a fast-growing sector, growing 20.9 percent in 2006. Source: 2007 OTA Manufacturer Survey
5. According to the National Restaurant Association's 2007 Restaurant Industry Forecast, chefs ranked organic food as third on a list of the top 20 items for 2007.
6. A new 26-foot step-side van with a customized kitchen is worth about $120,000, compared to the $1.5 million price tag that would accompany a new bricks-and-mortar restaurant location.
7. The industry is heavily concentrated in urban areas, particularly in the central parts of large cities. This industry is thriving in cities such as L.A, Portland, New York, Austin and San Francisco.
8. According the IBISWorld, the industry is most heavily concentrated in the Far West, the Great Lakes region, the Mid East (which includes New York), and the South East.
9. Major Market Segments:
   Street locations/corners 55.0%         Other locations/venues/events 18.0%
   Industrial/construction work sites 15.0%    Shopping malls 12.0%
10. According to a report by the National League of Cities, food trucks made approximately $650 million in 2012—and that figure is expected to quadruple to $2.7 billion by the year 2018.
11. According to the National League of Cities, food truck revenue is expected to increase 76 percent over the next five years.

**Infographics:**
http://blog.ncrsilver.com/2014/09/26/getrolling-america-food-truck-facts-infographic/

## 5.3   Industry Trends

We will determine the trends that are impacting our consumers and indicate ways in which our customers' needs are changing and any relevant social, technical or other changes that will impact our target market. Keeping up with trends and reports will help management to carve a niche for our business, stay ahead of the competition and deliver products that our customers need and want.

Our plan is to capitalize on the following trends:
1. With an aging, baby boomer population with significant disposable income, projections for specialty food sales are positioned for continued growth.
2. There has been a significant movement in the food industry toward the production of low-fat and vegetarian foods that suit today's healthier eating habits.
3. Organic products for children continue to be among the fastest-growing segments

within the organic industry, according to the Organic Trade Association (OTA).
4. Americans are developing a bigger appetite for more upscale and healthier foods because of higher discretionary incomes, better educations, more frequent travel, more fine dining, and more exposure to ethnic foods.
5. Average American families are becoming increasingly adventurous in their diets.
6. There is a growing demand for specialty food items and a significant percentage of people demanding naturally grown, organic specialty foods.
7. With the increase in dual-income families, both the husband and wife are working, there is greater need for convenience in shopping for daily necessities.
8. On-trend organic food items include convenient, healthful snack foods such as rice chips, snack bars and fruit bars.
9. Some organic food items for kids are shared among child and adult usage, such products include milk, yogurt/yogurt smoothies, frozen fruit, frozen vegetables and applesauce.
10. Kid-friendly packaging designs with a natural/organic edge are becoming more prevalent.
11. Organic rice milks and soy milks are the fastest growing categories, followed closely by nutritional bars.
12. Growing interest in physical fitness has sparked noteworthy increases in sales of performance-oriented food products and supplements, which are being treated more and more as dessert options.
13. Workout buffs who pay heed to the advice of fitness nutritionists eat six to seven smaller desserts a day, interspersing vitamin-packed whey-protein shakes and energy bars with conventional desserts as the guiding wisdom is that the body works more efficiently, and actually burns more calories, if it is fed smaller amounts on a more continuous basis.
14. Low-fat claims are the most important for consumers in terms of health.
15. Consumers of all ages and health conditions will likely reward manufacturers that are able to imbue their products with health properties while maintaining their good taste.
16. People are either buying these food trucks in anticipation of a layoff or to supplement their incomes.
17. Food truck vendors are adding locally grown ingredients and ethnically popular condiment flavorings to cater to the taste preferences of local communities.
18. Continued increased focus on healthy lifestyles and food purveyors providing customers with healthy choices and customization.
19. The use of 'green' menus, as well as biodegradable service-ware reflects a commitment to the well-being of the environment and the customers' health.
20. The increasing popularity of Ready-to-Drink (RFD) chilled coffee beverages.
21. Customers want to be able to personalize their food and beverages with special toppings and flavor additives.
22. Vendors are looking for faster and more convenient ways to service time-starved customers.
23. Driving sales is the popularity of high protein foods and interest in natural and organic products.
24. New products available are mostly brand favorites reformulated with a reduced

fat content or increased protein content. New products in flavors such as honey and brown sugar, barbeque, Cajun, spicy and teriyaki have hit the market in the last year.
25. According to consumer research, convenient packaging, preparation and usage information are high priorities.
26. Corporate players, such as Jack in the Box and Sizzler, are developing food trucks to expand their company footprint during a tight economy, build their brand image and develop the catering side of the business.
27. Interest in food trucks is being stirred by the second season of "The Food Truck Wars" coming this summer to the Food Network.
28. There is a new wave of Asian flavors that are spicier and more complex, driven by Northern Thai cuisine, Japanese okonomiyaki pancakes and tangy Filipino foods, according to Sterling-Rice Group, Boulder, Colo.

## 5.4  Key Industry Terms

We will use the following term definitions to help our company to understand and speak the common language of our industry, and aid efficient communication.

**Canopy**
The canopy is a part that covers the cart. Depending on its size, it can protect the coffee, food and employees from the sun. Canopies can often be customized with your business name, which makes your cart easily recognizable.

**Casters**
Casters are the wheels attached to the bottom of the cart. Casters can be stationary or swivel and will make the cart portable.

**Chicago-style Hot Dog**
A steamed, boiled or grilled—but never broiled—all-beef hot dog on a poppy seed bun, originating from the city of Chicago, Illinois. The hot dog is topped with mustard, onion, sweet pickle relish, a dill pickle spear, tomato slices or wedges, pickled sport peppers, a dash of celery salt, and sometimes, but not always, cucumber slices. Ketchup is never used.

**Comfort Foods**
Reflect those menu items that have a degree of "flavor familiarity', contain 'locally grown' ingredients, contribute to 'eating indulgence' (without guilt), and provide a 'one-up' eating experience.

**Counter-style Cart**
A cart that includes a service counter for customers. The counter can simply be a place to set hot dogs while the customer pays or adds condiments, or it can provide a space for customers to eat either standing or sitting on stools.

**"COGS" (cost of goods sold).**
Describes the amount of money a food truck spends on supplies and food ingredients – such as beverages, seasonings, meats, fruits and vegetables – used to prepare the menu items they sell. The COGS should ideally account for no more than 35 percent of sales.

**Fleet**
Having more than one hot dog cart in various locations.

**Hand Sink Cart**
A small portable hand sink. This is necessary for hand washing, but you may also be able to use it to wash equipment in between preparing your customers' coffee beverages.

**Ice Caddie**
Keeps ice cool. Optional piece of equipment that is used to provide iced beverages.

**Commissary**
A commercial enterprise that sells food and equipment to the general public.

**Espresso**
A dark, rich, full-bodied coffee made when finely ground dark-roasted coffee is processed with a special machine that forces a small amount of water at high pressure through a special filter.

**The Food Code**
Established by the FDA as a guideline for local and state governments as a way to regulate the mobile food industry and protect the health and safety of consumers, residents and employees.

**Gourmet Coffee (Also known as 'Specialty' or Premium' Coffee)**
Made from Arabica beans usually harvested by hand in mountainous areas.

**Italian Hotdog**
A type of hotdog popular in north jersey and the boardwalk of the jersey shore. The basic ingredients are a cooked hot dog and a combination of fried peppers (green or red), onions, and potatoes cooked in soybean oil. The hot dog is then placed in pizza bread, and topped with the vegetables and potatoes and some like it with mustard or ketchup.

**Mobile Cart**
Most often considered "mobile food facilities," and therefore they must have a health department approved commissary to obtain a permit for legal operation.

**Mobile Support Unit   (MSU)**
A vehicle or cart that is used in conjunction with a commissary. A cart on wheels that travels to mobile food facilities as needed to replenish supplies, clean the interior of the unit, and/or dispose of liquid and solid wastes.

**Occasion Management**
Providing the right configuration of product to promote for a specific event, like the Super Bowl.

**Organic Products/"Certified Organic"**
To include the term organic on packaging, a manufacturer must create its product in accordance with USDA rules. The USDA's National Organic Program certifies products as organic based on farming, handling, manufacturing, distribution and labeling practices. Requirements include: no antibiotics or growth hormones for animals, animals must be raised on organic feed and have free range to graze, crops must be raised with no synthetic pesticides or fertilizers containing synthetic chemicals, no sewage-sludge fertilizer, no bio-engineered foods or irradiation, and no GMOs (genetically modified organisms). Farming practices should enhance and preserve soil and water. A government inspector must certify the farm after visit; farmers must keep detailed records on crops.

**Made with Organic Ingredients**

Products with at least 70% organic ingredients may say "Made with Organic Ingredients" and list up to three ingredients. This category may not use the "USDA Organic" seal on the label.

**Pastry Display Window**
A window in the front of the car that allows customers to view pastries and other offerings.

**Revocation**
When a license is taken away or revoked for infractions of any rules imposed on vendors by the state or city in which they operate.

**Sanitary**
Free from contamination.

**Sanitize**
To treat by a process that destroys most microorganisms, including all pathogens.

## 5.5 Industry News

Some cities. like Atlanta, are setting up multiple food truck parks. This involves rounding up other local food trucks and setting up a mobile food court that also would share a bar and have live entertainment. Some food truck parks also feature a weekend Farmer's Market.

Fast casual Baja Fresh Mexican Grill recently purchased the Calbi BBQ Truck with plans to franchise it.

Food trucks offering fare from grilled cheese to cupcakes have launched recently, all relying on word of mouth and Twitter to gather crowds at a moment's notice.

Mobile Food Trucks now have their own Food Network Cable Show:
www.foodnetwork.com/the-great-food-truck-race/index.html

## 5.6 Industry Growth Strategy

| Initiative | Tactics | |
|---|---|---|
| Build Awareness | Advertising | |
| Expand Distribution | Incentives | Discounts |
| | Sales Reps | |
| Build Buying Rate | Frequent Buyer Cards | Bulk Purchase Discounts |
| Build Penetration | Broad Advertising | Sampling Programs |
| | High-value incentives | |
| Build Extended Usage | New Usage Ideas | |
| Increase Loyalty | Frequent Buyer Cards | Rebates |
| | Volume Discounts | Product Improvements |
| Strengthen | Demonstrations | |

| | | |
|---|---|---|
| Merchandising | Signage | Display Housekeeping |
| | Point-of-Purchase Displays | Financial Incentives |
| Improve Product Quality | Reduce defect rate | Add Features |
| | Improve Reliability | Enhance Customer Service |
| Decease Product Costs | Increase production efficiency | Eliminate unnecessary features |
| | Negotiate lower supplier costs | Utilize cheaper materials |
| | Realize economies of scale | Master learning curve |
| Introduce New Brand | Awareness | Consistency |
| Attract Competitor customers | Incentive offers | Product Comparisons |
| | High value trail promotion | |
| Enter a New Market | Sampling | Incentives |
| | Build awareness | New application ideas |
| Increase Referrals | Incentives | Refer-a-friend Programs |
| Reposition the Brand | Packaging | Pricing |
| | Endorsements | Partnerships |
| New Distribution Channel | Online marketing | Mobile Services |
| Increase Pricing | Better image | |
| Strengthen Brand | Customer brand involvement | |
| Accelerate R & D | Develop new product development processes. | |

# 6.0 Strategy and Implementation Summary

Our strategy to succeed is to give people a combination of great tasting, healthy, interesting, organic food, and in an environment, that is appealing to 'trendy' people. Additional methods of enhancing our Mobile Food Truck name recognition will be local newspaper advertising with coupons, special sampling promotions, companion promotions and discounts with other merchants, messaging via social networks and offers to local schools for discounts to students with good grades and seniors.

Effectively advertising our food truck business will significantly affect our success. Since a food truck is a mobile business, we will take care when planning the route, we intend to travel, and focus on neighborhoods with business parks, cultural attractions or other well-populated areas. We will build a customer base that knows when and where to find our food truck route via Twitter and Facebook. Local advertising that reaches our target audience will be utilized. Direct mailings, billboards, radio spots and coupons are some of the techniques we will employ. "Buy one get one free" coupons will be used as an attention-getting program that lets customers believe they are getting a bargain and provides a way to track traffic to our business. Although this will give away inventory, we will be able to sell additional items, meet new customers and expose them to additional products. Offering customers, a free beverage after several visits to our truck, will also create ongoing business, while rewarding customers for their loyalty.

Additional sales revenue and name recognition for our food truck will be generated by sponsoring sports, social, educational and fund-raising activities within the local communities. The principals have numerous fund-raising ideas and plans for community involvement that will help make the business a money-maker.

_____ (company name) will promote the launch of the food truck route. We will have live music and sample menu items in a designated parking lot for the opening weekend. We will advertise in the university daily student newspaper as well as the local area advertising flyer. In the advertisements for the market opening, we will have a ___ (20?) % off coupon for purchases over _____ (twenty?) dollars. We will continue this discount for the first month of operation.

_____ (company name) will give back to the community. We will participate in community projects like the area's food bank and community programs for children. We will also host a number of community events, such as charity brunches, and car washes benefiting local humane societies.

Our strategy will exploit our advantages over the competition (convenience, and high quality) with carefully-tracked milestones for growth.

Initial marketing efforts for opening will be geared towards generating name recognition and making a clear distinction between our healthy Mobile Food Truck and other local competitors. Follow-up marketing programs will encourage repeat visits and assist customers in understanding and appreciating the nutritional value of our products.

We will gear prices towards our competitors in the nearest cities and online, with a small "convenience" premium for offering them locally. This will offset our distribution costs. Local discounts, daily menu specials, and new organic products will satisfy customers they are getting a good value. Our emphasis on consistently good and reliable service will make new customers repeat customers.

Our sales strategy is based on serving our niche markets better than the competition and leveraging our competitive advantages. These advantages include superior attention to understanding and satisfying customer health needs and taste preferences, creating a one-stop meal solution, and value pricing.

The objectives of our marketing strategy will be to recruit new customers, retain existing customers, get good customers to spend more and return more frequently. Establishing a loyal customer base is very important because such core customers will not only generate the most lifetime sales, but also provide valuable referrals.

We will generate word-of-mouth buzz through direct-mail campaigns, exceeding customer expectations, developing a Web site, getting involved in community events, and donating our services at charity functions in exchange for press release coverage. Our sales strategy will seek to convert potential and first-time customers into long-term relationships and referral agents. The combination of our competitive advantages, targeted marketing campaign and networking activities, will enable _____ (company name) to continue increasing our market share.

## 6.1.0 Promotion Strategy

Promotion strategies will be focused to the target market segment. Given the importance of word-of-mouth/referrals among the area residents, we shall strive to efficiently service all our customers to gain their business regularly, which is the recipe for our long-term success. We shall focus on direct resident marketing, publicity, sampling, and advertising as proposed. Our promotion strategy will focus on generating referrals from existing customers and professionals, community involvement and direct mail campaigns with enclosed route maps and time schedules.

Our promotional strategies will also make use of the following tools:
- **Advertising**
    - Yearly anniversary parties to celebrate the success of each year.
    - Yellow Pages ads in the book and online.
    - Flyers promoting special promotion events with coupons.
    - Doorknob hangers, if not prohibited by neighborhood associations.

- **Local Marketing / Public Relations**
    - Client raffle for gift certificates or discount coupons
    - Participation in local civic groups.
    - Press release coverage of our sponsoring of events at the local community center for families and residents.

- 0 Article submissions to magazines describing the benefits of our healthy meals, catering and other foodservice programs.
- O Sales Brochure to convey our program specialties to prospective customers.
- 0 Present free seminars to schools on the benefits of healthy snacks and handout free samples and merchandise with our name and logo.

- **Local Media**
    - o Direct Mail - We will send quarterly postcards and annual direct mailings to residents with a ___ (10?) mile radius of our commissary. It will contain an explanation of the benefits of our services.
    - o Radio Campaign - We will make "live on the air" presentations of our trial service coupons to the disk jockeys, hoping to get the promotions broadcasted to the listening audience. We will also make our food expertise available for talk radio programs.
    - o Newspaper Campaign - Placing several ads in local community newspapers to launch our initial campaign. We will include a trial coupon.
    - o Website – We will collect email addresses for a monthly newsletter.
    - o Cable TV advertising on local health shows.

## 6.1.1  Grand Opening

Our Grand Opening celebration will be a very important promotion opportunity to create word-of-mouth advertising results.  We will create an event that will lead first-time guests to become our regular customers.
Source:
www.dummies.com/how-to/content/ten-tips-for-preventing-food-truck-failure.html

**We will do the following things to make the open house a successful event:**
1. Enlist local business support to contribute a large number of door prizes.
2. Use a sign-in sheet to create an email/mailing list.
3. Create free children ID cards.
4. Schedule appearance by local celebrities.
5. Create a festive atmosphere with balloons, beverages and music.
6. Get the local radio station to broadcast live from the event and handout fun gifts.
7. Offer an membership club application fee waiver.
8. Giveaway our logo imprinted T-shirts as a contest prize.
9. Allow potential customers to view your facility and ask questions.
10. Print promotional flyers and pay a few kids to distribute them locally.
11. Arrange for face painting, storytelling, clowns, and snacks for everyone.
12. Arrange for local politician to do the official opening ceremony so all the local newspapers came to take pictures and do a feature story.
13. Arrange that people can tour our facility on the open day in order to see our facilities, collect sales brochures and find out more about our services.
14. Allocate staff members to perform specific duties, handout business cards and sales brochures and instruct them to deal with any questions or queries.
16. Organize a drawing with everyone writing their name and phone numbers on the

back of business cards and give a voucher as a prize to start a marketing list.
17. Hand out free samples of menu items.
18. Distribute coupons.

## 6.1.2 Value Proposition

Our value proposition will summarize why a consumer should use our mobile food truck products and services. We will enable quick access to our broad line of quality foods and innovative foodservices, out of our mobile truck in the _____ (city) area.

Our value proposition will convince prospects that our healthy products and innovative recipes will add more value and better solve their need for a convenient, one-stop food truck with quick serve foodservice capabilities. We will use this value proposition statement to target customers who will benefit most from using our mobile services. These are families and workers who demand time-saving convenience, fast service, healthy premium quality foods, and the ability to customize the final product with condiments to meet their individual taste preferences. Our value proposition will be concise and appeal to the customer's strongest decision-making drivers, which are access convenience, a time-efficient purchase experience, product quality, health benefits, ethnic influences, value pricing and development of personal relationships.

### Recap of Our Value Proposition:

**Trust** – We are known as a trusted business partner with strong customer and vendor endorsements. We have earned a reputation for quality, integrity, and delivery of successful event solutions.

**Quality** – We offer a quality eating experience and chef professional backgrounds in _____ at competitive rates.

**Convenience** - We service our customers where they want to be serviced.

**Experience** – Our ability to bring people with years of culinary experience with deep technical knowledge is at the core of our success.

**True Vendor Partnerships** – Our true vendor partnerships enable us to offer the quality resources of much larger organizations with greater flexibility.

**Customer Satisfaction and Commitment to Success** – Through partnering with our customers and delivering quality solutions, we have been able to achieve an impressive degree of repeat business. Since ____ (year), more than ____% of our business activity is generated by existing customers. Our philosophy is that "our clients' success is our success." Our success is measured in terms of our clients' success through the solutions we build for them.

## 6.1.3 Positioning Statement

_____ (company name) will aim to attract area residents who desire healthy meal solutions, when and where they want them, and top-quality quick serve specialties.

Our positioning strategy will be the result of conducting in-depth consumer market research to find out what benefits consumers want and how our products and services can meet those needs. Due to the increase in two-income families, many service-oriented professions are leaning toward differentiating themselves on the basis of convenience. This is also what we intend to do. For instance, we plan to have extended, "people" hours on various days of the week and offer a pick-up and home delivery service. Our food truck company will be the leader in both customer service and the use of quality fresh ingredients.

We also plan to develop specialized services that will enable us to pursue a niche focus on specific interest based programs, such as Corporate Catering Services. These objectives will position us at the _____ (mid-level/high-end) of the market and will allow the company to realize a healthy profit margin in relation to its low-end, discount rivals and achieve long-term growth.

## 6.1.4 Unique Selling Proposition (USP)

Our unique selling proposition will answer the question why a customer should choose to do business with our mobile food truck company versus any and every other option available to them in the marketplace. Our USP will be a description of a unique important benefit that our Mobile Food Truck offers to customers, so that price is no longer the key to our sales.

**Our USP will include the following:**
Who our target audience is: _____
What we will do for them: _____
What qualities, skills, talents, traits do we possess that others do not: _____
What are the benefits we provide that no one else offers: _____
Why that is different from what others are offering: _____
Example: We only use organic ingredients or authentic ethnic seasonings.
Why that solution matters to our target audience: _____

## 6.1.5 Distribution Strategy

Customers can contact the _____ (company name) by telephone, fax, internet and by dropping in. Our nearest competitors are ___ (#) miles away in either direction. The truck will also stock special request items for regular area residents.

1. **Order by Phone**
   Customers can contact us 24 hours a day, 7days a week at _____.
   Our Customer Service Representatives will be available to assist customers Monday through Friday from ___ a.m. to ___ p.m. EST.
2. **Order by Fax**
   Customers may fax their orders to _____ anytime.
   They must provide: Account number, Billing and shipping address, Purchase

order number, if applicable, Name and telephone number, Product number/description, Unit of measure and quantity ordered and Applicable sales promotion source codes.

3. **Order Online**
Customers can order online at www._____.com. Once the account is activated, customers will be able to place orders, browse the catalog, check stock availability and pricing, check order status and view both order and patient history.

**We plan to pursue the following distribution channels:** (select)
1. Our own retail outlets _____
2. Independent retail outlets _____
3. Chain store retail outlets _____
4. Wholesale outlets _____
5. Independent distributors _____
6. Independent commissioned sales reps _____
7. In-house sales reps _____
8. Direct mail using own catalog or flyers _____
9. Catalog broker agreement _____
10. In-house telemarketing _____
11. Contracted telemarketing call center _____
12. Cybermarketing via own website _____
13. Online sales via amazon, eBay, etc. _____
14. TV and Cable Direct Marketing _____
15. TV Home Shopping Channels (QVC) _____
16. Mobile Truck and Cart Units _____
17. Franchised Business Units _____
18. Trade Shows _____
19. High-end Flea Markets _____
20. Consignment Shops _____
21. Home Party Sales Plans _____
22. Trunk Sales _____
23. Fundraisers _____
24. Farmer's Markets _____
26. Kiosks and Vending Machines _____
27. Sublet Retail Space _____

# 6.1.6 Sales Rep Plan

We will use sales reps to sell to corporate event planners.
1. In-house or Independent _____
2. Salaried or Commissioned _____
3. Salary or Commission Rate _____
4. Salary Plus Commission Rate _____
5. Special Performance Incentives _____

6. Negotiating Parameters — Price Breaks/Added Services/ _____

7. Performance Evaluation Criteria — No. of New Customers/Sales Volume/ _____

8. Number of Reps _____
9. Sales Territory Determinants — Geography/Demographics/ _____

10. Sales Territories Covered _____
11. Training Program Overview _____
12. Training Program Cost _____
13. Sales Kit Contents _____
14. Primary Target Market _____
15. Secondary Target Market _____

Rep Name          Compensation Plan          Assigned Territory
_____
_____

## 6.2 Competitive Advantages

A **competitive advantage** is the thing that differentiates a business from its competitors. It is what separates our business from everyone else. It answers the questions: "Why do customers buy from us versus a competitor?", and "What do we offer customers that is unique?". We will use the following competitive advantages to set us apart from our competitors. The distinctive competitive advantages which _____ (company name) brings to the marketplace are as follows: (Note: Select only those you can support)

1. A mobile service that conveniently serves the foot and drive-by traffic in the _____ (community name) area.
2. We are a community oriented company that will give back to the community in terms of support for the area's food bank and community programs for children.
3. Residents and visitors are willing to pay a premium for premium meals and the convenience of being able to get what they want without having to travel.
4. Our customers purchase our meals because they are convenient, authentic, nutritious and delicious.
5. We generate repeat business because our prices are reasonable and the meals are consistently good and nutritious.
6. We will train our staff to answer most customers questions, so that their time is valued.
7. Our website will enable online ordering and pre-ordering, and the issuance of reminder notices for automatic or programmed event scheduling.
8. We constantly are search of the latest technology to update our operations and reinforce the image in customer minds that we are among the most progressive foodservice professionals in the area.
9. We will utilize a software package that provides document management services

and advanced management tools, such as basic and intermediate reporting functions, cost-benefit analysis, inventory management and audit functionality, in addition to electronic records storage and retrieval.
10. We offer discounts and other incentives for referrals.
11. We have the technological and professional staffing capabilities to provide our customers with the highest possible level of personalized service.
12. We have an ethnically diverse and multilingual staff, which is critical for a service-oriented business.
13. We have formed alliances that enable us to provide one-stop shopping or an array of home replacement meals through a single access point.
14. We developed a specialized training program for the staff, so they will be proficient at administering our service programs.
15. Our superior customer service, delivered through our trained staff, sets us apart and provides our competitive advantage
16. We guarantee minimal waiting to be serviced.
17. We have the resources to research new ingredients and cooking methods, and make informed recommendations.
18. We have an inventory management system that reduces out-of-stock situations, and assures that needed ingredients are in stock.
19. We regularly conduct focus groups to understand changing customer expectations.
20. We utilize reliable equipment with back-up alternatives.
21. We hire and train our employees to be responsive and empathetic to customer needs.
22. We are able to convert our overhead cost savings into a better meal value for the customer.

## 6.2.1 Branding Strategy

Our branding strategy involves what we do to shape what the customer immediately thinks our business offers and stands for. The purpose of our branding strategy is to reduce customer perceived purchase risk and improve our profit margins by allowing use to charge a premium for our mobile foodservices.

We will invest $____ every year in maintaining our brand name image, which will differentiate our mobile food truck business from other companies. The amount of money spent on creating and maintaining a brand name will not convey any specific information about our products, but it will convey, indirectly, that we are in this market for the long haul, that we have a reputation to protect, and that we will interact repeatedly with our customers. In this sense, the amount of money spent on maintaining our brand name will signal to consumers that we will provide products and services of consistent quality.

We will use the following ways to build trust and establish our personal brand:
1. Build a consistently published blog and e-newsletter with informational content.
2. Create comprehensive social media profiles.

3. Contribute articles to related online publications.
4. Earn Career Certifications

**Resources:**
https://www.abetterlemonadestand.com/branding-guide/

Our key to marketing success will be to effectively manage the building of our brand platform in the market place, which will consist of the following elements:

**Brand Vision** - our envisioned future of the brand is to be the favored source for fast quality meal solutions to manage the desire for something made with fresh ingredients and reasonably priced.

**Brand Attributes** - Partners, problem solvers, nutritious, reasonably priced, fast service, responsive, flexible and easy to work with.

**Brand Essence** - the shared soul of the brand, the spark of which is present in every experience a customer has with our mobile foodservice, will be "Problem Solving Convenience" and "Nutritious." This will be the core of our organization, driving the type of people we hire and the type of behavior we expect.

**Brand Image** - the outside world's overall perception of our organization will be that we are mobile foodservice pros who are conveniently alleviating the complications of what and where to eat.

**Brand Promise** - our concise statement of what we do, why we do it, and why customers should do business with us will be, "To experience fast quality food at value-driven prices.

**We will use the following methodologies to implement our branding strategy:**
1. Develop processes, systems and quality assurance procedures to assure the consistent adherence to our quality standards and mission statement objectives.
2. Develop business processes to consistently deliver upon our value proposition.
3. Develop training programs to assure the consistent professionalism and responsiveness of our employees.
4. Develop marketing communications with consistent, reinforcing message content.
5. Incorporate testimonials into our marketing materials that support our promises.
6. Develop marketing communications with a consistent presentation style. (Logo design, company colors, slogan, labels, packaging, stationery, etc.)
7. Exceed our brand promises to achieve consistent customer loyalty.
8. Use surveys, focus groups and interviews to consistently monitor what our brand means to our customers.
9. Consistently match our brand values or performance benchmarks to our customer requirements.
10. Focus on the maintenance of a consistent number of key brand values that are tied to our company strengths.
11. Continuously research industry trends in our markets to stay relevant to customer needs and wants.
12. Attach a logo-imprinted product label and business card to all products, marketing communications and invoices.
13. Develop a memorable and meaningful tagline that captures the essence of our

brand.
14. Prepare a one-page company overview and make it a key component of our sales presentation folder.
15. Hire and train employees to put the interests of customers first.
16. Develop a professional website that is updated with fresh content on a regular basis.
17. Use our blog to circulate content that establishes our niche expertise and opens a two-way dialogue with our customers.
18. Uses the content, design and layout of the menu to convey consistently your brand image.
19. Require all employees to wear uniforms with the company logo.
20. Attractive and tasteful uniforms will also help our staff's morale. The branding will become complete with the addition of our corporate logo, or other trim or accessories which echo the style and theme of our establishment.
21. Create an effective slogan with the following attributes:
    a. Appeals to customers' emotions.
    b. Shows off how our service benefits customers by highlighting our customer service or care.
    c. Has 8 words or less and is memorable
    d. Can be grasped quickly by our audience.
    e. Reflects our business' personality and character.
    f. Shows sign of originality.
22. Create a Proof Book that contains before and after photos, testimonial letters, our mission statement, copies of industry certifications and our code of ethics.
23. Make effective use of trade show exhibitions and email newsletters to help brand our image.

**The communications strategy we will use to build our brand platform will include the following items:**

Website - featuring product line information, research, testimonials, cost benefit analysis, frequently asked questions, and planned menu and location information. This website will be used as a tool for both our sales team and our customers.

Presentations, brochures and mailers geared to the facility level, explaining the benefits of our mobile foodservice business as part of a comprehensive plan.

Presentations and brochures geared to the corporate account decision maker explaining the benefits of our program in terms of positive enjoyment outcomes, reduced costs, and reduced risk of negative survey events.

A presentation and recruiting brochure geared to prospective sales people and cooks that emphasizes the benefits of joining our organization.

Training materials that help every employee deliver our brand message in a consistent manner.

## 6.2.2  Brand Positioning Statement

We will use the following brand positioning statement to summarize what our brand

means to our targeted market:
To _____ (target market)
_____ (company name) is the brand of _____ (product/service frame of reference) that enables the customer to _____ (primary performance benefit) because ____ (company name) _____ (products/services) _____ (are made with/offer/provide) the best _____ (key attributes)

## 6.3 Business SWOT Analysis

**Definition:** SWOT Analysis is a powerful technique for understanding our Strengths and Weaknesses, and for looking at the Opportunities and Threats faced.

**Strategy:** We will use this SWOT Analysis to uncover exploitable opportunities and carve a sustainable niche in our market. And by understanding the weaknesses of our business, we can manage and eliminate threats that would otherwise catch us by surprise. By using the SWOT framework, we will be able to craft a strategy that distinguishes our business from our competitors, so that we can compete successfully in the market.

Strengths (select)

What food wagon products and services are we best at providing?
What unique resources can we draw upon?

1. Our base of operations is in the heart of an upscale neighborhood and is in close proximity to a popular _____ with ample parking facilities.
2. Our central facility can efficiently service our Mobile Food Trucks.
3. The nearest competition is __ miles and has a minimal inventory of organic health foods.
4. Our truck has been extensively renovated, with many upgrades.
5. Our truck has the ability to change inventory with the seasonal requirements.
6. Experienced management team from the _____ (?) industry.
7. Strong networking relationships with many different organizations, including _____.
8. Excellent staff are experienced, highly trained and customer attentive.
9. Wide diversity of ice cream product/service offerings.
10. High customer loyalty.
11. The proven ability to establish excellent personalized client service.
12. Strong relationships with suppliers, that offer flexibility and respond to special customer requirements.
13. Good referral relationships.
14. Client loyalty developed through a solid reputation with repeat customers.
15. Our business has a focused target market of _____ (Working People?).
16. Lower start-up costs than restaurant.
17. _____

Weaknesses

In what areas could we improve?
Where do we have fewer resources than others?
1. Lack of developmental capital to complete Phase I start-up.
2. New comer to the area.
3. Lack of marketing experience.
4. The struggle to build brand equity.
5. A limited marketing budget to develop brand awareness.
6. Finding dependable and people oriented staff.
7. We need to develop the information systems that will improve our productivity and inventory management.
8. Don't know the needs and wants of the local population.
9. The owner must deal with the mobile service experience learning curve.
10. Challenges caused by the seasonal nature of the business.
11. Open just a few hours a day,
12. Can only serve what fits inside its miniature kitchen.
13. Cannot compete with the volume of customers that a brick and mortar restaurant serves.
14. Food truck owner-operators must pay to outfit and insure two kitchens – their mobile kitchen and brick and mortar kitchen.
15. Food trucks are vulnerable to mechanical problems.
16. Food trucks are also especially vulnerable to the weather.
17. Mobility makes it harder for our customers to find us.
18. Must master social networking skills.
19. _____

## Opportunities

What opportunities are there for new and/or improved services?
What trends could we take advantage of?
1. Seasonal changes in inventory.
2. Could take market share away from existing competitors.
3. Greater need for mobile home services by time starved dual income families.
4. Growing market with a significant percentage of the target market still not aware that _____ (company name) exists.
5. The ability to develop many long-term customer relationships.
6. Expanding the range of product/service packaged offerings.
7. Greater use of direct advertising to promote our services.
8. Establish referral relationships with local businesses serving the same target market segment.
9. Networking with non-profit organizations.
10. The aging population will need and expect a greater range of home services.
11. Increased public awareness of the importance of 'green' matters.
12. Strategic alliances offering sources for referrals and joint marketing activities to extend our reach.
13. _____ (supplier name) is offering co-op advertising.

14. A competitor has overextended itself financially and is facing bankruptcy.
15. Introduction of beverages/snacks combined with ice cream would increase the chances of a combined and multi-dining options to become a one-stop healthy food source.
16. _____

## Threats

What trends or competitor actions could hurt us?
What threats do our weaknesses expose us to?
1. Another Mobile Food Truck could move into this area.
2. Further declines in the economic forecast.
3. Inflation affecting operations for gas, labor, and other operating costs.
4. Keeping trained efficient staff and key personnel from moving on or starting their own business venture.
5. Imitation competition from similar indirect service providers.
6. Price differentiation is a significant competition factor.
7. The government could enact legislation that could affect reimbursements.
8. We need to do a better job of assessing the strengths and weaknesses of all of our competitors.
9. Sales of organic and low-fat meal solutions by mass discounters.
10. Increased competition from new and healthy dessert alternatives.
11. Must stay profitable through poor weather and off seasons.
12. _____

## Recap:

We will use the following strengths to capitalize on recognized opportunities:
1. _____
2. _____

We will take the following actions to turn our weaknesses into strengths and prepare to defend against known threats.
1. _____
2. _____

# 6.4.0 Marketing Strategy

Our marketing strategy is based on establishing _____ (company name) as the convenient one-stop resource of choice for people in need of quality quick-service meals at value-driven prices.

We will start our business with our known personal referral contacts and then continue our campaign to develop recognition among other groups. We will develop and maintain a database of our contacts in the field. We will work to maintain and exploit our existing relationships throughout the start-up process and then use our marketing tools and social networking connections to communicate with other potential referral sources.

The marketing strategy will create awareness, interest and appeal from our target market. Its ultimate purpose is to encourage repeat purchases and get customers to refer friends and professional contacts. To get referrals we will provide excellent service and build relationships with customers by caring about what the customer needs and wants.

Our marketing strategy will revolve around two different types of media, sales brochures and a website. These two tools will be used to make customers aware of our broad range of Mobile Food Truck offerings. One focus of our marketing strategy will be to drive customers to our website for information about our food specialties and route schedules.

A combination of local media and event marketing will be utilized. _____ (company name) will create an identity oriented marketing strategy with executions particularly in the local media. Our marketing strategy will utilize prime time radio spots, print ads, press releases, yellow page ads, flyers, twitter, Facebook and newsletter distribution. We will make effective use of direct response advertising, and include coupons in all print ads. We will also place small display ads in local free magazines.

We will use comment cards, newsletter sign-up forms and surveys to collect customer email addresses and feed our client relationship management (CRM) software system. This system will automatically send out, on a predetermined schedule, follow-up materials, such as article reprints, seminar invitations, email messages, surveys and e-newsletters. We will offset some of our advertising costs by asking our suppliers and other local merchants to place ads in our newsletter.

## Current Situation
We will study the current marketing situation on a weekly basis to analyze trends and identify sources of business growth. As onsite owners, we will be on hand daily to insure customer service. Our services include products of the highest quality and a prompt response to feedback from customers. Our extensive and detailed financial statements, produced monthly, will enable us to stay competitive and exploit presented opportunities.

## Marketing Budget
Our marketing budget will be a flexible $_____ per quarter. The marketing budget

can be allocated in any way that best suits the time of year.
Marketing budget per quarter:

| | | | | |
|---|---|---|---|---|
| Newspaper Ads | $_____ | Radio advertisement | $_____ |
| Web Page | $_____ | Customer raffle | $_____ |
| Direct Mail | $_____ | Sales Brochure | $_____ |
| Home Shows | $_____ | Seminars | $_____ |
| Superpages | $_____ | Google Adwords | $_____ |
| Giveaways | $_____ | Vehicle Signs | $_____ |
| Business Cards | $_____ | Flyers | $_____ |
| Labels/Stickers | $_____ | Videos/DVDs | $_____ |
| Samples | $_____ | Newsletter | $_____ |
| Yard Signs | $_____ | Email Campaigns | $_____ |
| Sales Reps Comm. | $_____ | Social Networking | $_____ |
| Other | $_____ | | |

Total: $ _____

Our objective in setting a marketing budget has been to keep it between ____ (3?) and ____ (5?) percent of our estimated annual gross sales.

## Marketing Mix

Customers will primarily come from word-of-mouth and our referral program. The overall market approach involves creating brand awareness through targeted advertising, public relations, co-marketing efforts with select alliance partners, direct mail, email campaigns (with constant contact.com), and a website.

## Video Marketing Clips

We will link to our website a series of YouTube.com based video clips that talk about our range of Mobile Food Truck meal options, and demonstrate our expertise with certain ethnic recipes. We will create business marketing videos that are both entertaining and informational.

The video will include:
- **Client testimonials** - We will let our best customers become our instant sales force because people will believe what others say about you more readily than what you say about yourself
- **Product Demonstrations** - Train and pre-sell our potential customers on our most popular meal options just by talking about and showing them. Often, our potential customers don't know the full range and depth of our catering services because we haven't taken the time to show and tell them.
- **Include Business Website Address**
- **Food truck and commissary video tour**
- **Owner Interview:** Explanation of our mission statement and unique selling proposition
- **Frequently Asked Questions** - We will answer questions that we often get, and anticipate rejections we might get and give great reasons to convince potential customers that we are the best Mobile Food Truck in the area.

**Include a Call to Action** - We have the experience and the know-how to cater your next family or business event. So call us, right now, and let's get started.

**Seminar** - Include a portion of a seminar on the health benefits of eating organic foods.

**Comment on industry trends and product news** - We will appear more in-tune and knowledgeable in our market if we can talk about what's happening in our industry and marketplace.

Resources:    www.businessvideomarketing.tv    www.hotpluto.com
www.hubspot.com/video-marketing-kit
www.youtube.com/user/mybusinessstory

Analytics Report
http://support.google.com/youtube/bin/static.py?hl=en&topic=1728599&guide=1714169&page=guide.cs

Note:    Refer to Video Marketing Tips in rear marketing worksheets section.

Examples:
www.youtube.com/watch?v=ujX8jKQSkIg
www.youtube.com/watch?v=43tgft908HA&NR=1


## Top 11 places where we will share our videos online:

**YouTube**                                   **www.youtube.com**
This very popular website allows you to log-in and leave comments and ratings on the videos. You can also save your favorite videos and allows you to tag posted videos. This makes it easier for your videos to come up in search engines.

**Google Video**                              **http://video.google.com/**
A video hosting site. Google Video is not just focused on sharing videos online, but this is also a market place where you can buy the videos you find on this site using Google search engine.

**Yahoo! Video**                              **http://video.yahoo.com/**
Uploading and sharing videos is possible with Yahoo Video!. You can find several types of videos on their site and you can also post comments and ratings for the videos.

**Revver**                                    **http://www.revver.com/**
This website lets you earn money through ads on your videos and you will have a 50/50 profit split with the website. Another great deal with Revver is that your fans who posted your videos on their site can also earn money.

**Blip.tv**                                   **http://blip.tv/**
Allows viewers to stream and download the videos posted on their website. You can also use Creative Commons licenses on your videos posted on the website. This allows you to decide if your videos should be attributed, restricted for commercial use and be used under specific terms.

**Vimeo**                                     **http://www.vimeo.com/**
This website is family safe and focuses on sharing private videos. The interface of the website is similar to some social networking sites that allow you to customize your profile page with photos from Flickr and embeddable player. This site allows users to socialize through their videos.

**Metacafe**                                  **http://www.metacafe.com/**
This video sharing site is community based. You can upload short-form videos and share

it to the other users of the website. Metacafe has its own system called VideoRank that ranks videos according to the viewer reactions and features the most popular among the viewers.

**ClipShack**      http://www.clipshack.com/

Like most video sharing websites, you can post comments on the videos and even tag some as your favorite. You can also share the videos on other websites through the html code from ClipShack and even sending it through your email.

**Veoh**      http://www.veoh.com/

You can rent or sell your videos and keep the 70% of the sales price. You can upload a range of different video formats on Veoh and there is no limit on the size and length of the file. However, when your video is over 45 minutes it has to be downloaded before the viewer can watch it.

**Jumpcut**      http://download.cnet.com/JumpCut/3000-18515_4-10546353.html

Jumpcut allows its users to upload videos using their mobile phones. You will have to attach the video captured from your mobile phone to an email. It has its own movie making wizard that helps you familiarize with the interface of the site.

**DailyMotion**      www.dailymotion.com

As one of the leading sites for sharing videos, Dailymotion attracts over 114 million unique monthly visitors (source: comScore, May 2014) 1.2 billion videos views worldwide (source: internal). Offers the best content from users, independent content creators and premium partners. Using the most advanced technology for both users and content creators, provides high-quality and HD video in a fast, easy-to-use online service that also automatically filters infringing material as notified by content owners.

Offering 32 localized versions, their mission is to provide the best possible entertainment experience for users and the best marketing opportunities for advertisers, while respecting content protection.

## Trade Shows

We will exhibit at as many local trade shows per year as possible. These include Home and Garden Shows, County Fairs, open exhibits in shopping malls, business spot-lights with our local Chamber of Commerce, business expos, food festivals and more. The objective is to get our company name and catering service out to as many people as possible. When exhibiting at a trade show, we will put our best foot forward and represent ourselves as professionals. We will be open, enthusiastic, informative and courteous. We will exhibit our catering services with sales brochures, logo-imprinted giveaways, sample products to taste, a photo book for people to browse through and a computer to run our video presentation through. We will use a 'free drawing' for a gift basket prize and a sign-in sheet to collect names and email addresses. We will also develop a questionnaire or survey that helps us to assemble an ideal customer profile and qualify the leads we receive. We will train our booth attendants to answer all type of questions and to handle objections. We will also seek to present educational seminars at the show to gain increased publicity, and name and expertise recognition. Most importantly, we will develop and implement a follow-up program to stay-in-touch with prospects.

Resources:      www.tsnn.com      www.expocentral.com
     www.acshomeshow.com/      http://tradeshowprnews.com/

**Food Truck Festivals**                   **http://foodtruckfestivalsofne.com/**

The 2015 FTFNE tour is the largest group of consecutive food truck festivals to ever hit the Northeast. They have teamed up with some of the biggest food trucks in the region to launch a festival tour coming to cities and towns throughout New England, making sure that there will be a festival somewhere in the region virtually every weekend from June through October.

## Business Cards

Our business card will include our company logo, complete contact information, name and title, association logos, slogan or markets serviced, licenses and certifications. The center of our bi-fold card will contain a listing of the services we offer. We will give out multiple business cards to friends, family members, and to each customer, upon the completion of the service. We will also distribute business cards in the following ways:

1. Attached to invoices, surveys, flyers and door hangers.
2. Included in customer product packages.
3. We will leave a stack of business cards in a Lucite holder with the local Chamber of Commerce and any other businesses offering free counter placement.

We will use fold-over cards because they will enable us to list all our services and complete contact instructions on the inside of the card. We will also give magnetic business cards to new customers for posting on the refrigerator door.

We will place the following referral discount message on the back of our business cards:
> - Our business is very dependent upon referrals. If you have associates who could benefit from our quality foodservices, please write your name at the bottom of this card and give it to them. When your friend presents this card at their first appointment, he or she will be entitled to 10% off discount. And, on your next invoice, you will also get a 10% discount as a thank you for your referral. The card will feature our 'free sampling program' and info about our specialty service.

Resource:      www.vistaprint.com

## Direct Mail Package

To build name recognition and to announce the start of our Mobile Food Truck Service, we will offer a mail package consisting of a tri-fold brochure containing a coupon for a free cup of _____ to welcome our new customers. From those identified local residential customers we shall ask them to complete a survey and ask them of their perception of the mobile service, any specific product or dessert items that they would like to see added to our menu, etc. Those customers returning completed surveys would receive a gift or discount.

## Online Directory Listings

The following directory listings use proprietary technology to match customers with industry professionals in their geographical area. The local search capabilities for specific niche markets offer an invaluable tool for the customer. These directories help member businesses connect with purchase-ready buyers, convert leads to sales, and maximize the value of customer relationships. Their online and offline communities provide a quick and easy no-cost solution for customers to find a mobile ice cream company quickly. We intend to sign-up with all no cost directories and evaluate the ones that charge a fee.

1. www.findlafoodtrucks.com
2. www.allscream.com/
3. http://twitter.com/#!/foodtruckdir
4. www.twitter.com/streeteateries
5. www.foodtrucksmap.com
6. www.foodtruckdirectory.com
7. www.food-truck.com
8. www.mobilecravings.com
9. www.midtownlunch.com (NYC)
10. www.bingfoodcarts.com (Portland)
11. www.roaminghunger.com/la (Los Angeles)
12. http://www.sacfoodtrucks.net/p/blog-page.html

**Food Truck Fiesta**          **http://foodtruckfiesta.com/about/**

Launched in July 2010, Food Truck Fiesta answers the call of many hungry Washingtonians for a quick way to locate their favorite food trucks. Food Truck Fiesta offers, and automated and real-time view of Washington DC's food trucks plotted on a Google map. Commentary is provided on the many days of drama in the food truck world.

**Other General Directories Include:**

| | |
|---|---|
| Listings.local.yahoo.com | Switchboard Super Pages |
| YellowPages.com | MerchantCircle.com |
| Bing.com/businessportal | Local.com |
| Yelp.com | BrownBook.com |
| InfoUSA.com | iBegin.com |
| Localeze.com | Bestoftheweb.com |
| YellowBot.com | HotFrog.com |
| InsiderPages.com | MatchPoint.com |
| CitySearch.com | YellowUSA.com |
| Profiles.google.com/me | Manta.com |
| Jigsaw.com | LinkedIn.com |
| Whitepages.com | PowerProfiles.com |

| | |
|---|---|
| Get Listed | http://getlisted.org/enhanced-business-listings.aspx |
| Universal Business Listing | https://www.ubl.org/index.aspx |
| | www.UniversalBusinessListing.org |

**Universal Business Listing (UBL)** is a local search industry service dedicated to acting as a central collection and distribution point for business information online. UBL provides business owners and their marketing representatives with a one-stop location for broad distribution of complete, accurate, and detailed listing information.

## Local Publications

We will place low-cost classified ads in neighborhood publications to advertise our organic ice cream foodservice menu options. We will also submit public relations and informative articles to improve our visibility and establish our expertise and trustworthiness. These publications include the following:
1. Neighborhood Newsletters and Church Bulletins
2. Local Restaurant Association Newsletter
3. Local Chamber of Commerce Newsletter
4. Realtor Magazines
5. Homeowner Association Newsletters

Resource: Hometown News  www.hometownnews.com
Pennysaver  www.pennysaverusa.com

## New Homeowners

We will reach out to new movers in our immediate neighborhood. Marketing to new movers will help bring in more long-term customers. And, because new movers are five times more likely to become loyal, this marketing program, will generate new, fresh customers who are likely to turn in to the regular customers. The value of a new loyal customer will be significant, as a new loyal customer who comes in ___ (#) times a month can be worth up to $_____ a year for standard services. Furthermore, many studies suggest that new movers typically stay in their new homes for an average of 5.6 years. We will also participate in local Welcome Wagon activities for new residents, and assemble a mailing list to distribute sales literature from county courthouse records and Realtor supplied information. We will use a postcard mailing to promote a special get-acquainted offer to new residents.

We will adhere the following routine when marketing to new local homeowners:
1. Send out a friendly welcome letter / flyer / brochure welcoming each new family to the community along with information on our pest control services.
2. Include a gift certificate or a new client discount coupon / certificate to entice the new family to try our service, risk free with no obligation.
3. Send out a new client discount or offer an initial free evaluation.
4. Send out a postcard with a discount or coupon.

**Resources:**
Welcome Wagon  www.WelcomeWagon.com
Welcome Mat Services  www.WelcomeMatServices.com
Welcomemat Services uses specialized, patent-pending technology to store and log customer demographics for use by the local companies it supports.

## Bench Ads
These ads will provide us with an affordable way to improve our visibility.
Resource: www.BenchAds.net

## Networking
Networking will be a key to success because referrals and alliances formed can help to improve our community image and keep our practice growing. We will strive to build

long-term mutually beneficial relationships with our networking contacts and join the following types of organizations:
1. We will form a LeTip Chapter to exchange business leads.
2. We will join the local BNI.com referral exchange group.
3. We will join the Chamber of Commerce to further corporate relationships.
4. We will join the Rotary Club, Lions Club, Kiwanis Club, Church Groups, etc.
5. We will do volunteer work for American Heart Assoc. and Habitat for Humanity.
6. We will become an affiliated member of the local board of Realtors and the Women's Council of Realtors.
7. We will become a member of local Parent Teachers Association.
8. We will join local garden and women's clubs and senior citizen groups.

We will use our metropolitan _____ (city) Chamber of Commerce to target prospective business contacts. We will mail letters to each prospect describing our mobile ice cream services. We will follow-up with phone calls.

## Newsletter

We will develop a one-page menu/newsletter to be handed out to customers to take home with them as they visit the truck. The monthly menu/newsletter will be used to build our brand and update customers on pricing and special promotional developments. It will also serve as a reminder of what sets our Mobile Food Truck apart; homemade quality, fast service, convenience and freshness. The newsletter would contain local "hot spot' information and other tips. The menu/ newsletter will be produced in-house and for the cost of paper and computer time. We will include the following types of information:
1. Our involvement with charitable events.
2. New Service/Product Introductions/ Staff Changes
3. Featured employee/customer of the month.
4. New industry technologies.
5. Customer endorsements/testimonials.
6. Classified ads from local sponsors and suppliers.
7. Announcements / Upcoming events.

Resources:     Microsoft Publisher         www.aweber.com

**We will adhere to the following newsletter writing guidelines:**
1. We will provide content that is of real value to our subscribers.
2. We will provide solutions to our subscriber's problems or questions.
3. We will communicate regularly on a weekly basis.
4. We will create HTML Messages look professional and allow us to track how many people click on our links and/or open our emails.
5. We will not pitch our business opportunity in our Ezine very often.
6. We will focus our marketing dollars on building our Ezine subscriber list.
7. We will focus on relationship building and not the conveying of a sales message.
8. We will vary our message format with videos, articles, checklists, quotes, pictures and charts.

9. We will recommend occasionally affiliate products in some of our messages to help cover our marketing costs.
10. We will consistently follow the above steps to build a database of qualified prospects and customers.

**Resources:**
www.constantcontact.com
www.mailchimp.com
http://lmssuccess.com/10-reasons-online-business-send-regular-newsletter-customers/
www.smallbusinessmiracles.com/how/newsletters/
www.fuelingnewbusiness.com/2010/06/01/combine-email-marketing-and-social-media-for-ad-agency-new-business/


## Vehicle Signs/Wraps

We will place magnetic and vinyl signs on our vehicles and include our company name, phone number, company slogan and website address, if possible. We will create a cost-effective moving billboard with high-quality, high-resolution vehicle wraps. We will wrap a portion of the vehicle or van to deliver excellent marketing exposure.

Resource: www.awthentikgraphics.com/

Ex: http://bostinno.com/2015/06/06/does-this-local-food-truck-have-the-best-truck-design-in-the-country/

**Design Tips:**
1. Avoid mixing letter styles and too many different letter sizes.
2. Use the easiest to recognize form of your logo.
3. The standard background is white.
4. Do not use a background color that is the same as or close to your vehicle color.
5. Choose colors that complement your logo colors.
6. Avoid the use too many colors.
7. Use dark letter colors on a light background or the reverse.
8. Use easy to read block letters in caps and lower case.
9. Limit content to your business name, slogan, logo, phone number and website-address.
10. Include your license number if required by law.
11. Magnetic signs are ideal for door panels (material comes on 24" wide rolls).
12. Graphic vehicle window wraps allow the driver to still see out.
13. Keep your message short so people driving by can read it at a glance.
14. Do not use all capital letters.
15. Be sure to include your business name, phone number, slogan and web address.

## Vehicle Wraps

Vehicle wrapping will be one of our preferred marketing methods. According to company research, wrapped vehicles have more impact than billboards, create a positive image for the company and prompt the public to remember the words and images featured in the company's branding. Vehicle wrapping is also an inexpensive marketing strategy. A typical truck wrap costs about $2,500, and is a one-time payment for an ad that spans the life of a truck's lease.

## Advertising Wearables
We will give all preferred club members an eye-catching T-shirt or sweatshirt with our company name and logo printed across the garment to wear about town. We will also give them away as a thank you for customer referral activities. We will ask all employees to wear our logo-imprinted shirts.

## Stage Events
We will stage events to become known in our community. This is essential to attracting referrals. We will schedule regular events, such as seminar talks, demonstrations, catered open house events and fundraisers. We will offer seminars through organizations to promote the concept and benefits of our healthy meals and fast nutritious snacks. We will use event registration forms, our website and an event sign-in sheet to collect the names and email addresses of all attendees. This database will be used to feed our automatic customer relationship follow-up program and newsletter service.
Resource:     www.eventbrite.com

## Sales Brochures
The sales brochure will enable us to make a solid first impression when pursing business. Our sales brochure will include the following contents and become a key part of our sales presentation folder and direct mail package:

- Contact Information
- Customer Testimonials
- Competitive Advantages
- Trial Coupon
- Specialties
- Business Description
- List of Products/Health Benefits
- Owner Resume/Bio
- Map of truck route.

**Sales Brochure Design**
1. Speak in Terms of Our Prospects Wants and Interests.
2. Focus on all the Benefits, not Just Features.
3. Put the company logo and Unique Selling Proposition together to reinforce the fact that your company is different and better than the competition.
4. Include a special offer, such as a discount, a free report, a sample, or a free trial to increase the chances that the brochure will generate sales.

**We will incorporate the following Brochure Design Guidelines:**
1. Design the brochure to achieve a focused set of objectives (marketing of programs) with a target market segment (residential vs. commercial).
2. Tie the brochure design to our other marketing materials with colors, logo, fonts and formatting.
3. List capabilities and how they benefit clients.
4. Demonstrate what we do and how we do it differently.
5. Define the value proposition of our engineering installing services

6. Use a design template that reflects your market positioning strategy.
7. Identify your key message (unique selling proposition)
8. List our competitive advantages.
9. Express our understanding of client needs and wants.
10. Use easy to read (scan) headlines, subheadings, bullet points, pictures, etc.
11. Use a logo to create a visual branded identity.
12. The most common and accepted format for a brochure is a folded A3 (= 2 x A4), which gives 4 pages of information.
13. Use a quality of paper that reflects the image we want to project.
14. Consistently stick to the colors of our corporate style.
15. Consider that colors have associations, such as green colors are associated with the environment and enhance an environmental image.
16. Illustrations will be appropriate and of top quality and directly visualize the product assortment, product application and production facility.
17. The front page will contain the company name, logo, the main application of your product or service and positioning message or Unique Selling Proposition.
18. The back page will be used for testimonials or references, and contact details.

**Catering Sales Presentation Folder Contents**

| | | | |
|---|---|---|---|
| 1. | Resumes | 2. | Dish Photos |
| 3. | Contract/Application | 4. | Frequently Asked Questions |
| 5. | Sales Brochure | 6. | Business Cards |
| 7. | Testimonials/References | 8. | Program Descriptions |
| 9. | Informative Articles | 10. | Referral Program |
| 11. | Company Overview | 12. | Operating Policies |
| 13. | Article Reprints | 14. | Press Releases |

# Coupons

We will use coupons with limited time expirations to get prospects to try our healthy replacement desserts. We will also accept the coupons of our competitors to help establish new client relationships. We will run ads directing people to our Web site for a $___ coupon certificate. This will help to draw in new customers and collect e-mail addresses for the distribution of a monthly newsletter. Research indicates that we can use our coupons to spark online searches of our website and drive sales. This will help to draw in new clients and collect e-mail addresses for the distribution of a monthly newsletter. We will include a coupon with each sale, or send them by mail to our mailing list.

Examples:
http://www.simplyfreshdelivered.com/coupons.html
https://www.valpak.com/coupons/printable/gagas-rollin-diner-of-vallejo-ca/122794

**We will use coupons selectively to accomplish the following:**
1. To introduce a new product or service.
2. To attract loyal customers away from the competition
3. To prevent customer defection to a new competitor.
4. To help celebrate a special event.

5. To thank customers for a large order and ensure a repeat order within a certain limited time frame.

Resource:
http://mobile-cuisine.com/marketing/why-a-food-truck-may-offer-coupons/
http://www.foodtruckcoupons.com/

**Buy One Get One Free!**
Coupons will be an excellent promotional tool because they can be very effective, and they are easy to track. When we receive a number of coupons back from our customers we will tally up our results. The key will be to up-sell the purchase once we have them in the door. The coupon redeemers will hopefully bring friends or family. We will also tell these customers about the meal combos and treats we have available.

**Types of Coupons:**
1. Courtesy Coupons          Rewards for repeat business
2. Cross-Marketing Coupons   Incentive to try other products/services.
3. Companion Coupon          Bring a friend incentive.

Websites like Groupon.com, LivingSocial, Eversave, and BuyWithMe sell discount vouchers for services ranging from custom _____ to ____ consultations. Best known is Chicago-based Groupon. To consumers, discount vouchers promise substantial savings — often 50% or more. To merchants, discount vouchers offer possible opportunities for price discrimination, exposure to new customers, online marketing, and "buzz." Vouchers are more likely to be profitable for merchants with low marginal costs, who can better accommodate a large discount and for patient merchants, who place higher value on consumers' possible future return visits.

Examples:
www.groupon.com/lists/new-york-city/new-york-food-trucks-10-drive-by-kitchens

## Cross-Promotions
We will develop and maintain partnerships with local businesses that cater to the needs of seniors and working mothers, such as beauty salons and day care centers, and conduct cross-promotional marketing campaigns by exchanging customer email lists and endorsements.

## Premium Giveaways
We will distribute logo-imprinted promotional products at events, also known as giveaway premiums, to foster top-of-mind awareness (www.promoideas.org). These items include logo-imprinted T-shirts, business cards with magnetic backs, mugs with contact phone number and calendars that feature important date reminders.

## Local Newspaper Ads
We will use these ads to announce the opening of our facility and get our name established. We will adhere to the rule that frequency and consistency of message are

essential. We will include a list of our specialty services. We will include a coupon to track the response in zoned editions of 'Shopper' Papers, Theater Bills and Community Newsletters. We will use the ad to announce any weekly or monthly ice cream specials.

**Our newspaper ads will utilize the following design tips:**
1. We will start by getting a media kit from the publisher to analyze their demographic information as well as their reach and distribution.
2. Don't let the newspaper people have total control of our ad design, as we know how we want our company portrayed to the market.
3. Make sure to have 1st class graphics since this will be the only visual distinction we can provide the reader about our business.
4. Buy the biggest ad we can afford, with full-page ads being the best.
5. Go with color if affordable, because consumers pick color ads over black 82% of the time.
6. Ask the paper if they have specific days that more of our type of buyer reads their paper.
7. If we have a hit ad on our hands, we will make it into a circular or door-hanger to extend the life of the offer.
8. Don't change an ad because we are getting tired of looking at it.
9. We will start our headline by telling our story to pull the reader into the ad.
10. We will use "Act Now" to convey a sense of urgency to the reader.
11. We will use our headline to tell the reader what to do.
12. The headline is a great place to announce a free offer.
13. We will write our headline as if we were speaking to one person, and make it personal.
14. We will use our headline to either relay a benefit or intrigue the reader into wanting more information.
15. Use coupons giving a dollar amount off, not a percentage, as people hate doing the math.

| Publication Type | Ad Size | Timing | Circulation | Section | Fee |
|---|---|---|---|---|---|
| | | | | | |
| | | | | | |

## Doorhangers

Our doorhangers will feature our 'Free Cup of _____' if the customer purchases before a certain date. The doorhanger will include a listing of all our product categories and foodservice delivery options. We will also attach our business card to the doorhanger and distribute the doorhangers multiple times to the same subdivision.

## Mobile Coupon Program

We plan to drive truck sales with a mobile coupon program. Customers who text the word "____" for our company name to shortcode _____ (#) will receive mobile coupons and other information regarding premium meal options and promotions. The first mobile coupon will reward customers with $1 off any tasty meal combination.

Customers will receive additional offers through yearend, including special offers on ____. The mobile texting campaign will be a way to engage customers through an innovative promotion. Mobile coupons resonate among customers tapped into social media and the latest trends. Mobile coupons and discounts are a top incentive for consumers, a study from ABI Research found. Some 63% of respondents said a coupon would be the most effective incentive to get them to respond to a mobile marketing message. P-O-P signage and social media marketing on YouTube, Twitter, Facebook and blogs will be used to support this campaign.

Resource:   Cellit Mobile Marketing   www.cellitmarketing.com/

## Article Submissions

We will pitch articles to consumer magazines, local newspapers, business magazines and internet articles directories to help establish our specialized expertise and improve our visibility. Hyperlinks will be placed within written articles and can be clicked on to take the customer to another webpage within our website or to a totally different website. These clickable links or hyperlinks will be keywords or relevant words that have meaning to our Mobile Food Truck. We will create keyword-rich article titles that match the most commonly searched keywords for our topic. In fact, we will create a position whose primary function is to link our mobile food truck with opportunities to be published in local publications.

**Publishing requires an understanding of the following publisher needs:**
1. Review of good work.
2. Editor story needs.
3. Article submission process rules
4. Quality photo portfolio
5. Exclusivity requirements.
6. Target market interests

**Our Article Submission Package will include the following:**
1. Well-written materials
2. Good Drawings
3. High-quality Photographs
4. Well-organized outline.

**Examples of General Publishing Opportunities:**
1. Document a new solution to old problem
2. Publish a research study
3. Mistake prevention advice
4. Present a different viewpoint
5. Introduce a local angle on a hot topic.
6. Reveal a new trend.
7. Share specialty niche expertise.
8. Share wine health benefits

Article Title Examples:   "The Health Benefits of Organic Foods"
"The World's Strangest _____ Ingredients"
"The History of Mobile Food Trucks"
"What's Up with the New Breed of Food Trucks?"

**Internet article directories include:**

http://ezinearticles.com/             http://www.mommyshelpercommunity.com
http://www.wahm-articles.com          http://www.ladypens.com/
http://www.articlecity.com            http://www.amazines.com
http://www.articledashboard.com       http://www.submityourarticle.com/articles

http://www.webarticles.com
http://www.article-buzz.com
www.articletogo.com
http://article-niche.com
www.internethomebusinessarticles.com
http://www.articlenexus.com

http://www.articlecube.com
http://www.free-articles-zone.com
http://www.content-articles.com
http://superpublisher.com
http://www.site-reference.com
www.articlebin.com

## Online Classified Ad Placements

The following free classified ad sites, will enable our business to thoroughly describe the benefits of our Mobile Food Truck products and services:

1. **Craigslist.org**
2. Ebay Classifieds
3. Classifieds.myspace.com
4. KIJIJI.com
5. //Lycos.oodle.com
6. Webclassifieds.us
7. USFreeAds.com
8. www.oodle.com
9. Backpage.com
10. stumblehere.com
11. Classifiedads.com
12. gumtree.com
13. Inetgiant.com
14. www.sell.com
15. Freeadvertisingforum.com
16. Classifiedsforfree.com
17. www.olx.com
18. www.isell.com
19. Base.google.com
20. www.epage.com
21. Chooseyouritem.com
22. www.adpost.com
23. Adjingo.com
24. Kugli.com

**Sample CraigsList.org Classified Ad#1**

_____ (company name) Can Turn Your Next Family Celebration into a Special Catered Party. We strive to provide our Customers with the best party planning in _____ Area! Free estimates, affordable prices, quality organic ingredients and dependable service. We are the Mobile Party Caterers to hire for a very special birthday celebration! Call _____. or e-mail _____ for further info or to schedule an estimate. References are available upon request. Visit our website _____ for our Customers' reviews and to see photos of our catered party celebrations.

**Sample CraigsList.org Classified Ad#2**

MOBILE Food & YOGURT Smoothie TRUCK FOR ALL EVENTS!!!
Try something new this year by having our mobile food truck cater and compliment your next party/event. Children as well as grown adults crave and love our hot meals, appetizers and smoothies! Whether it's a huge BLOCK PARTY, PRIVATE PARTY, or COMPANY EVENT, _____ (company name) provides un-matched mobile food truck services. Our party packages start as low as $____. Give us a call soon as possible to book your party/event because the weekend slots full up fast. You can reach us by phone at __. If it's more convenient, email us at _____. When you get an opportunity visit our website at www._____.com to see what we offer. Thank you in advance for your interest and make it a great day!

**Two-Step Direct Response Classified Advertising**

We will use 'two-step direct response advertising' to motivate readers to take a step or action that signals that we have their permission to begin marketing to them in step two. Our objective is to build a trusting relationship with our prospects by offering a free unbiased, educational report in exchange for permission to continue the marketing process. This method of advertising has the following benefits:

1. Shorter sales cycle.
2. Eliminates need for cold calling.
3. Establishes expert reputation.
4. Better qualifies prospects
5. Process is very trackable.
6. Able to run smaller ads.

**Sample Two-Step Lead Generating Classified Ad:**
FREE Report Reveals "The Secrets to Hiring the Best Mobile Catering Service" or…"Learn How 'All Natural' Compares to '100% Organic".
Call 24 hour recorded message and leave your name and address or visit our website at _____ and enter your contact information. Your report will be sent out immediately.

Note: The respondent has shown they have an interest in our mobile foodservices. We will send this lead the report with excellent and impartial advice. We will also include a section in the report on our complete range of organic products and contact information, along with a coupon for a free food sampling, initial consultation and a sales brochure.

## Yellow Page Ads

Research indicates that the use of the traditional Yellow Page Book is declining, but that new residents or people who don't have many personal acquaintances will look to the Yellow Pages to establish a list of potential businesses to call upon. Even a small 2" x 2" boxed ad can create awareness and attract the desired target client, above and beyond the ability of a simple listing. We will use the following design concepts:

1. We will use a headline to sell people on what is unique about our mobile foodservice operations.
2. We will include a service guarantee to improve our credibility.
3. We will include a coupon offer and a tracking code to monitor the response rate and decide whether to increase or decrease our ad size in subsequent years.
4. We will choose an ad size equal to that of our competitors, and evaluate the response rate for future insertion commitments.
5. We will include our hours of operation, motto or slogan and logo.
6. We will include our competitive advantages.
7. We will list under the same categories as our competitors.

Resource:     www.superpages.com     www.yellowpages.com

**Ad Information:**
Book Title: _____          Coverage Area: _____
Yearly Fee: $_____             Ad Size: _____ page
Renewal date: _____            Contact: _____

## Cable Television Advertising

Cable television will offer us more ability to target certain market niches or demographics with specialty programming. We will use our marketing research survey to determine which cable TV channels our customers are watching. It is expected that many

watch the Home & Garden TV channel, and that people with surplus money watch the Golf Channel and the Food Network. Our plan is to choose the audience we want, and to hit them often enough to entice them to take action. We will also take advantage of the fact that we will be able to pick the specific areas we want our commercial to air. Ad pricing will be dependent upon the number of households the network reaches, the ratings the particular show has earned, and the supply and demand for a particular network.
Resource:
Spot Runner         www.spotrunner.com

**Ad Information:**

Length of ad "spot": __ seconds          Development costs: $____ (onetime fee)
Length of campaign: __ (#) mos.          Runs per month: Three times per day
Cost per month.: $_____                 Total campaign cost: $_____.

## Radio Advertising

We will use non-event based radio advertising. This style of campaign is best suited for non-promotional sales driven retail businesses, such as our mobile food truck. We will utilize a much smaller schedule of ads on a consistent long-range basis (48 to 52 weeks a year) with the We will use non-event based radio advertising. This style of campaign is best suited for non-sales driven retail businesses, such as our company. We will utilize a much smaller schedule of ads on a consistent long-range basis (48 to 52 weeks a year) with the objective of continuously maintaining top-of-mind-awareness. This will mean maintaining a sufficient level of awareness to be either the number one or number two choice when a triggering-event, such as a party, moves the consumer into the market for services and forces "a consumer choice" about which company in the consumer's perception might help them the most. This consistent approach will utilize only one ad each week day (260 days per year) and allow our company to cost-effectively keep our message in front of consumers once every week day. The ad copy for this non-event campaign, called a positioning message, will not be time-sensitive. It will define and differentiate our business' "unique market position", and will be repeated for a year.
Note: On the average, listeners spend over 3.5 hours per day with radio.

Radio will give us the ability to target our audience, based on radio formats, such as news-talk, classic rock and the oldies. Radio will also be a good way to get repetition into our message, as listeners tend to be loyal to stations and parts of the day.

1. We will use radio advertising to direct prospects to our Web site, advertise a limited time promotion or call for an informational flooring brochure.
2. We will try to barter our services for radio ad spots.
3. We will use a limited-time offer to entice first-time customers to use our mobile foodservices.
4. We will explore the use of on-air community bulletin boards to play our public announcements about community sponsored events.
5. We will also make the radio station aware of our expertise in the mobile foodservice field and our availability for interviews.
6. Our choice of stations will be driven by the market research information we collect via our surveys.
7. We will capitalize on the fact that many stations now stream their programming

on the internet and reach additional local and even national audiences, and if online listeners like what they hear in our streaming radio spot, they can click over to our website.
8. Our radio ads will use humor, sounds, compelling music or unusual voices to grab attention.
9. Our spots will tell stories or present situations that our target audience can relate to, such as how to read product labels for the real story.
10. We will make our call to action, a website address or vanity phone number, easy to remember and tie it in with our company name or message.
11. We will approach radio stations about buying their unsold advertising space for deep discounts. (Commonly known at radio stations' as "Run of Station")
On radio, this might mean very early in the morning or late at night. We will talk to our advertising representatives and see what discounts they can offer when one of those empty spaces comes open.

Resources:   Radio Advertising Bureau      www.RAB.com
             Radio Locator                 www.radio-locator.com
             Radio Directory               www.radiodirectory.com

**Ad Information:**

Length of ad "spot": __ seconds          Development costs: $____ (onetime fee)
Length of campaign: __ (#) mos.          Runs per month: Three times per day
Cost per month.: $_____                 Total campaign cost: $_____.

## E-mail Marketing

We will use the following email marketing tips to build our mailing list database, improve communications, boost customer loyalty and attract new and repeat business.

1. Define our objectives as the most effective email strategies are those that offer value to our subscribers: either in the form of educational content or promotions. To drive sales, a promotional campaign is the best format. To create brand recognition and reinforce our expertise in our industry we will use educational newsletters.
2. A quality, permission-based email list will be a vital component of our email marketing campaign. We will ask customers and prospects for permission to add them to our list at every touch-point or use a sign-in sheet.
3. We will listen to our customers by using easy-to-use online surveys to ask specific questions about customers' preferences, interests and satisfaction.
4. We will send only relevant and targeted communications.
5. We will reinforce our brand to ensure recognition of our brand by using a recognizable name in the "from" line of our emails and including our company name, logo and a consistent design and color scheme in every email.

**Resources:**

https://cbtnews.com/8-tips-drive-successful-email-marketing-campaign/
https://www.inman.com/2017/06/05/4-tips-for-effective-email-marketing/
https://due.com/blog/ways-take-good-care-email-list/

Every ___ (five?) to ____ (six?) weeks, we will send graphically-rich, permission-based, personalized, email marketing messages to our list of customers who registered on our website, in our truck or at a show. The emails will alert customers in a ___ (50?)-mile radius to promotions as well as other local events sponsored by our company. This service will be provided by either ExactTarget.com or ConstantContact.com. The email will announce a special promotional event and contain a short sales letter. The message will invite recipients to click on a link to our website to checkout more information about the event, then print out the page and bring it with them to the event. The software offered by these two companies will automatically personalize each email with the customer's name. The software also provides detailed click-through behavior reports that will enable us to evaluate the success of each message. The software will also allow us to dramatically scale back its direct mail efforts and associated costs. Our company will send a promotional e-mail about a promotion that the customer indicated was important to them in their preferred membership application. Each identified market segment will get notified of new products, specials and offers based on past buying patterns and what they've clicked on in our previous e-newsletters or indicated on their surveys. The objective is to tap the right customer's need at the right time, with a targeted subject line and targeted content. Our general e-newsletter may appeal to most customers, but targeted mailings that reach out to our various audience segments will build even deeper relationships, and drive higher sales.

Resource:
www.constantcontact.com/pricing/email-marketing.jsp
http://www.verticalresponse.com/blog/10-retail-marketing-ideas-to-boost-sales/
www.constantcontact.com/pricing/email-marketing.jsp

**Google Reviews**
We will use our email marketing campaign to ask people for reviews. We will ask people what they thought of our mobile food truck business or catering services and encourage them to write a Google Review if they were impressed. We will incorporate a call to action (CTA) on our email auto signature with a link to our Google My Review page.
Source:
https://superb.digital/how-to-ask-your-clients-for-google-reviews/

Resources:
https://support.google.com/business/answer/3474122?hl=en
https://support.google.com/maps/answer/6230175?co=GENIE.Platform%3DDesktop&hl=en
www.patientgain.com/how-to-get-positive-google-reviews

Example:
We will tell our customers to:
1. Go to https://www.google.com/maps
2. Type in your business name, select the listing
3. There's a "card" (sidebar) on the left-hand side. At the bottom, they can click 'Be the First to Write a Review' **or** 'Write a Review' if you already have one review.

Source:
https://www.reviewjump.com/blog/how-do-i-get-google-reviews/

## Voice Broadcasting

A web-based voice broadcast system will provide a powerful platform to generate thousands of calls to clients and customers or create customizable messages to be delivered to specific individuals. Voice broadcasting and voice mail broadcast will allow our company to instantly send interactive phone calls with ease while managing the entire process right from the Web. We will instantly send alerts, notifications, reminders, GOTV - messages, and interactive surveys with ease right from the Web. The free VoiceShot account will guide us through the process of recording and storing our messages, managing our call lists, scheduling delivery as well as viewing and downloading real-time call and caller key press results. The voice broadcasting interface will guide us through the entire process with a Campaign Checklist as well as tips from the Campaign Expert. Other advanced features include recipient targeting, call monitoring, scheduling, controlling the rate of call delivery and customized text to speech (TTS).

Resource: http://www.voiceshot.com/public/outboundcalls.asp

## Facebook.com

We will use Facebook to move our businesses forward and stay connected to our customers in this fast-paced world. Content will be the key to staying in touch with our customers and keeping them informed. The content will be a rich mix of information, before and after photos, interactive questions, current trends and events, industry facts, education, promotions and specials, humor and fun. We will use the following step system to get customers from Facebook.com:

1. We will open a free Facebook account at Facebook.com.
2. We will begin by adding Facebook friends. The fastest way to do this is to allow Facebook to import our email addresses and send an invite out to all our customers.
3. We will post a video to get our customers involved with our Facebook page. We will post a video called "How to Plan a Successful Catered Party." The video will be first uploaded to YouTube.com and then simply be linked to our Facebook page. Video will be a great way to get people active and involved with our Facebook page.
4. We will send an email to our customers base that encourages them to check out the new video and to post their feedback about it on our Facebook page. Then we will provide a link driving customers to our Facebook page.
5. We will respond quickly to feedback, engage in the dialogue and add links to our response that direct the author to a structured mini-survey.
6. We will optimize our Facebook profile with our business keyword to make it an invaluable marketing tool and become the "go-to" expert in our industry
7. On a monthly basis, we will send out a message to all Facebook fans with a special offer, as Fan pages are the best way to interact with customers and potential customers on Facebook,
8. We will use Facebook as a tool for sharing success stories and relate the ways in which we have helped our customers.

9. We will use Facebook Connect to integrate our Facebook efforts with our regular website to share our Facebook Page activity. This will also give us statistics about our website visitors, and add social interaction to our site.

Resources:
http://www.facebook.com/advertising/
http://mobile-cuisine.com/features/facebook-marketing-tips-for-food-trucks/
http://www.socialmediaexaminer.com/how-to-set-up-a-facebook-page-for-business/
http://smallbizsurvival.com/2009/11/6-big-facebook-tips-for-small-business.html

Examples:
www.facebook.com/pages/Simply-Steves-Mobile-Food-Truck/177464262278388

**Facebook Profiles** represent individual users and are held under a person's name. Each profile should only be controlled by that person. Each user has a wall, information tab, likes, interests, photos, videos and each individual can create events.

**Facebook Groups** are pretty similar to Fan Pages but are usually created for a group of people with a similar interest and they are wanting to keep their discussions private. The members are not usually looking to find out more about a business - they want to discuss a certain topic.

**Facebook Fan Pages** are the most viral of your three options. When someone becomes a fan of your page or comments on one of your posts, photos or videos, that is spread to all their personal friends. This can be a great way to get your information out to lots of people...and quickly! In addition, one of the most valuable features of a business page is that you can send "updates" about new products and content to fans and your home building brand becomes more visible.

**Facebook Live** lets people, public figures and Pages share live video with their followers and friends on Facebook.
Source:
https://live.fb.com/about/
Resources:
https://www.facebook.com/business/a/Facebook-video-ads
http://smartphones.wonderhowto.com/news/facebook-is-going-all-live-video-streaming-your-phone-0170132/

**Facebook Business Page**
Resources:
https://www.facebook.com/business/learn/set-up-facebook-page
https://www.pcworld.com/article/240258/how_to_make_a_facebook_page_for_your_small_business.html
https://blog.hubspot.com/blog/tabid/6307/bid/5492/how-to-create-a-facebook-business-page-in-5-simple-steps-with-video.aspx

**Small Business Promotions**
This group allows members to post about their products and services and is a public group designated as a Buy and Sell Facebook group.
Source:   https://www.facebook.com/groups/smallbusinesspronotions/
Resource:
https://www.facebook.com/business/a/local-business-promotion-ads
https://www.facebook.com/business/learn/facebook-create-ad-local-awareness
www.socialmediaexaminer.com/how-to-use-facebook-local-awareness-ads-to-target-customers/

**Facebook Ad Builder**
https://waymark.com/signup/db869ac4-7202-4e3b-93c3-80acc5988df9/?partner=fitsmallbusiness

**Facebook Lead Ads        www.facebook.com/business/a/lead-ads**
A type of sponsored ad that appears in your audience's timeline just like other Facebook ads.  However, the goal with lead ads is literally to capture the lead's info without them leaving Facebook.  These ads don't link to a website landing page, creating an additional step.

**Best social media marketing practices:**
1. Assign daily responsibility for Facebook to a single person on your staff with an affinity for dialoguing.
2. Set expectations for how often they should post new content and how quickly they should respond to comments – usually within a couple hours.
3. Follow and like your followers when they seem to have a genuine interest in your area of health and wellness expertise.
4. Post on the walls of not only your own Facebook site, but also on your most active, influential posters with the largest networks.
5. Periodically post a request for your followers to "like" your page.
6. Monitor Facebook posts to your wall and respond every two hours throughout your business day.

**We will use Facebook in the following ways to market our mobile food truck:**
1. Promote our blog posts on our Facebook page
2. Post a video of our service people in action.
3. Make time-sensitive offers during slow periods
4. Create a special landing page for coupons or promotional giveaways
5. Create a Welcome tab to display a video message from our owner.
   Resource:  Pagemodo.
6. Support a local charity by posting a link to their website.
7. Thank our customers while promoting their businesses at the same time.
8. Describe milestone accomplishments and thank customers for their role.
9. Give thanks to corporate accounts.
10. Ask customers to contribute stories about _____ occurrences.
11. Use the built-in Facebook polling application to solicit feedback.

12. Use the Facebook reviews page to feature positive comments from customers, and to respond to negative reviews.
13. Introduce customers to our staff with resume and video profiles.
14. Create a photo gallery of unusual ____ (requests/jobs?) to showcase our expertise.

**We will also explore location-based platforms like the following:**
- FourSquare
- Facebook Places
- GoWalla
- Google Latitude

As a mobile food truck serving a local community, we will appreciate the potential for hyper-local platforms like these. Location-based applications are increasingly attracting young, urban influencers with disposable income, which is precisely the audience we are trying to attract. People connect to geo-location apps primarily to "get informed" about local happenings.

Foursquare.com
A web and mobile application that allows registered users to post their location at a venue ("check-in") and connect with friends. Check-in requires active user selection and points are awarded at check-in. Users can choose to have their check-ins posted on their accounts on Twitter, Facebook, or both. In version 1.3 of their iPhone application, foursquare enabled push-notification of friend updates, which they call "Pings". Users can also earn badges by checking in at locations with certain tags, for check-in frequency, or for other patterns such as time of check-in.]
Resource:
https://foursquare.com/business/
https://support.foursquare.com/hc/en-us/articles/201065050-How-do-I-add-create-a-place-

We will offer specials to those who frequent our mobile food business and check in regularly. We will offer the "mayor" to receive a free dish or desert. We will also utilize foursquare to get many people to check in at once, also called a "swarm." If we can get a certain predetermined and posted number of check-ins, everyone will get our discount of the day.
Source: www.morebusiness.com/7-tips-to-improve-your-food-cart-marketing-strategy


Instagram
Instagram.com is an online photo-sharing, video-sharing and social networking service that enables its users to take pictures and videos, apply digital filters to them, and share them on a variety of social networking services, such as
Facebook, Twitter, Tumblr and Flickr. A distinctive feature is that it confines photos to a square shape, similar to Kodak Instamatic and Polaroid images, in contrast to the 16:9 aspect ratio now typically used by mobile device cameras. Users are also able to record and share short videos lasting for up to 15 seconds.

**Resources:**
http://nextrestaurants.com/social-media/instagram-works-for-food-trucks/

http://nextshark.com/3-ways-food-trucks-are-using-instagram-to-build-loyal-customers/
http://eatst.foodnetwork.ca/blog/label/food-trucks-using-instagram
http://www.wordstream.com/blog/ws/2015/01/06/instagram-marketing

We will use Instagram in the following ways to help amplify the story of our brand, get people to engage with our content, and get people to visit our site:
1. Let our customers and fans know about specific product availability.
2. Tie into trends, events or holidays to drive awareness.
3. Let people know we are open and our menu is spectacular.
4. Run a monthly contest and pick the winning hashtagged photograph to activate our customer base and increase our exposure.
5. Encourage the posting and collection of happy onsite customer photos.

Examples:
http://ink361.com/app/users/ig-665618581/lafamiglia187/photos

Note: Commonly found in tweets, a hashtag is a word or connected phrase (no spaces) that begins with a hash symbol (#). They're so popular that other social media platforms including Facebook, Instagram and Google+ now support them. Using a hashtag turns a word or phrase into a clickable link that displays a feed (list) of other posts with that same hashtag. For example, if you click on #_____ in a tweet, or enter #_____ in the search box, you'll see a list of tweets all about _____ .


## Snapchat.com

This is a photo messaging app for iPhone and Android mobile devices. Users can take a picture or video and add text, drawings, and a variety of filters. They set a designated time limit, 1-10 seconds, and send to selected contacts from their list. Users can also set a "story" – a Snap that pins to their profile and is viewable for 24 hours after posting. Snapchat photos display for a maximum of 10 seconds (for 24 hours, in the case of a snap story) before becoming permanently inaccessible. The user may choose to save their snaps, but this will only save it to their local device. If the receiver uses the screenshot function on their phone, or chooses to replay a snap, the sender is notified. The point of Snapchat is to be fun and quirky, enticing and engaging your contacts with visual snippets of whatever you are doing. Teen and millennial users enjoy using Snapchat where they would traditionally send a text message. In many cases it's easier and more stimulating to send a quick clip of the property you are viewing, for example, than it would be to send a text description.

Snapchat is not useful as a lead generating tool, but it is exceptionally useful for client engagement and retention. When we meet with a client and exchange mobile contact information, we will ask if they use Snapchat and if we can add them to keep them updated on locations and menu changes. The beauty of the Snap is that is draws the client into the environment and makes them want to experience more. We will use this limitation to our advantage and make our client feel compelled to request and attend more food festivals. Snapchat is also a phenomenal tool to engage with existing clients. It will make buyers feel connected to the food truck owner, which is conducive to converting sales and retaining these clients in the future. While the primary user demographic is in the millennial age range, the app is popular with many adults as well. Incorporating Snapchat into our client communication strategy will aid our ability to form long term client relationships.

Resources:
https://blog.hootsuite.com/smart-ways-to-use-snapchat-for-business/
http://smallbiztrends.com/2014/10/how-businesses-can-use-snapchat.html
http://nymag.com/selectall/2017/04/the-snapchat-101-the-best-coolest-smartest-weirdest-accounts.html

## MySpace Advertising

MySpace.com offers a self-service, graphical "display" advertising platform that will enable our company to target our marketing message to our audience by demographic characteristics. With the new MySpace service, we will be able to upload our own ads or make them quickly with an online tool, and set a budget of $25 to $10,000 for the campaigns. We can choose to target a specific gender, age group and geographic area. We will then pay MySpace each time someone clicks on our ad. Ads can link to other MySpace pages, or external websites. MyAds will let us target our ads to specific groups of people using the public data on MySpace users' profiles, blogs and comments. MySpace will enable our company to target potential customers with similar interests to our existing customer base, as revealed via our marketing research surveys. Also the bulletin function on MySpace will allow us to update customers on company milestone achievements and coming events. We will also post a short video to our home page and encourage the sharing of the video with other MySpace users.
Examples:
https://myspace.com/lulubssandwiches

## LinkedIn.com

LinkedIn ranks high in search engines and will provide a great platform for sending event updates to business associates. To optimize our LinkedIn profile, we will select one core keyword. We will use it frequently, without sacrificing consumer experience, to get our profile to skyrocket in the search engines. Linkedin provides options that will allow our detailed profile to be indexed by search engines, like Google. We will make use of these options, so our business will achieve greater visibility on the Web. We will use widgets to integrate other tools, such as importing your blog entries or Twitter stream into your profile, and go market research and gain knowledge with Polls. We will answer questions in Questions and Answers to show our expertise, and ask questions in Questions and Answers to get a feel for what customers and prospects want or think. We will publish our LinkedIn URL on all our marketing collateral, including business cards, email signature, newsletters, and web site.  We will grow our network by joining industry and alumni groups related to our business. We will update our status examples of recent work, and link our status updates with our other social media accounts. We will start and manage a group or fan page for our product, brand or business. We will share useful articles that will be of interest to customers, and request LinkedIn recommendations from customers willing to provide testimonials. We will post our presentations on our profile using a presentation application. We will ask our first-level contacts for introductions to their contacts and interact with LinkedIn on a regular basis to reach those who may not see us on other social media sites. We will link to articles posted elsewhere, with a summary of why it's valuable to add to our credibility and list our newsletter subscription information and archives. We will post discounts and package deals. We will buy a LinkedIn direct ad that our target market will see. We will find vendors and contractors through connections.

Examples:
http://www.linkedin.com/in/desifoodtruck

## Podcasting

Our podcasts will provide both information and advertising. Our podcasts will allow us to pull in a lot of customers. Our monthly podcasts will be heard by ___ (#) eventual subscribers. Podcasts can now be downloaded for mobile devices, such as an iPod. Podcasts will give our company a new way to provide information and an additional way to advertise. Podcasting will give our business another connection point with customers. We will use this medium to communicate on important issues, what is going on with a planned event, and other things of interest to our health-conscious customers. The programs will last about 10 minutes and can be downloaded for free on iTunes. The purpose is not to be a mass medium. It is directed at a niche market with an above-average educational background and very special interests. It will provide a very direct and a reasonably inexpensive way of reaching our targeted audience with relevant information about our mobile ice cream products and services.

Resources:
www.apple.com/itunes/download/.
www.cbc.ca/podcasting/gettingstarted.html
http://tastetrekkers.com/episode-73-best-food-trucks/


## Press Release Overview:

We will use market research surveys to determine the media outlets that our demographic customers read and then target them with press releases. We will draft a cover letter for our media kit that explains that we would like to have the newspaper print a story about the start-up of our new local business or a milestone that we have accomplished. And, because news releases may be delivered by feeds or on news services and various websites, we will create links from our news releases to content on our website. These links which will point to more information or a special offer, will drive our clients into the sales process. They will also increase search engine ranking on our site. We will follow-up each faxed package to the media outlet with a phone call to the lifestyle section editor.

**Resources:**
http://mobile-cuisine.com/marketing/press-release-food-truck/

http://www.mr-trailers.com/2015/03/14/press-release-template/

## Media Kit

We will compile a media kit with the following items:
1. A pitch letter introducing our Mobile Food Truck business.
2. A press release with news story facts about our impact on real people diets.
3. Biographical fact sheet or sketches of key personnel.
4. Listing of product and service features and benefits to customers.
5. Photos of satisfied customers.
6. Endorsements and Testimonials.

Resource: http://mobile-cuisine.com/marketing/writing-a-press-release-for-your-food-truck/

## Press Releases

We will use well-written press releases to not only catch a reader's attention, but also to clearly and concisely communicate our business' mission, goals and capabilities.

The following represents a partial list of some of the reasons we will issue a free press release on a regular basis:
1. Announce Mobile Food Truck Grand Opening Event
2. Planned Open House Event
3. Addition of new product releases or service introduction.
4. Support for a Non-profit Cause or other local charity, such as a Food Drive.
5. Presentation of a free seminar or workshop on making organic ice cream.
6. Report Survey Results
7. Publication of an article or book on health food industry trends.
8. Addition of a new staff member.
9. Receiving an Association Award.
10. Sponsorship of a school ice cream party.
11. The creation of a new holiday inspired flavor and flavor name.
12. Send a free ice cream cake to the local radio station for a local DJs birthday

Examples:
https://www.foodtrucksin.com/blog/free-press-your-new-food-truck

Note: We will read the local paper regularly and get a feel for who reports on what. Then we will offer to be a resource for articles any time the editor wishes to speak to a local business owner. By giving them the support they need, we will generate substantial PR exposure over time.

### We will use the following techniques to get our press releases into print:
1. Find the right contact editor at a publication, that is, the editor who specializes in health and lifestyle issues.
2. Understand the target publication's format, flavor and style and learn to think like its readers to better tailor our pitch.
3. Ask up front if the journalist is on deadline.
4. Request a copy of the editorial calendar--a listing of targeted articles or subjects broken down by month or issue date, to determine the issue best suited for the

content of our news release or article.
5. Make certain the press release appeals to a large audience by reading a couple of back issues of the publication we are targeting to familiarize ourselves with its various sections and departments.
6. Customize the PR story to meet the magazine's particular style.
7. Avoid creating releases that look like advertising or self-promotion.
8. Make certain the release contains all the pertinent and accurate information the journalist will need to write the article and accurately answer the questions "who, what, when, why and where".
9. Include a contact name and telephone number for the reporter to call for more information.

**PR Distribution Checklist**
We will send copies of our press releases to the following entities:
1. Send it to clients to show accomplishments.
2. Send to prospects to help prospects better know who you are and what you do.
3. Send it to vendors to strengthen the relationship and to influence referrals.
4. Send it to strategic partners to strengthen and enhance the commitment and support to our firm.
5. Send it to employees to keep them in the loop.
6. Send it to Employees' contacts to increase the firm's visibility exponentially.
7. Send it to elected officials who often provide direction for their constituents.
8. Send it to trade associations for maximum exposure.
9. Put copies in the lobby and waiting areas.
10. Put it on our Web site, to enable visitors to find out who we are and what our firm is doing, with the appropriate links to more detailed information.
11. Register the Web page with search engines to increase search engine optimization.
12. Put it in our press kit to provide members of the media background information about our firm.
13. Include it in our newsletter to enable easy access to details about company activities.
14. Include it in our brochure to provide information that compels the reader to contact our firm when in need of legal counsel.
15. Hand-it out at trade shows and job fairs to share news with attendees and establish credibility.

**Media List**

| Journalist | Interests | Organization | Contact Info |
|---|---|---|---|

Distribution: www.1888PressRelease.com   www.ecomwire.com
www.prweb.com   www.WiredPRnews.com
www.PR.com   www.eReleases.com
www.24-7PressRelease.com   www.NewsWireToday.com
www.PRnewswire.com   www.onlinePRnews.com

www.PRLog.org
www.businesswire.com    www.marketwire.com
www.primezone.com    www.primewswire.com
www.xpresspress.com/    www.ereleases.com/index.html
www.Mediapost.com

Journalist Lists:    www.mastheads.org    www.easymedialist.com
www.helpareporter.com

Media Directories
Bacon's –    www.bacons.com/    AScribe –    www.ascribe.org/
Newspapers – www.newspapers.com/    Gebbie Press – www.gebbieinc.com/

Support Services
PR Web -    http://www.prweb.com
Yahoo News –    http://news.yahoo.com/
Google News –    http://news.google.com/

Resource:
**HARO** ("Help A Reporter Out")    www.helpareporter.com/
An online platform that provides journalists with a robust database of sources for upcoming stories. It also provides business owners and marketers with opportunities to serve as sources and secure valuable media coverage.

## Contest

Before opening our Mobile Food Truck, we will hold a contest for nearby elementary and middle school students to name the truck. We will give the shop naming contest winner $_____ (100.00) and $_____ (200.00) to their school. More importantly, we will give a certificate for a free cone to each and every entrant. A subsequent contest will be used to create and name an original sundae treat.

## Postcards

1. We will use a monthly, personalized, newsletter styled postcard, that includes healthy dessert suggestions, to stay-in-touch with prospects and customers.
2. Postcards will offer cheaper mailing rates, staying power and attention grabbing graphics, but require repetition, like most other advertising methods.
3. We will develop an in-house list of potential customers for routine communications from open house events, seminar registrations, direct response ads, etc.
4. We will use postcards to encourage users to visit our website, and take advantage of a special promotional replacement dessert offer.
5. We will grab attention and communicate a single-focus message in just a few words.
6. The visual elements of our postcard (color, picture, symbol) will be strong to help get attention and be directly supportive of the message.
7. We will facilitate a call to immediate action by prominently displaying our phone number and website address.
8. We will include a clear deadline, expiration date, limited quantity, or

consequence of inaction that is connected to the offer to communicate immediacy and increase response.

Resource: www.Postcardmania.com

## Flyers

1. We will seek permission to post flyers on the bulletin boards in local businesses, community centers, housing development offices and local schools.
2. We will also insert flyers into our direct mailings.
3. We will use our flyers as part of a handout package at open house events.
4. The flyers will feature a coupon for a free cup of organic ice cream.
5. The flyers will contain a listing of our product categories and foodservice specialties, along with the benefits our catering services.
5. We will circulate flyers to the following local agencies and organizations:
   - Churches and Synagogues         - Parent Support Groups
   - Nat'l Council of Jewish Women   - National Org. for Women
   - Senior and Child Daycare Centers

## Referral Program

We understand the importance of setting up a formal referral network through contacts with the following characteristics:

1. We will give a premium reward based simply on people giving referral names on the club membership registration form.
2. Send an endorsed testimonial letter from a loyal customer to the referred prospect.
3. Include a separate referral form as a direct response device.
4. Provide a space on the response form for leaving positive comments that can be used to build a testimonial letter, that will be sent to each referral.
5. We will clearly state our incentive rewards, and terms and conditions.
6. We will distribute a newsletter to stay in touch with our customers and include articles about our referral program success stories.
7. We will encourage our staff at weekly meetings to seek referrals from their personal contacts.

**Sources:**
1. Referrals from other retailers, particularly those of other niche specialties.
2. Give speeches on a complicated niche area that other practitioners may feel is too narrow for them to handle, thus triggering referrals.
3. Structured Client Referral Program.
4. Newsletter Coupons.

**Methods:**
1. Always have ready a 30-second elevator speech that describes what you do and who you do it for.
2. Use a newsletter to keep our name in front of referrals sources.
3. Repeatedly demonstrate to referral sources that we are also thinking about their

practice or business.
4. Regularly send referrals sources articles on unique yet important topics that might affect their businesses.
5. Use Microsoft Outlook to flag our contacts to remind us it is time to give them some form of personal attention.
6. Ask referral sources for referrals.
7. Get more work from a referral source by sending them work.
8. Immediately thank a referral source, even for the mere act of giving his name to a third party for consideration.
9. Remember referral sources with generous gift baskets and gift certificates.
10. Schedule regular lunches with former school classmates and new contacts.

We will offer an additional donation of $ _____ to any organization whose member use a referral coupon to become a client. The coupon will be paid for and printed in the organization's newsletter.

**Referral Tracking Form**

| Referral Source Name | Presently Referring Yes/No | No. of Clients Referred | Anticipated Revenue | Actions to be Taken | Target Date |
|---|---|---|---|---|---|
|  |  |  |  |  |  |
|  |  |  |  |  |  |

**Sample Referral Program**
We want to show our appreciation to established customers and business network partners for their kind referrals to our business. ____ (company name) wants to reward our valued and loyal customers who support our _____ Programs by implementing a new referral program. Ask any of our team members for referral cards to share with your family and friends to begin saving towards your next ____ (product/service) purchase. We will credit your account $___ (?) for each new customer you refer to us as well as give them 10% off their first visit. When they come for their first visit, they should present the card upon arrival. We will automatically set you up a referral account.

Examples:
http://sidewalksofny.com/food-truck-tours.php

**The Referral Details are as Follows:**
1. You will receive a $__ (?) credit for every customer that you refer for _____ (products/services). Credit will be applied to your referral account on their initial visit.
2. We will keep track of your accumulated reward dollars and at any time we can let you know the amount you have available for use in your reward account.
3. Each time you visit ____ (company name), you can use your referral dollars to pay up to 50% of your total charge that day
4. Referral dollars are not applicable towards the purchase of _____ products.
5. All referral rewards are for __ products and cannot be used towards ___ services.

## Referral Coupon Template

Company Name: _____
Address: _____
Phone: _____ Website: _____

Print and present this coupon with your first order and the existing customer who referred you will receive a credit for $_____ .

| **Current customer** | **Referred customer** |
|---|---|
| Name: _____ | Name: _____ |
| Address: _____ | Address: _____ |
| Phone: _____ | Phone: _____ |
| Email: _____ | Email: _____ |
| Date referred: | |

**Office use only**
Credit memo number: _____
Credit issued date: _____  Credit applied by: _____

## Invite-A-Friend

We will setup an aggressive invite-a-friend referral program. We will encourage new members or newsletter subscribers, during their initial registration process, to upload and send an invitation to multiple contacts in their email address books. We will encourage them by providing an added incentive, such as a free _____ .

## Blogging

We will use our blog to keep customers and prospects informed about products, events and services that relate to our ice cream business, new releases, contests, and specials. Our blog will show readers that we are a good source of expert information that they can count on. With our blog, we can quickly update our customers anytime our company releases a new product, the holding of a contest or are placing organic food items on special pricing. We will use our blog to share customer testimonials and meaningful product usage stories and recipes. We will use the blog to supply advice on creative applications for our mobile ice cream products and catering services. Our visitors will be able to subscribe to our RSS feeds and be instantly updated without any spam filters interfering. We will also use the blog to solicit product usage recommendations and future product addition suggestions. Additionally, blogs are free and allow for constant ease of updating.

**Our blog will give our company the following benefits:**
1. A cost-effective marketing tool.
2. An expanded network.
3. A promotional platform for new _____ services.
4. An introduction to people with similar interests.
5. Builds credibility and expertise recognition.

**We will use our blog for the following purposes:**
1. To share customer testimonials, experiences and meaningful success stories.
2. Update our clients anytime our company releases a new service.
3. Supply advice on _____ options.
4. Discuss research findings.
5. To publish helpful content.
6, To welcome feedback in multiple formats.
7. Link together other social networking sites, including Twitter.
8. To improve Google rankings.
9. Make use of automatic RSS feeds.

**We will adhere to the following blog writing guidelines:**
1. We will blog at least 2 or 3 times per week to maintain interest.
2. We will integrate our blog into the design of our website.
3. We will use our blog to convey useful information and not our advertisements.
4. We will make the content easy to understand.
5. We will focus our content on the needs of our targeted audience.

**Our blog will feature the following on a regular basis:**
1. Useful articles and assessment coupons.
2. Give away of a helpful free report in exchange for email addresses
3. Helpful information for our professional referral sources, as well as clients, and online and offline community members.
5. Use of a few social media outposts to educate, inform, engage and drive people back to our blog for more information and our free report.

To get visitors to our blog to take the next action step and contact our firm we will do the following:
1. Put a contact form on the upper-left hand corner of our blog, right below the header.
2. Put our complete contact information in the header itself.
3. Add a page to our blog and title it, "Become My Client.", giving the reader somewhere to go for the next sign-up steps.
4. At the end of each blog post, we will clearly tell the reader what to do next; such as subscribe to our RSS feed, or to sign up for our newsletter mailing list.

Resources:     www.blogger.com     www.blogspot.com     www.wordpress.com
Examples:
http://foodtruckin.blogspot.com/

## Blog Article Submissions
We will submit information about our mobile food truck's experiences, menu, routes and event appearances to local bloggers who focus on this topic. We will locate these bloggers by doing a Google search for 'mobile food truck bloggers', and then narrow the search by adding our city name.

**Examples:**

http://blogs.ajc.com/food-and-more/2014/09/27/fall-2014-dining-guide-a-dozen-top-food-trucks/
http://bostonfoodtruck.wordpress.com/
http://blog.pennlive.com/life/2014/05/two_more_mobile_food_trucks_-.html


## Bandit Signs
We plan to use sign holders or bandit signs, placed along key roads close to our business, to promote special events. The signs will feature our specialty, name and contact information.

## Portable Sales Tents
We will sponsor and set-up temporary sales tents and tables at local festivals and health fairs to handout our business cards and sales brochures, and offer free vision screenings.

## Customer Reward/Loyalty Program
For the carryout customer and as a means of building business by word-of-mouth customers will be encouraged and rewarded as repeat customers. This will be accomplished by offering a free lunch dessert to those customers who sign-up for our frequent buyer card and purchase ___ (10?) lunches within a ___ (#) month period. These loyalty punch cards will be very effective in the mobile ice cream business. It gets customers to come back for their ice cream cravings because they seek to qualify for the bonus reward. It will be important not to require too many visits before the customer receives the bonus or it won't work. To get a free cone or sundae a good number of visits will be about 5 or 6 purchases.

**Resources:**
http://mobile-cuisine.com/loyalty-rewards-program/
http://shawngraham.me/blog/a-6-step-guide-to-building-a-customer-loyalty-program-for-your-local-market
http://streetfightmag.com/2012/06/12/6-pos-systems-with-loyalty-program-integration/

**Frequent Buyer Program Types:**
1. Punch Cards — Receive something for free after ? Purchases.
2. Dollar-for-point Systems — Accrue points toward a free product.
3. Percentage of Purchase — Accrue points toward future purchases.


## Membership Club
It will easy to join our free membership club. We will simply print out the application form, and ask the customer to fill it in and take it to our truck. We will give the customer a shopping bag containing our membership card, discount voucher, the latest newsletter and other useful information.

Exclusive membership benefits include:
**Super Wednesdays**

Receive up to ___ (20?) % discount off the recommended retail price of healthy choice ice cream on the first Wednesday of every month.

**Up-to-date Health Information**

Our award winning Good Health Newsletter will be sent to customers three times a year, along with special discount coupons which will guarantee as much as ___ (20?) % discount off the recommended retail price.

**Red Hot Rewards**

With every purchase customers will earn exclusive reward points which go towards gift vouchers that can be redeemed on further purchases.

# Seminars

Seminars will present the following marketing and bonding opportunities:
1. Signage and branding as a presenting sponsor.
2. Opportunity to distribute name and logo imprinted handouts.
3. Media exposure through advertising and public relations.
4. The opportunity for one-on-one interaction with a targeted group of consumers to demonstrate an understanding of their needs and our matching expert solutions.
5. Use of sign-in sheet to collect names and email addresses for database build.

**Possible seminar funding sources:**
1. Small registration fee to cover the cost of hand-outs and refreshments.
2. Get sponsorship funding from partner/networking organizations.
3. Sponsorship classified ads in the program guide or handouts.

We will establish our expertise and trustworthiness by offering free seminars on the following types of topics:
1. Understanding the Health Benefits of Organic Foods
2. Party Planning Tips for Mobile Catered Parties
3. How to Achieve Weight Loss with the Right Meals

**Seminar target groups include the following:**
1. Fitness Club Members
2. Seniors
3. Parents with Obese Children
4. People with Special Diets

**Seminar marketing approaches include:**
1. Posting to website and enabling online registrations.
2. Email blast using www.constantcontact.com
3. Include seminar schedule in newsletter.
4. Classified ads using craigslist.org

**Seminar Objectives:**

| Seminar Topic | Target Audience | Handout | Target Date |
|---|---|---|---|
| | | | |
| | | | |

# Twitter

We will use 'Twitter.com' as a way to produce new business from existing customers and generate prospective customers online. Twitter is a free social networking and micro-blogging service that allows its users to send and read other users' updates (otherwise known as tweets), which are text-based posts of up to 140 characters in length. Updates are displayed on the user's profile page and delivered to other users who have signed up to receive them. The sender can restrict delivery to those in his or her circle of friends, with delivery to everyone being the default. Users can receive updates via the Twitter website, SMS text messaging, RSS feeds, or email. Twitter will give us the ability to have ongoing two-way conversations with our customers, which will allow us to get better at what we do and offer, while giving us the ability to express our own unique 'personality'. We will use our Twitter account to respond directly to questions, distribute news, solve problems, post updates, circulate information about fundraisers, hold trivia question contests for a chance to win a gift certificate and offer special discounts, known as 'Tweet Deals', on selected meals and catering services. Our posts on Twitter will include our URL (address), our new offers, dessert recipe tips and new service offerings. On a long-term basis, using Twitter consistently and efficiently will help push our website up the rankings on Google. The intangible, that will only have a positive effect, are the hundreds of impressions that each tweet will get, not to mention the positive statements that will be posted about our service, staff, selection and product knowledge. Using TweetReach, we expect our special promotional offers to receive thousands of impressions. We will also add our website, company logo, personal photo and/or blog on our profile page.

We will provide the following instructions to register as a 'Follower' of _____ (company name) on Twitter:
1. In your Twitter account, click on 'Find People' in the top right navigation bar, which will redirect to a new page.
2. Click on 'Find on Twitter' which will open a search box that says 'Who are you looking for?'
3. Type '_____ (company name) / _____ (owner name)' and click 'search'. This will bring up the results page.
4. Click the blue '_____' name to read the bio or select the 'Follow' button.

Examples:
http://twitter.com/#!/KogiStreetTeam


## Business Logo
Our logo will graphically represent who we are and what we do, and it will serve to help brand our image. It will also convey a sense of uniqueness and professionalism. The logo will represent our company image and the message we are trying to convey. Our business logo will reflect the philosophy and objectives of our Mobile Food Truck business. Our logo will incorporate the following design guidelines:
1. It will relate to our industry, our name, a defining characteristic of our company or a competitive advantage we offer.
2. It will be a simple logo that can be recognized faster.
3. It will contain strong lines and letters which show up better than thin ones.

4. It will feature something unexpected or unique without being overdrawn.
5. It will work well in black and white (one-color printing).
6. It will be scalable and look pleasing in both small and large sizes.
7. It will be artistically balanced and make effective use of color, line density and shape.
8. It will be unique when compared to competitors.
9. It will use original, professionally rendered artwork.
10. It can be replicated across any media mix without losing quality.
11. It appeals to our target audience.
12. It will be easily recognizable from a distance if utilized in outdoor advertising.

Resources:	www.freelogoservices.com/	www.hatchwise.com
www.logosnap.com	www.99designs.com
www.fiverr.com	www.freelancer.com
www.upwork.com

Logo Design Guide:
www.bestfreewebresources.com/logo-design-professional-guide
www.creativebloq.com/graphic-design/pro-guide-logo-design-21221

# Fundraisers

Community outreach programs involving charitable fundraising and showing a strong interest in the local school system will serve to elevate our status in the community as a "good corporate citizen" while simultaneously increasing truck traffic. We will execute a successful fundraising program for our Mobile Food Truck and build goodwill in the community, by adhering to the following guidelines:

1. Keep It Local
   When looking for a worthy cause, we will make sure it is local so the whole neighborhood will support it.
2. Plan It
   We will make sure that we are organized and outline everything we want to accomplish before planning the fundraiser.
3. Contact Local Media
   We will contact the suburban newspapers to do stories on the event and send out press releases to the local TV and radio stations.
4. Contact Area Businesses
   We will contact other businesses and have them put up posters in their trucks and pass out flyers to promote the event.
5. Get Recipient Support
   We will make sure the recipients of the fundraiser are really willing to participate and get out in the neighborhood to invite everyone into our truck for the event, plus help pass out flyers and getting other businesses to put up the posters.
6. Give Out Bounce Backs
   We will give a "bounce-back" coupon that allows for both a discount and an additional donation in exchange for customer next purchase. (It will have an expiration date of two weeks to give a sense of urgency.)

7. Be Ready with plenty of product and labor on hand for the event.

**Fundraiser Action Plan Checklist:**
1. Choose a good local cause for your fundraiser.
2. Calculate donations as a percentage for normal sales.
3. Require the group to promote and support the event.
4. Contact local media to get exposure before and after the event.
5. Ask area businesses to put up flyers and donate printing of materials.
6. Use a bounce-back coupon to get new customers back.
7. Be prepared with sufficient labor and product.

**Resources:**
http://foodtruckconnection.com/fundraisers/
http://www.fundraiserhelp.com/food-truck-fundraiser.htm
http://greenzonwheelz.com/food-truck-fundraisers-a-great-option-for-your-fundraising-needs/

# Billboards

We will use billboard advertising to create brand awareness and strong name recognition. We will design Billboards that are eye-catching and informative, and use easy to read fonts like Verdana. We will include our business name, location, a graphic, standout border and no more than eight words. In designing the billboard we will consider the fact that the eye typically moves from the upper left corner to the lower right corner of a billboard. We will use colors that can be viewed by color blind people, such as yellow, black and blue, and pictures to contrast with the sky and other surroundings. We will keep the layout uncluttered and the message simple, and include a direct call to action. Depending on the billboards size and location, the cost will range from $1,000 to $5,000 per month. We will try to negotiate a discount on a long-term contract.

Resources:    Outdoor Advertising Association of America         www.oaaa.org
              EMC Outdoor, Inc.                                 www.emcoutdoor.com

# Theater Advertising

Theater advertising is the method of promoting our business through in-theatre promotions. The objective of theater advertising is to expose the movie patron to our advertising message in various ways throughout the theater. Benefits include; an engaged audience that can't change the channel, an audience that is in a quiet environment, an audience that is in a good mood and receptive, advertising that is targeted to our local geographic area, full color video advertising on a 40 foot screen, and a moving and interactive ad with music and voiceover.

Resources:   Velocity Cinema Advertising      www.movieadvertising.com/index.html
             NCM                              www.nationalcinemedia.com/intheatreadvertising/
             ScreenVision                     www.screenvision.com
             AMC Theaters                     www.amctheatres.com
             Regal Entertainment Group        www.regmovies.com

# Mobile Marketing

We will create a new mobile marketing strategy that spotlights our new flagship product, And the importance of targeting a younger segment to expand our customer base.
We will use mobile advertising to tap into a younger tech-savvy segment of the market to grow our brand in the coming years.

First, consumers will opt-in by sending a text to our SMS platform and in return they will receive an offer for a free burrito via their mobile phones. Once a customer redeems the text message offer, the software will provide us with a report that details what radio station that customer was listening to, the daypart, and which program they were listening to, that prompted the customer to respond to the offer. Our trained staff will be the key in assisting customers with the promotion and up-selling. We will work with Opt It, Inc. to execute its first text messaging campaign. We want the portion of our customer base that does not typically clip coupons out of the Sunday paper to have easy access to the great deals we offer. We believe there will be a large number of people who opted-in on our Web site to receive mobile offers even before the promotion begins. Now, instead of promoting what's happening in a few weeks, we can have managers text local people to let them know about an event that's happening in a few hours.

In a texting component, customers will be able to text "____" to _____ (#) and receive mobile coupons. The second part of the message asks customers if they would like to register their e-mail addresses to receive weekly communications from _____ (company name). The first mobile coupon will reward customers with $___ off any family package. Customers will continue to receive additional offers, including special offers on holiday gift items. This will purely be an opt in campaign, and will let us create an ongoing conversation with our customers.

Resource:      Mobile Marketing Association     www.mmaglobal.com
                  BxP Marketing visit     www.bxpmarketing.com.

## Google Maps
We will first make certain that our business is listed in Google Maps. We will do a search for our business in Google Maps. If we don't see our business listed, then we will add our business to Google Maps. Even if our business is listed in Google Maps, we will create a Local Business Center account and take control of our listing, by adding more relevant information. Consumers generally go to Google Maps for two reasons: Driving Directions And to Find a Business.
Resource:    http://maps.google.com/

## Bing Maps                   www.bingplaces.com/
This will make it easy for customers to find our business.

## Google Places
Google Places helps people make more informed decisions about where to go for Mobile Food Trucks. Place Pages connect people to information from the best sources across the web, displaying photos, reviews and essential facts, as well as real-time updates and offers from business owners. We will make sure that our Google Places listing is up to

date to increase our online visibility. Google Places is linked to our Google Maps listing, and will help to get on the first page of Google search page results when people search for an Mobile Food Truck in our area.

Resource: www.google/com/places

## Yelp.com

We will use Yelp.com to help people find our local business. Visitors to Yelp write local reviews, over 85% of them rating a business 3 stars or higher In addition to reviews, visitors can use Yelp to find events, special offers, lists and to talk with other Yelpers. As business owners, we will setup a free account to post offers, photos and message our customers. We will also buy ads on Yelp, which will be clearly labeled "Sponsored Results". We will also use the Weekly Yelp, which is available in 42 city editions to bring news about the latest business openings and other happenings.

Examples:

http://www.yelp.com/biz/simply-steves-mobile-food-truck-minneapolis

## Epinions.com

This site helps people make informed buying decisions. It is a premier consumer reviews platform on the Web and a reliable source for valuable consumer insight, unbiased advice, in-depth product evaluations and personalized recommendations. Epinions is a service of Shopping.com, Inc., a leading provider of comparison shopping services. Shopping.com's mission is to help consumers anywhere use the power of information to find, compare and buy anything.

## Manta.com

Manta is the largest free source of information on small companies, with profiles of more than 64 million businesses and organizations. Business owners and sales professionals use Manta's vast database and custom search capabilities to quickly find companies, easily connect with prospective customers and promote their own services. Manta.com, founded in 2005, is based in Columbus, Ohio.

Resource: http://www.manta.com/getlisted/

Examples:

http://www.manta.com/c/mt4qsqy/brian-s-lunch-truck

## Zomato.com (Urbanspoon.com)

Urbanspoon is a leading provider of time-critical dining data, and an all-around factor the multi-billion dollar restaurant information industry. Twitter @urbanspoon

Examples:

www.urbanspoon.com/c/12/Miami-restaurants.html

http://www.urbanspoon.com/t/160/21/Harrisburg/Food-Truck-restaurants

Resource:

http://www.urbanspoon.com/cities/160/suggestions/new

## Pay-Per-Click Advertising

Google AdWords, Yahoo! Search Marketing, and Microsoft adCenter are the three largest network operators, and all three operate under a bid-based model. Cost per click (CPC) varies depending on the search engine and the level of competition for a particular keyword. Google AdWords are small text ads that appear next to the search results on Google. In addition, these ads appear on many partner web sites, including NYTimes.com (The New York Times), Business.com, Weather.com, About.com, and many more. Google's text advertisements are short, consisting of one title line and two content text lines. Image ads can be one of several different Interactive Advertising Bureau (IAB) standard sizes. Through Google AdWords, we plan to buy placements (ads) for specific search terms through this "Pay-Per-Click" advertising program. This PPC advertising campaign will allow our ad to appear when someone searches for a keyword related to our business, organization, or subject matter. More importantly, we will only pay when a potential customer clicks on our ad to visit our website. For instance, since we operate an Mobile Food Truck in ___ (city), ____ (state), we will target people using search terms such as "Lunch Truck, Food Wagon, Food Truck, mobile carts, corporate catered events, catering truck, catered birthday party, tacos, gyro, in ____ (city), ____ (state)". With an effective PPC campaign our ads will only be displayed when a user searches for one of these keywords. In short, PPC advertising will be the most cost-effective and measurable form of advertising for our Mobile Food Truck.

Resources:
http://adwords.google.com/support/aw/?hl=en
www.wordtracker.com


## Yahoo Local Listings

We will create our own local listing on Yahoo. To create our free listing, we will use our web browser and navigate to http://local.yahoo.com. We will first register for free with Yahoo, and create a member ID and password to list our business. Once we have accessed http://local.yahoo.com, we will scroll down to the bottom and click on "Add/Edit a Business" to get onto the Yahoo Search Marketing Local Listings page. In the lower right of the screen we will see "Local Basic Listings FREE". We will click on the Get Started button and log in again with our new Yahoo ID and password. The form for our local business listing will now be displayed. When filling it out, we will be sure to include our full web address (http://www.companyname.com). We will include a description of our Mobile Food Truck meals and foodservices in the description section, but avoid hype or blatant advertising, to get the listing to pass Yahoo's editorial review. We will also be sure to select the appropriate business category and sub categories.

Resource:
www.yahoo.com/style/a-taste-of-the-countrys-best-food-trucks-117032284796.html
http://divcreative.com/2013/10/22/yahoos-social-media-tips-for-food-trucks/


## Point-of-Purchase Displays (POP)

The term point-of-purchase, or POP, typically refers to the promotional graphics focused on influencing consumer behavior at the moment of the purchasing decision. These graphics serve to impact a buying decision in favor of a specific brand or product, where the purchase is imminent. POP is increasingly becoming one of the more important aspects of advertising and promotion, because of its efficiency in targeting the consumer in the actual buying environment, the decline of network television viewership and newspaper readership, and the stark reality of recession-sized ad budgets. Because of its impact, we will work with our distributor to secure the following types of items from food manufacturers:

1. Banners
2. Ceiling danglers
3. Themed wall coverings
4. Directional posters
5. Floor Decals
6. Props

## Advertorials

An advertorial is an advertisement written in the form of an objective article, and presented in a printed publication—usually designed to look like a legitimate and independent news story. We will use quotes as testimonials to back up certain claims throughout our copy and break-up copy with subheadings to make the material more reader-friendly. We will include the "call to action" and contact information with a 24/7 voicemail number and a discount coupon. The advertorial will have a short intro about a client's experience with our Mobile Food Truck and include quotes, facts, and statistics. We will present helpful information about party planning.

## Affiliate Marketing

We will create an affiliate marketing program to broaden our reach. We will first devise a commission structure, so affiliates have a reason to promote our business. We will give them ___ (10)% of whatever sales they generate. We will go after event planner bloggers or webmasters who get a lot of web traffic for our keywords. These companies would then promote our mobile ice cream products and services, and they would earn commissions for the sales they generated. We will work with the following services to handle the technical aspects of our program.

ConnectCommerce https://www.connectcommerce.com/
Commission Junction https://members.cj.com
ShareASale http://www.shareasale.com/
Share Results
LinkShare https://cli.linksynergy.com/cli/publisher/registration/
Affiliate Scout http://affiliatescout.com/
Affiliate Seeking http://www.affiliateseeking.com/
Clix Galore http://www.clixgalore.com/

## Gift with Purchase (GWP)

A GWP is an item that is presented to our client when he or she spends above a specified amount on products or services. The Gift with purchase or free item could be anything from recipe booklets, company voucher, product samples, etc. We will attach our marketing logo and business card to the gift and use it as means to thank the customer for their patronage. We will also explore the dramatic impact of a surprise gift with purchase, because an unexpected bonus item is often very appreciated and remembered.

## HotFrog.com

HotFrog is a fast growing free online business directory listing over 6.6 million US businesses. HotFrog now has local versions in 34 countries worldwide.

Anyone can list their business in HotFrog for free, along with contact details, and products and services. Listing in HotFrog directs sales leads and enquiries to your business. Businesses are encouraged to add any latest news and information about their products and services to their listing. HotFrog is indexed by Google and other search engines, meaning that customers can find your HotFrog listing when they use Google, Yahoo! or other search engines.

Resource:
http://www.hotfrog.com/AddYourBusiness.aspx
Examples:
http://www.hotfrog.com/find/food-truck

## Local.com

Local.com owns and operates a leading local search site and network in the United States. Its mission is to be the leader at enabling local businesses and consumers to find each other and connect. To do so, the company uses patented and proprietary technologies to provide over 20 million consumers each month with relevant search results for local businesses, products and services on Local.com and more than 1,000 partner sites. Local.com powers more than 100,000 local websites. Tens of thousands of small business customers use Local.com products and services to reach consumers using a variety of subscription, performance and display advertising and website products.

Resource: http://corporate.local.com/mk/get/advertising-opportunities

## Autoresponder

An autoresponder is an online tool that will automatically manage our mailing list and send out emails to our customers at preset intervals. We will write a short article that is helpful to potential Mobile Food Truck buyers. We will load this article into our autoresponder. We will let people know of the availability of our article by posting to newsgroups, forums, social networking sites etc. We will list our autoresponder email address at the end of the posting so they can send a blank email to our autoresponder to receive our article and be added to our mailing list. We will then email them at the interval of our choosing with special offers. We will load the messages into our autoresponder and set a time interval for the messages to be mailed out.

Resource: www.aweber.com


## Corporate Incentive/Employee Rewards Program

Our Employee Rewards Program will motivate and reward the key resources of local corporations – the people who make their business a success. We will use independent sales reps to market these programs to local corporations. It will be a versatile program, allowing the corporate client to customize it to best suit the following goals:

1. Welcome New Hires

2. Introduce an Employee Discount Program for our food truck menu items.
3. Reward increases in sales or productivity with an Employee Incentive Program
4. Thank Retirees for their service to the company
5. Initiate a Loyalty Rewards Program geared towards the customers of our corporate customers or their employees.

## Database Marketing

Database marketing is a form of direct marketing using databases of customers or prospects to generate personalized communications in order to promote a product or service for marketing purposes. The method of communication can be any addressable medium, as in direct marketing. With database marketing tools, we will be able to implement customer nurturing, which is a tactic that attempts to communicate with each customer or prospect at the right time, using the right information to meet that customer's need to progress through the process of identifying a problem, learning options available to resolve it, selecting the right solution, and making the purchasing decision. We will use our databases to learn more about customers, select target markets for specific campaigns, through customer segmentation, compare customers' value to the company, and provide more specialized offerings for customers based on their transaction histories, demographic profile and surveyed needs and wants. This database will gives us the capability to automate regular promotional mailings, to semi-automate the telephone outreach process, and to prioritize prospects as to interests, timing, and other notable delineators. The objective is to arrange for first meetings, which are meant to be informal introductions, and valuable fact-finding and needs-assessment events.

We will use sign-in sheets, coupons, surveys and newsletter subscriptions to collect the following information from our clients:

1. Name
2. Telephone Number
3. Email Address
4. Home Address
5. Birth Date
6. Other Relevant Dates

We will utilize the following types of contact management software to generate leads and stay in touch with customers to produce repeat business and referrals:

1. Act — www.act.com
2. Front Range Solutions — www.frontrange.com
3. The Turning Point — www.turningpoint.com
4. Acxiom — www.acxiom.com/products_and_services/

We will utilize contact management software, such as ACT and Goldmine, to track the following:

1. Dates for follow-ups.
2. Documentation of prospect concerns, objections or comments.
3. Referral source.
4. Marketing Materials sent.
5. Log of contact dates and methods of contact.
6. Ultimate disposition.

## Cause Marketing

Cause marketing or cause-related marketing refers to a type of marketing involving the cooperative efforts of a "for profit" business and a non-profit organization for mutual benefit. The possible benefits of cause marketing for business include positive public relations, improved customer relations, and additional marketing opportunities.

Cause marketing sponsorship by American businesses is rising at a dramatic rate, because customers, employees and stakeholders prefer to be associated with a company that is considered socially responsible. Our business objective will be to generate highly cost-effective public relations and media coverage for the launch of a marketing campaign focused on _____ (type of cause), with the help of the _____ (non-profit organization name) organization.

Resources: www.causemarketingforum.com/
www.cancer.org/AboutUs/HowWeHelpYou/acs-cause-marketing

## Courtesy Advertising

We will engage in courtesy advertising, which refers to a company or corporation "buying" an advertisement in a nonprofit dinner program, event brochure, and the like. Our company will gain visibility this way while the nonprofit organization may treat the advertisement revenue as a donation. We will specifically advertise in the following non-profit programs, newsletters, bulletins and event brochures: _____

## BBB Accreditation

We will apply for BBB Accreditation to improve our perceived trustworthiness. BBB determines that a company meets BBB accreditation standards, which include a commitment to make a good faith effort to resolve any consumer complaints. BBB Accredited Businesses pay a fee for accreditation review/monitoring and for support of BBB services to the public. BBB accreditation does not mean that the business' products or services have been evaluated or endorsed by BBB, or that BBB has made a determination as to the business' product quality or competency in performing services. We will place the BBB Accreditation Logo in all of our ads.

Examples:
www.bbb.org/fort-worth/Business-Reviews/not-elsewhere-classified/sassy-hot-dogs-in-fort-worth-tx-235970482/

## Sponsor Events

The sponsoring of events, such as sports tournaments, will allow our company to engage in what is known as experiential marketing, which is the idea that the best way to deepen the emotional bond between a company and its customers is by creating a memorable and interactive experience. We will ask for the opportunity to prominently display our company signage and the set-up of a booth from which to handout sample products and sales literature. We will also seek to capitalize on networking, speech giving and workshop presenting opportunities.

## Sponsorships

We will sponsor a local team, such as our child's little league baseball team, the local soccer club or a bowling group. We will then place our company name on the uniforms or shirts in exchange for providing the equipment and/or uniforms.

## Patch.com

A community-specific news and information platform dedicated to providing comprehensive and trusted local coverage for individual towns and communities.
Patch makes it easy to: Keep up with news and events, Look at photos and videos from around town, Learn about local businesses, Participate in discussions and Submit announcements, photos, and reviews.
Examples:
http://roseville-ca.patch.com/topics/Mobile+Food+Trucks
http://elkgrove.patch.com/articles/elk-grove-to-consider-new-food-truck-laws

## Mobile iPhone Apps

We will use new distribution tools like the iPhone App Store to give us unprecedented direct access to consumers, without the need to necessarily buy actual mobile *ads* to reach people. Thanks to Apple's iPhone and the App Store, we will be able to make cool mobile apps that may generate as much goodwill and purchase intent as a banner ad. We will research Mobile Application Development, which is the process by which application software is developed for small low-power handheld devices, such as personal digital assistants, enterprise digital assistants or mobile phones. These applications are either pre-installed on phones during manufacture, or downloaded by customers from various mobile software distribution platforms. iPhone apps make good marketing tools. The bottom line is iPhones and smartphones sales are continually growing, and people are going to their phones for information. Apps will definitely be a lead generation tool because it gives potential clients easy access to our contact and business information and the ability to call for more information while they are still "hot". Our apps will contain: directory of staffers, publications on relevant issues, office location, videos, etc.

We will especially focus on the development of apps that can accomplish the following:
1. **Mobile Reservations:** Customers can use this app to access mobile reservations linked directly to your in-house calendar. They can browse open slots and book appointments easily, while on the go.
2. **Appointment Reminders:** You can send current customers reminders of regular or special appointments through your mobile app to increase your yearly revenue per customer.
3. **Style Libraries**
   Offer a style library in your app to help customers to pick out a _____ style. Using a simple photo gallery, you can collect photos of various styles, and have customers browse and select specific _____.
4. **Customer Photos**

Your app can also have a feature that lets customers take photos and email them to you. This is great for creating a database of customer photos for testimonial purposes, advertising, or just easy reference.

5. **Special Offers**

    Push notifications allow you to drive activity on special promotions, deals, events, and offers. If you ever need to generate revenue during a down time, push notifications allow you to generate interest easily and proactively.

6. **Loyalty Programs**

    A mobile app allows you to offer a mobile loyalty program (buy ten ___, get one free, etc.). You won't need to print up cards or track anything manually – it's all done simply through users' mobile devices.

7. **Referrals**

    A mobile app can make referrals easy. With a single click, a user can post to a social media account on Facebook or Twitter about their experience with your business. This allows you to earn new business organically through the networks of existing customers.

8. **Product Sales**

    We can sell food products through our mobile app. Customers can browse products, submit orders, and make payments easily, helping you open up a new revenue stream.

Resources:	http://www.apple.com/iphone/apps-for-iphone/
	http://iphoneapplicationlist.com/apps/business/
	http://mashable.com/2014/08/08/gastrodamus/

Software Development:	http://www.mutualmobile.com/
	http://www.avenuesocial.com/mob-app.php#
	http://www.biznessapps.com/

## Mobile Food Truck App Examples:

Food Truck Fiesta	http://foodtruckfiesta.com/iphone-app-food-truck-fiesta/
A real-time automated food truck tracking system in Washington, DC.

FoodTrucksIn.com
Provides the locations of over 6,200 mobile food trucks across the country, and is regarded as having the complete list of food truck locations.

FreshCheq  https://problemsolutionhq.leadpages.co/freshcheq-food-truck-landing-page/
Helps to automate food safety tasks and produce quick, cloud based reports on food temperatures and sanitary conditions over time.

Intuit Mint	www.mint.com/
A couple of great features of this food truck business app are: Expense tracking, Goal planning, Automatic purchase categorizing, Budget setting and Auto bill paying.

Trello Productivity App	https://trello.com/platforms

This app is fast, flexible, and even fun to use, and helps to organize all the components for food truck projects into columns and cards that are easy to drag around, add supporting details to, comment on, and assign from person to person on the food truck team.

Quick Response Codes

QR Codes are a type of matrix barcode (or two-dimensional code) that is designed to be read by smartphones. The code consists of black modules arranged in a square pattern on a white background. The information encoded may be text, a URL, or other data. Many Android, Nokia, and Blackberry handsets come with QR code readers installed. QR reader software is available for most mobile platforms. QR codes storing addresses and Uniform Resource Locators (URLs) may appear in magazines, on signs, buses, business cards, or almost any object about which users might need information. Users with a camera phone equipped with the correct reader application can scan the image of the QR code to display text, contact information, connect to a wireless network, or open a web page in the telephone's browser. This act of linking from physical world objects is termed hardlinking or object hyperlinking. Sectors of the general public are still getting acquainted with the practice of scanning the codes that appear with increasing frequency in advertisements, and thus consider an educational step or simple line of adjacent text to encourage a scan. The bar codes digitally store a lot of content in a small space, enabling smartphone code readers to connect the user with a website page, maps, phone numbers, email or other QR capability. Among the benefits to marketing and advertising is that the use of QR codes typically occurs at the moment when the reader is most interested in the subject matter and likely to act. In many applications, the objective is to provide an easy means for the reader to act now. A comScore survey data says QR code users are more likely to be male (60.5%), between the ages of 18 to 34 (53.4%) and have a household income in excess of $100,000 (36.1%). Magazines and newspapers are the preferred vehicle for scanning QR codes (49.4%), followed by product packaging (34.3%).

Flash Buying

Flash Buy will be a group where every local business can play a part. This will be an effort for us to plan a visit to a locally-owned business on a particular day, pay for the goods/services, and help the chosen business reach an epic day of profits. For example, we will plan for local business group members to visit our store on a certain date. Group members will go there, any time that they wish throughout the selected day, receive a modest discount, and this will spark a rise in profits. This will be an opportunity for other businesses to become aware of and experience our mobile food truck, and create word-of-mouth advertising.

Transit Ads

According to the Metropolitan Transportation Authority, MTA subways, buses and railroads provide billions of trips each year to residents. Marketing our mobile food truck in subway cars and on the walls of subway stations will be a great way to advertise our business to a large, captive audience.

## Restroom billboard advertising (Bathroom Advertising)

We will target a captive audience by placing restroom billboard advertising in select high-traffic venues with targeted demographics. A simple, framed ad on the inside of a bathroom stall door or above a urinal gets at least a minute of viewing, according to several studies. The stall door ads are a good choice for venues with shorter waiting times, such as small businesses, while large wall posters are well-suited to airports or movie theatres where people are more likely to be standing in line near the entrance or exit. Many new restroom based ad agencies that's specialize in restroom advertisement have also come about, such as; Zoom Media, BillBoardZ , Flush Media , Jonny Advertising, Insite Advertising, Inc, Wall AG USA, ADpower, NextMedia, and Alive Promo (American Restroom Association, 9/24/2009).

Resources:
http://www.indooradvertising.org/
http://www.stallmall.com/
http://www.zoommedia.com/

## Tumblr.com

Tumblr will allow us to effortlessly share anything. We will be able to post text, photos, quotes, links, music, and videos, from our browser, phone, desktop, email, or wherever we happen to be. We will be able to customize everything, from colors, to our theme's HTML.

Examples:
https://www.tumblr.com/search/mobile%20food%20trucks
http://foodtrucknyc.tumblr.com/

## Gift Certificates

We will offer for sale Gift Certificates via our website. This will provide an excellent way to be introduced to new clients and improve our cash flow position. An e-commerce platform for small businesses. BoomTime protects info with 256-bit SSL encryption when transmitting certain kinds of information, such as financial services information or payment information. An icon resembling a padlock is displayed on the bottom of most browser windows during SSL transactions, which you can also verify by looking at the address bar, which will start with "https://" instead of just "http://". The information you provide will be stored securely on BoomTime servers. BoomTime is PCI DSS compliant, which outlines a standard for security procedures for merchants and service providers that store, process, or transmit cardholder data.

Resources:
- Boom Time — https://ps1419.boomtime.com/lgift
- Gift Cards — www.giftcards.com
- Gift Card Café — www.TheGiftCardCafe.com

Allows companies to create their own special deals and discount services, and send it to just the contacts in their client database.

Examples:

https://www.giftrocket.com/gift-card/xplosive-mobile-food-truck-seattle
http://columbusfoodadventures.com/tickets/gift-certificates
http://www.giftly.com/gift-card/tumbleweeds-gourmet-mobile-food-truck-bozeman

thumbtack.com
A directory for finding and booking trustworthy local services, which is free to consumers.

Resource:
www.thumbtack.com/postservice
Examples:
https://www.thumbtack.com/ny/rochester/mobile-food-trucks/
https://www.thumbtack.com/oh/columbus/catering/food-truck

## Publish e-Book

Ebooks are electronic books which can be downloaded from any website or FTP site on the Internet. Ebooks are made using special software and can include a wide variety of media such as HTML, graphics, Flash animation and video. We will publish an e-book to establish our mobile food truck expertise, and reach people who are searching for ebooks on how to make better use our products and/or services. Included in our ebook will be links back to our website, product or affiliate program. Because users will have permanent access to it, they will use our ebook again and again, constantly seeing a link or banner which directs them to our site. The real power behind ebook marketing will be the viral aspect of it and the free traffic it helps to build for our website. ebook directories include: www.e-booksdirectory.com/
www.ebookfreeway.com/p-ebook-directory-list.html
quantumseolabs.com/blog/seolinkbuilding/top-5-free-ebook-directories-subscribers/
Resource: www.free-ebooks.net/

**e-books are available from the following sites:**

| | |
|---|---|
| Amazon.com | Createspace.com |
| Lulu.com | Kobobooks.com |
| BarnesandNoble.com | Scribd.com |
| AuthorHouse.com | |

Resource:
www.smartpassiveincome.com/ebooks-the-smart-way/

## Business Card Exchanges

We will join our Chamber of Commerce or local retail merchants' association and volunteer to host a mixer or business card exchange. We will take the opportunity to invite social and business groups to our store to enjoy beer and wine tastings, and market to local businesses that will be looking for employee benefits and customer holiday gifts in the coming months. We will also build our email database by collecting the business cards of all attendees.

## Banner Advertising
We will use banners as an affordable way to draw attention to our business. We will place one on the side or front of our food truck, or on a prominent building and have it point to our truck. We will use colorful storefront banners with catchy phrases to grab the attention of local foot and vehicle traffic.
Resource:   http://www.fastsigns.com/
Ex:        "Free Drink with Taco Meal"

## Hubpages.com
HubPages has easy-to-use publishing tools, a vibrant author community and underlying revenue-maximizing infrastructure. Hubbers (HubPages authors) earn money by publishing their Hubs (content-rich Internet pages) on topics they know and love, and earn recognition among fellow Hubbers through the community-wide HubScore ranking system. The HubPages ecosystem provides a search-friendly infrastructure which drives traffic to Hubs from search engines such as Google and Yahoo, and enables Hubbers to earn revenue from industry-standard advertising vehicles such as Google AdSense and the eBay and Amazon Affiliates program. All of this is provided free to Hubbers in an open online community.
Resource:    http://hubpages.crabbysbeach.com/blogs/
             http://hubpages.com/learningcenter/contents
Ex:         http://artofseattle.hubpages.com/hub/How-to-Eat-at-Food-Trucks

## Pinterest.com
The goal of this website is to connect everyone in the world through the 'things' they find interesting. They think that a favorite cook book, menu and price list, chef demonstration videos or recipe can reveal a common link between two people. With millions of new pins added every week, Pinterest is connecting people all over the world based on shared tastes and interests. What's special about Pinterest is that the boards are all visual, which is a very important marketing plus. When users enter a URL, they select a picture from the site to pin to their board. People spend hours pinning their own content, and then finding content on other people's boards to "re-pin" to their own boards. We will use Pinterest for remote personal shopping appointments. When we have a customer with specific needs, we will create a board just for them with items we sell that would meet their needs, along with links to other tips and content. We will invite our customer to check out the board on Pinterest, and let them know we created it just for them.
Resources:
 http://mobile-cuisine.com/social-media/how-to-use-pinterest-to-promote-a-
        food-truck-infographic/

**Pinterest usage recommendation include:**
1.   Conduct market research by showing photos of potential products or test launches, asking the customer base for feedback.
2.   Personalize the brand by showcasing style and what makes the brand different, highlighting new and exciting things through the use of imagery.

3.  Add links from Pinterest photos to the company webstore, putting price banners on each photo and providing a link where users can buy the products directly.

**Examples:**
https://www.pinterest.com/explore/food-truck/
https://www.pinterest.com/explore/food-truck-design/

Resources:
www.copyblogger.com/pinterest-marketing/
www.shopify.com/infographics/pinterest
www.pinterest.com/entmagazine/retail-business/
www.pinterest.com/brettcarneiro/ecommerce/
www.pinterest.com/denniswortham/infographics-retail-online-shopping/
www.cio.com/article/3018852/e-commerce/how-to-use-pinterest-to-grow-your-business.html

## Survey Marketing
We will conduct a door-to-door survey in our target area to illicit opinions to our proposed business. This will provide valuable feedback, lead to prospective clients and serve to introduce our mobile food truck business, before we begin actual operations.

## 'Green' Marketing
We will target environmentally friendly customers to introduce new customers to our business and help spread the word about going "green". We will use the following 'green' marketing strategies to form an emotional bond with our customers:
1.  We will use clearly labeled 'Recycled Paper' and Sustainable Packaging, such as receipts and storage containers.
2.  We will use "green", non-toxic cleaning supplies.
3.  We will install 'green' lighting and heating systems to be more eco-friendly.
4.  We will use web-based Electronic Mail and Social Media instead of using paper advertisements.
5.  We will find local suppliers to minimize the carbon footprint that it takes for deliveries.
6.  We will use products that are made with organic ingredients and supplies.
7.  We will document our 'Green' Programs in our sales brochure and website.
8.  We will be a Certified Energy Star Partner.
9.  We will install new LED warehouse lighting, exit signs, and emergency signs.
10. We will install motion detectors in low-traff7ic areas both inside and outside of warehouses.
11. We will implement new electricity regulators on HVAC units and compressors to lower energy consumption.
12. We will mount highly supervised and highly respected recycling campaigns.
13. We will start a program for waste product to be converted into sustainable energy sources.
14. We will start new company-wide document shredding programs.
15. We will use of water-based paints during the finishing process to reduce V.O.C.'s

to virtually zero.
16. Use of solar panels for non-critical sections and facilities in the complex.
17. Use of only hybrid or electric vehicles.

## Sticker Marketing

Low-cost sticker, label and decal marketing will provide a cost-effective way to convey information, build identity and promote our company in unique and influential ways. Stickers can be affixed to almost any surface, so they can go and stay affixed where other marketing materials can't; opening a world of avenues through which we can reach our target audience. Our stickers will be simple in design, and convey an impression quickly and clearly, with valuable information or coupon, printed optionally as part of its backcopy. Our stickers will handed out at trade shows and special events, mailed as a postcard, packaged with product and/or included as part of a mailing package. We will insert the stickers inside our product or hand them out along with other marketing tools such as flyers or brochures. Research has found that the strongest stickers are usually less than 16 square inches, are printed on white vinyl, and are often die cut. Utilizing a strong design, in a versatile size, and with an eye-catching shape, that is, relevant to our business, will add to the perceived value of our promotional stickers.

**We will adhere to the following sticker design tips:**
1. We will strengthen our brand by placing our logo on the stickers and using company colors and font styles.
2. We will include our phone number, address, and/or website along with our logo to provide customers with a call to action.
3. We will write compelling copy that solicits an emotional reaction.
4. We will use die-cut stickers using unusual and business relevant shapes to help draw attention to our business.
5. We will consider that size matters and that will be determined by where they will be applied and the degree of desired visibility to be realized.
6. We will be aware of using color on our stickers as color can help create contrast in our design, which enables the directing of prospect eyes to images or actionable items on the stickers.
7. We will encourage customers to post our stickers near their phones, on yellow page book covers, on event invitations, on notepads, on book covers, on gift boxes and product packaging, etc.
8. We will place our stickers on all the products we sell.

## USPS Every Door Direct Mail Program

Every Door Direct Mail from the U.S. Postal Service® is designed to reach every home, every address, every time at a very affordable delivery rate. Every business and resident living in the ____ zip code will receive an over-sized post card and coupon announcing the _____ (company name) grand opening 7-days before the grand opening:

**Price – USPS Marketing Mail™ Flats up to 3.3 oz**
EDDM Retail® USPS Marketing Flats $0.177 per piece

EDDM BMEU USPS Marketing Mail at $0.156 per piece

Resource:
https://www.usps.com/business/every-door-direct-mail.htm
https://eddm.usps.com/eddm/customer/routeSearch.action

## ZoomInfo.com

Their vision is to be the sole provider of constantly verified information about companies and their employees, making our data indispensible — available anytime, anywhere and anyplace the customer needs it. Creates just-verified, detailed profiles of 65 million businesspeople and six million businesses. Makes data available through powerful tools for lead generation, prospecting and recruiting.
Examples:
http://www.zoominfo.com/p/Tess-Wallerstedt/-2072307516

## Zipslocal.com

Provides one of the most comprehensive ZIP Code-based local search services, allowing visitors to access information through our online business directories that cover all ZIP Codes in the United States. Interactive local yellow pages show listings and display relevant advertising through the medium of the Internet, making it easy for everyone to find local business information

## Hold Biggest Fan Contest

Do you love _____ (company name)? Do you have a great story about how the team at ____ (company Name) helped you "get there" to achieve your goals? Well, then ____ (company name) wants to hear from you! _____ (company name) has launched the "Biggest Fan Contest" on its Facebook Page at the beginning of ____ (month), inviting current and former customers to share why they are _____'s (company name) "Biggest Fan." Participants are eligible to win a number of prizes including: _____.
To enter, visit www.facebook.com/_____ (company name), "like" the page, and click the "Biggest Fan Contest" tab on the righthand side. Participants are then asked to write a short blurb or upload a photo sharing why they love _____ (company name). If you have a story to tell or photo to share, enter today. Contest ends _____ (date).
See contest tab for full details.

## Yext.com

Enables companies to manage their digital presence in online maps, directories and apps. Over 400,000 businesses make millions of monthly updates across 85+ exclusive global partners, making Yext the global market leader. Digital presence is a fundamental need for all 50 million businesses in the world, and Yext's mission is perfect location information in every hand. Yext is based in the heart of New York City with 350 employees and was named to Forbes Most Promising Companies lists for 2015 and 2017, as well as the Fortune Best Places to Work 2015 list.

## Google+
We will pay specific attention to Google+, which is already playing a more important role in Google's organic ranking algorithm. We will create a business page on Google+ to achieve improved local search visibility. Google+ will also be the best way to get access to Google Authorship, which will play a huge role in SEO. Aside from having all the necessary information like hours and contact information, quality photos and visuals will be essential on our Google+ local page. To go above the basics, we will have a local Google photographer visit and create a virtual tour.

Resources:
https://plus.google.com/pages/create
http://www.google.com/+/brands/
https://www.google.com/appserve/fb/forms/plusweekly/
https://plus.google.com/+GoogleBusiness/posts
http://marketingland.com/beyond-social-benefits-google-business-73460
http://searchenginewatch.com/sew/how-to/2124899/seo-for-google-profiles-and-pages

Examples:
https://plus.google.com/110053090792356157038/posts
https://plus.google.com/+PrestigeFoodTrucksOrlando/posts


## Inbound Marketing
Inbound marketing is about pulling people in by sharing relevant mobile foodservice information, creating useful content, and generally being helpful. It involves writing everything from buyer's guides to blogs and newsletters that deliver useful content. The objective will be to nurture customers through the buying process with unbiased educational materials that turn consumers into informed buyers.
Resource:
www.Hubspot.com

## Google My Business Profile    www.google.com/business/befound.html
We will have a complete and active Google My Business profile to give our mobile food truck company a tremendous advantage over the competition, and help potential customers easily find our company and provide relevant information about our business.

## Sampling Program
We will give each sample with a mini-survey to enable customers to rate the menu item or mobile service, and supply constructive feedback.

## Reddit.com
An online community where users vote on stories. The hottest stories rise to the top, while the cooler stories sink. Comments can be posted on every story, including stories

about startup mobile food truck companies.
Examples:
https://www.reddit.com/r/foodtrucks/

## Testimonial Marketing

We will either always ask for testimonials immediately after a completed project or contact our clients once a quarter for them. We will also have something prepared that we would like the client to say that is specific to a service we offer, or anything relevant to advertising claims that we have put together. For the convenience of the client we will assemble a testimonial letter that they can either modify or just sign off on. Additionally, testimonials can also be in the form of audio or video and put on our website or mailed to potential clients in the form of a DVD or Audio CD. A picture with a testimonial is also excellent. We will put testimonials directly on a magazine ad, slick sheet, brochure, or website, or assemble a complete page of testimonials for our sales presentation folder.

Resources:
http://mobile-cuisine.com/catering/food-truck-catering-testimonials/

Examples:
http://www.mannafoodtruck.com/testimonials/

We will collect customer testimonials in the following ways:
1. Our website – A page dedicated to testimonials (written and/or video).
2. Social media accounts – Facebook fan pages offer a review tab, which makes it easy to receive and display customer testimonials.
3. Google+ also offers a similar feature with Google+ Local.
4. Local search directories – Ask customers to post more reviews on Yelp and Yahoo Local.
5. Customer Satisfaction Survey Forms

We will pose the following questions to our customers to help them frame their testimonials:
1. What was the obstacle that would have prevented you from buying this product?
2. "What was your main concern about buying this product?"
3. What did you find as a result of buying this product?
4. What specific feature did you like most about this product?
5. What would be three other benefits about this product?
6. Would you recommend this product? If so, why?
7. Is there anything you'd like to add?

## 6.4.1 Strategic Alliances

We will form strategic alliances to accomplish the following objectives:
1. To share marketing expenses.
2. To realize bulk buying power on wholesale purchases.
3. To engage in barter arrangements.
4. To collaborate with industry experts.
5. To set-up mutual referral relationships.

We will develop strategic referral alliances with the following service providers. We will conduct introductory 'cold calls' to their offices and make them aware of our menu selections and catering capabilities by distributing our brochures and business cards.

| | | | |
|---|---|---|---|
| 1. | Daycare Centers | 2. | Nursing Homes |
| 3. | Schools | 4. | Dance Schools |
| 5. | Martial Arts Academies | 6. | Restaurants |
| 7. | Day Spas | 8. | Boutiques |
| 9. | Health Clubs | 10. | Beauty Salons |
| 11. | Wedding Consultants | 12. | Banquet Halls |
| 13. | Event Planners | 14. | Youth Organizations |
| 15. | Party Planners | 16. | Catering employees |

We will assemble and present a sales presentation package that includes sales brochures, business cards, and a DVD presentation of basic healthy eating tips, and client testimonials. We will include coupons that offer a discount or other type of introductory deal. We will ask to set-up a take-one display for our sales brochures at the business registration counter.

We will promptly give the referring business any one or combination of the following reward options:
1. Referral fees
2. Free services
3. Mutual referral exchanges

We will monitor referral sources to evaluate the mutual benefits of the alliance and make certain to clearly define and document our referral incentives prior to initiating our referral exchange program.

## 6.4.2 Monitoring Marketing Results

To monitor how well _____ (company name) is doing, we will measure how well the advertising campaign is working by taking customer surveys. What we would like to know is how they heard of us and how they like and dislike about our services. In order to get responses to the surveys, we will be give discounts as thank you rewards.

**Response Tracking Methods**
    Coupons: ad-specific coupons that easily enable tracking

Landing Pages: unique web landing pages for each advertisement
800 Numbers: unique 1-800-# per advertisement
Email Service Provider: Instantly track email views, opens, and clicks
Address inclusion of dept # or suite #.

Our financial statements will offer excellent data to track all phases of sales. These are available for review on a daily basis. _____ (company name) will benchmark our objectives for sales promotion and advertising in order to evaluate our return on invested marketing dollars, and determine where to concentrate our limited advertising dollars to realize the best return. We will also strive to stay within our marketing budget.

**Key Marketing Metrics**
We will use the following two marketing metrics to evaluate the cost-effectiveness of our marketing campaign:
1. The cost to acquire a new customer: The average dollar amount invested to get one new client. Example: If we invest $3,000 on marketing in a single month and end the month with 10 new customers, our cost of acquisition is $300 per new customer.
2. The lifetime value of the average active customer. The average dollar value of an average customer over the life of their business with you. To calculate this metric for a given period of time, we will take the total amount of revenue our business generated during the time period and divide it by the total number of customers we had from the beginning of the time period.
3. We will track the following set of statistics on a weekly basis to keep informed of the progress of our practice:
    A. Number of total referrals.
    B. Percentage increase of total referrals (over baseline).
    C. Number of new referral sources.
    D. Number of new customers/month.
    E. Number of Leads

**Key Marketing Metrics Table**
We've listed some key metrics in the following table. We will need to keep a close eye on these, to see if we meet our own forecasted expectations. If our numbers are off in too many categories, we may, after proper analysis, have to make substantial changes to our marketing efforts.

| Key Marketing Metrics | 2017 | 2018 | 2019 |
|---|---|---|---|
| Revenue | | | |
| Leads | | | |
| Leads Converted | | | |
| Avg. Transaction per Customer | | | |
| Avg. Dollars per Customer | | | |
| Number of Referrals | | | |
| Number of PR Appearances | | | |
| Number of Testimonials | | | |

Number of New Club Members          _____
Number of Returns                   _____
Number of BBB Complaints            _____
Number of Completed Surveys         _____
Number of Blog readers              _____
Number of Twitter followers         _____
Number of Facebook Fans             _____

**Metric Definitions**
1. Leads: Individuals who step into the store to consider a purchase.
2. Leads Converted: Percent of individuals who actually make a purchase.
3. Average Transactions Per Customer: Number of purchases per customer per month. Expected to rise significantly as customers return for more and more _____ items per month
4. Average $ Per Customer: Average dollar amount of each transaction. Expected to rise along with average transactions.
5. Referrals: Includes customer and business referrals
6. PR Appearances: Online or print mentions of the business that are not paid advertising. Expected to be high upon opening, then drop off and rise again until achieving a steady level.
7. Testimonials: Will be sought from the best and most loyal customers. Our objective is ___ (#) per month) and they will be added to the website. Some will be sought as video testimonials.
8. New Loyalty Club Members: This number will rise significantly as more customers see the value in repeated visits and the benefits of club membership.
9. Number of Returns/BBB Complaints: Our goal is zero.
10. Number of Completed Surveys: We will provide incentives for customers to complete customer satisfaction surveys.

## 6.4.3    Word-of-Mouth Marketing

**We plan to make use of the following techniques to promote word-of-mouth advertising:**
1. Repetitive Image Advertising
2. Provide exceptional customer service.
3. Make effective use of loss leaders.
2. Schedule truck based activities, such as demonstrations or special events.
3. Make trial easy with a coupon or introductory discount.
4. Initiate web and magazine article submissions
5. Utilize a sampling program
6. Add a forward email feature to our website.
7. Share relevant and believable testimonial letters
8. Publish staff bios.
9. Make product/service upgrade announcements

10. Hold contests or sweepstakes
12. Have involvement with community events.
13. Pay suggestion box rewards
14. Distribute a monthly newsletter
15. Share easy-to-understand information (via an article or seminar).
16. Make personalized marketing communications.
17. Structure our referral program.
18. Sharing of Community Commonalities
19. Invitations to join our community of shared interests.
20. Publish Uncensored Customer Reviews
21. Enable Information Exchange Forums
22. Provide meaningful comparisons with competitors.
23. Clearly state our user benefits.
24. Make and honor ironclad guarantees
25. Provide superior post-sale support
26. Provide support in the pre-sale decision making process.
27. Host Free Informational Seminars or Workshops
28. Get involved with local business organizations.
29. Issue Press Release coverage of charitable involvements.
30. Hold traveling company demonstrations/exhibitions/competitions.

### 6.4.4 Customer Satisfaction Survey

We will design a customer satisfaction survey to measure the "satisfaction quotient" of our Mobile Food Truck customers. By providing a detailed snapshot of our current customer base, we will be able to generate more repeat and referral business and enhance the profitability of our company.

**Our Customer Satisfaction Survey will include the following basics:**
1. How do our customers rate our mobile food truck business?
2. How do our customers rate our competition?
3. How well do our customers rate the value of our products or services?
4. What new customer needs and trends are emerging?
5. How loyal are our customers?
6. What can be done to improve customer loyalty and repeat business?
7. How strongly do our customers recommend our business?
8. What is the best way to market our business?
9. What new value-added services would best differentiate our business from that of our competitors?
10. How can we encourage more referral business?
11. How can our pricing strategy be improved?

Our customer satisfaction survey will help to answer these questions and more. From the need for continual new products and services to improved customer service, our satisfaction surveys will allow our organization to quickly identify problematic and underperforming areas, while enhancing our overall customer satisfaction.

**Examples:**
https://www.surveymonkey.com/r/?sm=zfr4rcQeHOZ98mkREha3%2BA%3D%3D

**Resources:**
http://mobile-cuisine.com/marketing/customer-satisfaction-surveys/
http://smallbiztrends.com/2007/06/the-small-biz-7-survey.html
http://blog.elevateresearch.com/7-reasons-why-food-trucks-must-measure-customer-feedback
https://www.foodonatruck.com/food-truck-customer-survey/
https://twitter.com/MobileCuisine/status/705951163338907648
https://www.survata.com/
https://www.google.com/insights/consumersurveys/use_cases
www.surveymonkey.com
http://www.smetoolkit.org/smetoolkit/en/content/en/6708/Customer-Satisfaction-Survey-Template
http://smallbusiness.chron.com/common-questions-customer-service-survey-1121.html

# 6.4.5  Marketing Training Program

Our Marketing Training Program will include both an initial orientation and training, as well as ongoing continuing education classes. Initial orientation will be run by the owner until an HR manager is hired. For one week, half of each day will be spent in training, and the other half shadowing the operations manager.

Training will include:
- Learning the entire selection of products and services.
- Understanding our Mission Statement, Value Proposition, Position Statement and Unique Selling Proposition.
- Appreciating our competitive advantages.
- Understanding our core message and branding approach.
- Learning our store's policies; returns processing, complaint handling, etc.
- Learning our customer services standards of practice.
- Learning our customer and business referral programs.
- Learning our Membership Club procedures, rules and benefits.
- Becoming familiar with our company website, and online ordering options.
- Service procedures specific to the employee's role.

Ongoing workshops will be based on customer feedback and problem areas identified by mystery buyers, which will better train employees to educate customers. These ongoing workshops will be held _____ (once?) a month for _____ (three?) hours.

## 6.5 Sales Strategy

The development of our sales strategy will start by developing a better understanding of our customer needs. To accomplish this task, we will pursue the following research methods:
1. Join the associations that our target customers belong to.
2. Contact the membership director and establish a relationship to understand their member's needs, challenges and concerns.
3. Identify non-competitive suppliers who sell to our customer to learn their challenges and look for partnering solutions.
4. Work directly with our customer and ask them what their needs are and if our business may offer a possible solution.

The sales strategy of _____ (company name) is simple. The key to customer satisfaction is a community-friendly truck route that is easy to navigate and has knowledgeable people to help customers find what they want quickly. Customers will linger around the truck, learning new recipes, reading notices on the community bulletin board or speaking with friends.

Our most important sales strategy is developing an environment in which customers will return time-after-time because our market provides knowledgeable, friendly staff, quality products, and a menu that meets their health needs.

When customers visit our truck, they will know they will be buying from a sanitary vehicle that offers the best service in the industry. Our pricing strategy will focus on providing high quality, hard to find organic meal ingredients and healthy foodservices at a fair price. Because our closest competition is far away, we will be able to charge a premium for some products, but must be careful not to price our items too high or customers will continue to stock up on specialty organic foodstuffs when they visit large cities or will buy over the internet. We will make use of local discounts, daily specials, and new products to keep customers interested and to help them feel they are getting a good value. We intend to listen to our customers and collect their feedback through surveys and friendly conversation, to determine areas where we can expand and/or improve.

Our focus will be on making the foodservices we offer of the highest possible quality. Only when those services are well-established, will we consider expanding our range of products and services offered.

We will become a one-stop site for healthy home replacement meals and nutritious snacks. We will also be very active in the community, building a solid reputation with professionals and community leaders.

Our customers will be primarily obtained through word-of-mouth referrals, but we will also advertise introductory offers to introduce people to our programs. The combination of the perception of higher quality, exceptional health support and the recognition of superior value should turn referral leads into satisfied customers.

The company's sales strategy will be based on the following elements:
- Advertising in the Yellow Pages - two inch by two-inch ads describing our services will be placed in the local Yellow Pages.
- Placing classified advertisements in the regional editions of health magazines and on Craigslist.org.
- Word of mouth referrals - generating sales leads in the local community through customer referrals.

**Our basic sales strategy is to:**
- Develop a website for lead generation by _____ (date).
- Provide exceptional customer service.
- Accept payment by all major credit cards, cash, PayPal and check.
- Survey our customers regarding services they would like to see added.
- Sponsor charitable and other community events.
- Provide tours of the customized vehicle so people can personally witness our processes and build a trust bond with our mobile operations.
- Motivate employees with a pay-for-performance component to their straight salary compensation package, based on profits and customer satisfaction rates.
- Build long-term customer relationships by putting the interests of customers first.
- Establish mutually beneficial relationship with local businesses serving the health needs of local residents.

## 6.5.1 Customer Retention Strategy

**We will use the following post-project techniques to improve customer retention, foster referrals and improve the profitability of our practice:**

1. Keep the vehicle sparkling clean and well-organized.
2. Use only well-trained staff, and the highest quality equipment.
3. Actively solicit customer feedback and promptly act upon their inputs.
4. Tell customers how much you appreciate their business.
5. Call regular customers by their first names.
6. Send thank you notes.
7. Offer free new product samples.
8. Change displays and sales presentations on a regular basis.
9. Practice good phone etiquette
10. Respond to complaints promptly.
11. Reward referrals.
12. Publish a monthly opt-in direct response newsletter with customized content, dependent on recipient stated information preferences.
13. Develop and publish a list of frequently asked questions.

14. Issue Preferred Customer Membership Cards.
15. Hold informational seminars and workshops.
16. Provide an emergency hotline number.
17. Publish code of ethics and our service guarantees.
18. Help customers to make accurate competitor comparisons.
19. Build a stay-in-touch (drip marketing) communications calendar.
20. Keep marketing communications focused on our competitive advantages.
21. Offer repeat user discounts and incentives.
22. Be supportive and encouraging, and not judgmental.
23. Measure customer retention and look at recurring revenue and customer surveys.
24. Build a community of shared interests by offering a website forum or discussion group for professionals and customers to allow sharing of knowledge.
25. Offer benefits above and beyond those of our competitors.
26. Issue reminder emails and holiday gift cards.

**We will also consider the following Customer Retention Programs:**

| Type of Program | Customer Rewards |
|---|---|
| Frequency Purchase Loyalty Program | Special Discounts |
|  | Free Product or Services |
| 'Best Customer' Program | Special Recognition/Treatment/Offers |
| Affinity Programs | Sharing of Common Interests |
|  | Accumulate Credit Card Points |
| Customer Community Programs | Special Event Participation |
| Auto-Knowledge Building Programs | Purchase Recommendations based On Past Transaction History |
| Profile Building Programs | Recommendations Based on Stated Customer Profile Information. |

## 6.5.2  Sales Forecast

**Our sales projections are based on the following:**
1. Actual sales volumes of local competitors
2. Interviews with Mobile Food Truck owners and managers
3. Observations of truck sales and traffic at competitor sites.
4. Government and industry trade statistics
5. Local population demographics and projections.

Our sales forecast is an estimated projection of expected sales over the next three years, based on our chosen marketing strategy, general economic conditions and assumed competitive environment. ___ (company name) will focus on increasing ice cream sales to meet total sales forecast goals.

Sales are expected to be below average during the first year, until a regular customer base has been established. It has been estimated that it takes the average Mobile Food Truck a minimum of two years to establish a significant customer base. After the customer base is built, sales will grow at an accelerated rate from word-of-mouth referrals and continued networking efforts. We expect sales to steadily increase as our marketing campaign, employee training programs and contact management system are executed. By using advertising, especially discounted introductory coupons, as a catalyst for this prolonged process, ____(company name) plans to attract more customers sooner. Throughout the first year, it is forecasted that sales will incrementally grow until profitability is reached toward the end of year ____(one?). Year two reflects a conservative growth rate of ____ (20?) percent. Year three reflects a growth rate of ____ (25?) percent. We expect to be open for business on ____ (date), and start with __ (#) customers. With our unique mobile ice cream product and service offerings, along with our thorough and aggressive marketing strategies, we believe that sales forecasts are actually on the conservative side.

Table: Sales Forecast

| | Annual Sales | | |
|---|---|---|---|
| **Sales** | **2017** | **2018** | **2019** |
| Organic Hot Meals | | | |
| Sandwiches/Soup/Salad | | | |
| All Natural Beverages | | | |
| Healthy Snacks | | | |
| Gift Merchandise | | | |
| Miscellaneous | | | |
| **Total Unit Sales** | | | |
| | | | |
| **Direct Cost of Sales:** | | | |
| Organic Hot Meals | | | |
| Sandwiches/Soup/Salad | | | |
| All Natural Beverages | | | |
| Healthy Snacks | | | |
| Gift Merchandise | | | |
| Miscellaneous | | | |
| **Subtotal Direct Cost of Sales** | | | |

## 6.6 Merchandising Strategy

Merchandising is that part of our marketing strategy that is involved with promoting the sales of our merchandise, as by consideration of the most effective means of selecting, pricing, displaying, and advertising items for sale in our Mobile Food Truck business. Through proper product placement, space allocation, and on-location promotion, select sales space will be geared towards high profit margin products.

We will develop a merchandising strategy around the following design principles:
1. We will strive to feature merchandise that is not found in competitor trucks.
2. Use proper and informative signage to help sell merchandise.
3. We plan to group similar types of merchandise together for maximum visual appeal.

4. Product presentation will be designed to lead the customers through the entire display area.
5. We will designate a specific location for new product introductions.
6. We will reduce the clutter to increase customer convenience.
7. We will merchandise to the four corners of the truck by featuring destination categories the include coffee, foodservice and fountain drinks.
8. We will set up of special displays to coincide with a specific event, also known as occasion management.

The décor of the merchandising area is extremely important to sales. Display units are primary, but lighting, and countertops will all play important supporting roles.

We will monitor our sales figures and data to confirm that products in demand are well-stocked and slow-moving products are phased-out. We will     improve telephone skills of employees to boost phone orders for special occasion cakes and catering jobs.

We will attach our own additional business labels to all products to promote our line of services and location.

## 6.7   Pricing Strategy

**Our pricing strategy will take into view the following factors:**
1. Our overall marketing objectives
2. Customer demand
3. Service quality attributes
4. Competitor's Location and Pricing Strategy
5. Market and Economic Trends.
6. Level of Operating Expenses
7. Desired Profit Margin

We are not interested in being the low-price leader, as our pricing strategy plays a major role in whether we will be able to create and maintain customers for a profit. Our revenue structure must support our cost structure, so the salaries we pay to our staff are balanced by the revenue we collect.

**Sample Menu Pricing:**
Supreme Burger – with all the fixin's – $6 – add bacon for $1
Veggie Burger – with all the fixin's – $5
Fries basket for $3
American Cheese Sandwich - $3.50
Natural Fruit Smoothie - $3.50

Price List Comparison

| Competitor | Service/Product | Our Price | Competitor Price | B/(W) Competitor |
|---|---|---|---|---|
| | | | | |
| | | | | |

**We will adopt the following pricing guidelines:**
1. We must insure that our price plus service equation is perceived to be an exceptional value proposition.
2. We must refrain from competing on price, but always be price competitive.
3. We must develop value-added services, and bundle those with our products to create offerings that cannot be easily price compared.
4. We must focus attention on our competitive advantages.
5. Development of a pricing strategy based on our market positioning strategy, which is ____ (mass market value leadership/exceptional premium niche value?)
6. Our pricing policy objective, which is to _____ (increase profit margins/ achieve revenue maximization to increase market share/lower unit costs).
7. We will use marketplace intelligence and gain insights from competitor pricing.
8. We will solicit pricing feedback from customers using surveys and interviews.
9. We will utilize limited time pricing incentives to penetrate niche markets
10. We will conduct experiments at prices above and below the current price to determine the price elasticity of demand. (Inelastic demand or demand that does not decrease with a price increase, indicates that price increases may be feasible.)
11. We will keep our offerings and prices simple to understand and competitive, based on market intelligence.
12. We will consider a price for volume strategy on certain items, and study the effects of price on volume and of volume on costs, as in a recession, trying to recover these costs through a price increase can be fatal.

**Determining the costs of servicing business is the most important part of covering our expenses and earning profits. We will factor in the following pricing formula:**
Product Cost + Materials + Overhead + Labor + Profit + Tax = Price
**Materials** are those items consumed in the delivering of the service.
**Overhead costs** are the variable and fixed expenses that must be covered to stay in business. Variable costs are those expenses that fluctuate including vehicle expenses, rental expenses, utility bills and supplies. Fixed costs include the purchase of equipment, service ware, marketing and advertising, and insurance. After overhead costs are determined, the total overhead costs are divided among the total number of transactions forecasted for the year.
**Labor costs** include the costs of performing the services. Also included are Social Security taxes (FICA), vacation time, retirement and other benefits such as health or life insurance. To determine labor costs per hour, keep a time log. When placing a value on our time, we will consider the following: 1) skill and reputation; 2) wages paid by employers for similar skills and 3) where we live.
**Profit** is a desired percentage added to our total costs. We will need to determine the percentage of profit added to each service. It will be important to cover all our costs to

stay in business.

We will investigate available computer software programs to help us price our services and keep financial data for decision-making purposes. Close contact with customers will allow our company to react quickly to changes in demand. To ensure success, we will use periodic competitor and customer research to continuously evaluate our pricing strategy. We intend to review our profit margins every six months.

### 6.7.1 Profit Strategies

**We plan to pursue the following strategies to increase profits:**
1. Employee training increases productivity.
2. Inventory management lowers carrying costs.
3. Reduce shrinkage and breakage.
4. Comparison shop insurance coverage.
5. Comparison shop financing terms.
6. Monitor trends to lower 'dead stock' inventory.
7. Manage the inventory turnover ratio.
8. Manage credit policy and accounts receivable aging.
9. Manage Accounts Payable terms.
10. Manage the mix of brand name versus private label products.
11. Create pricing plans for different levels of value-added services.
12. Utilize loyalty programs to encourage repeat business.
13. Pool orders to obtain quantity discounts and reduced freight charges
14. Monitor operating expenses.
15. Install quality controls to reduce error rates.
16. Provide incentives for customers to increase transaction size.
17. Offer fee-based services.
18. Base salesperson's commission on transaction's contribution to profit.

## 6.8 Differentiation Strategies

We will use differentiation strategies to develop and market unique products for different customer segments. To differentiate ourselves from the competition, we will focus on the assets, creative ideas and competencies that we have that none of our competitors has. The goal of our differentiation strategies is to be able to charge a premium price for our unique products and services and/or to promote loyalty and assist in retaining our customers.

Due to the increase in two-income families, many service-oriented businesses are leaning toward differentiating themselves on the basis of convenience. We plan to have two shifts, an early morning shift for a healthy breakfast and an afternoon shift in which the Mobile Food Truck will be fully functional.

This will be a values-based company, and from the start, our idea will be to promote a healthier lifestyle through organic and natural foods. By concentrating on the sale of only healthy meals, _____ (company name) will be engaging in maximal product differentiation and at the same time restricting price competition.

Differentiation in our mobile food business will be achieved in the following types of ways, including:

|  | Explanation |
|---|---|
| ☐ Product features | _____ |
| ☐ Complementary services | _____ |
| ☐ Technology embodied in design | _____ |
| ☐ Location | _____ |
| ☐ Service innovations | _____ |
| ☐ Superior service | _____ |
| ☐ Creative advertising | _____ |
| ☐ Better supplier relationships | _____ |

Source: http://scholarship.sha.cornell.edu/cgi/viewcontent.cgi?article=1295&context=articles

Differentiating will mean defining who our perfect target market is and then catering to their needs, wants and interests better than everyone else. It will be about using surveys to determine what's most important to our targeted market and giving it to them consistently. It will not be about being "everything to everybody"; but rather, "the absolute best to our chosen targeted group".

In developing our differentiation strategy will we use the following form to help define our differences:

1. Targeted customer segments _____
2. Customer characteristics _____
3. Customer demographics _____
4. Customer behavior _____
5. Geographic focus _____
6. Ways of working _____
7. Service delivery approach _____
8. Customer problems/pain points _____
9. Complexity of customers' problems _____
10. Range of services _____

**We will use the following approaches to differentiate our products and services from those of our competitors to stand apart from standardised offerings:**

1. Superior quality
2. Unusual or unique product features
3. More responsive customer service

4. Rapid product or service innovation
5. Advanced technological features
6. Engineering design or styling
7. Additional product features
8. An image of prestige or status

**Specific Differentiators will include the following:**
1. Being a Specialist in one procedure
2. Utilizing advanced/uncommon technology
3. Possessing extensive experience
4. Building an exceptional facility
5. Consistently achieving superior results
6. Having a caring and empathetic personality
7. Giving customer s WOW experience, including a professional customer welcome package.
8. Enabling convenience and 24/7 online accessibility
9. Calling customers to express interest in their challenges.
10. Keeping to the appointment schedule.
11. Remembering customer names and details like they were family.
12. Assuring customer fears.
13. Building a visible reputation and recognition around our community
14. Acquiring special credentials or professional memberships
15. Providing added value services, such as taxi service, longer hours, financing plans, and post-sale services.

**The following differentiation strategies are based on current trends:**
1. We intend to capitalize on the trend toward more of a hospitality experience and demonstration theater, by enabling the customer to watch the face of the staff member as he or she prepares the meal.
2. We will create more unique flavors by engaging in co-branding arrangements with the makers of _____ ingredients, such as Nestle.
3. We will install a flat screen TV on the side of the truck, and continually play news programs directed at our target market.
4. We will focus on the creation of more healthy ice cream products, such as organic ingredients and soy-based ice cream.
5. We will design our Mobile Food Truck with the look of an old-fashioned ice cream truck to tap into nostalgic feelings.
6. We will package home replacement meals under our own private label name to build name recognition.
7. We will achieve horizontal differentiation by continuing to offer different seasoning profiles.
8. We will add hand-dipped ice cream from a local dairy farm.
9. We will install a drive-up window on one side of the truck and a walk-up window for added customer convenience on the other side.
10. We will feature a line of All Natural, sugar-free premium desserts.
11. We will bake on-site our own line of ____ (waffle cones?) with three distinctive

flavors: cinnamon, ginger and vanilla.
12. As part of a future line of breakfast items, we plan to introduce French Toast, Cinnamon Buns, Blueberry Muffins and Pop-Tart sandwiches.
13. Our counter servers will be trained to sing songs and provide other forms of fun entertainment, including magic tricks, for our kid customers, as consumers are willing to pay more for an 'experience'.
14. We also plan to roll out a "Grab and Go" freezer case where customers can quickly pick from a handful of the most popular flavors to take home, and avoid waiting in line to be served.
15. We will develop many new fruit drinks that will be aimed at nutrition-minded consumers, and a few will even be pitched as dessert replacements.

**Other differentiation strategies include:**
1. We will design a comfortable canopied seating area.
2. Online and fax ordering of foodservice items.
3. Delivery of foodservice items. (min = $25)
4. We will offer mobile services to senior living facilities and companies.
5. We will build an extensive profile on customers to capture information about their lifestyle, taste preferences and key occasion reminder dates.
6. We will develop a referral program that turns our customers into referral agents.
7. We will use regular client satisfaction surveys to collect feedback, improvement ideas, referrals and testimonials.
8. We will promote our "green" practices, such as establishing a recycling program, purchasing recycled-content goods and responsibly handling wastes.
9. We will customize our offerings according to the language, cultural influences, customs, interests and preferences of our local market to create loyalty and increase sales.
10. We will develop the expertise to satisfy the needs of targeted market segments with customized and exceptional support services.
11. We will develop original recipes for our own line of gourmet meals-to-go.
12. We will structure formally our new menu item sampling and complaint resolution programs.
Resource:
http://mobile-cuisine.com/marketing/4-food-truck-differentiation-tactics-work/

## 6.9 Milestones                                    (select)

The Milestones Chart is a timeline that will guide our company in developing and growing our business. It will list chronologically the various critical actions and events that must occur to bring our business to life. We will make certain to assign real, attainable dates to each planned action or event.

_____ (company name) has identified several specific milestones which will function as goals for the company. The milestones will provide a target for achievement as well as a mechanism for tracking progress. The dates were chosen based on realistic delivery times and necessary vehicle customization times. All critical path milestones will be completed within their allotted time frames to ensure the success of contingent milestones. The following table will provide a timeframe for each milestone.

Table: Milestones

| Milestones | Start Date | End Date | Budget | Responsibility |
|---|---|---|---|---|
| Business Plan Completion | | | | |
| Secure Permits/Licenses | | | | |
| Locate & Secure Space | | | | |
| Obtain Insurance Coverage | | | | |
| Secure Additional Financing | | | | |
| Get Start-up Supplies Quotes | | | | |
| Obtain County Certification | | | | |
| Purchase Office Equipment | | | | |
| Customize Vehicle | | | | |
| Define Marketing Programs | | | | |
| Install Equipment/Displays | | | | |
| Technology Systems | | | | |
| Set-up Accounting System | | | | |
| Develop Office Policies | | | | |
| Develop Procedures Manual | | | | |
| Arrange Support Service Providers | | | | |
| Finalize Media Plan | | | | |
| Create Facebook Brand Page | | | | |
| Conduct Blogger Outreach | | | | |
| Develop Personnel Plan | | | | |
| Develop Staff Training Programs | | | | |
| Hire/Train Staff | | | | |
| Implement Marketing Plan | | | | |
| Get Website Live | | | | |
| Conduct SEO Campaign | | | | |
| Form Strategic Alliances | | | | |
| Purchase Start-up Inventory/Supplies | | | | |
| Press Release Announcements | | | | |
| Advertise Grand Opening | | | | |
| Kickoff Advertising Program | | | | |
| Join Community Orgs./Network | | | | |
| Conduct Satisfaction Surveys | | | | |
| Evaluate/Revise Plan | | | | |
| Devise Growth Strategy | | | | |
| Monitor Social Media Networks | | | | |
| Respond to Reviews | | | | |
| Measure Return on Marketing $$$ | | | | |
| Revenues Exceed $_____ | | | | |
| Reach Profitability | | | | |
| **Totals:** | | | | |

# 7.0 Website Plan Summary

_____ (company name) is currently developing a website at the URL address www. (company name).com. We will primarily use the website to promote an understanding of the healthy foodservices we offer and to enable online order placement and route tracking. Existing customers and prospects will want to know more about the benefits of our healthy meal options with organic ingredients. Supplying the visitors to our websites with this information will make a huge difference in turning our website visitors into new customers.

The website will be developed to offer customers a product catalog for online orders. The overriding design philosophy of the site will be ease of use. We want to make the process of placing an order as easy and fast as possible thereby encouraging increased sales. We will incorporate special features such as a section that is specific to each customer so the customer can easily make purchases of repeat items. Instead of going through the website every month and locating their monthly needs, the site will capture regularly ordered items for that specific customer, significantly speeding up the ordering process. This ease-of-use feature will help increase sales as customers become more and more familiar with the site and appreciate how easy it is to place an order.

We will also provide multiple incentives to sign-up for various benefits, such as our newsletters and promotional sale notices. This will help us to build an email database, which will supply our automated customer follow-up system. We will create a personalized drip marketing campaign to stay in touch with our customers and prospects.

We will develop our website to be a resource for web visitors who are seeking knowledge and information about _____, with a goal to service the knowledge needs of our customers, and generate leads. Our home page will be designed to be a "welcome mat" that clearly presents our service offerings and provides links through which visitors can gain easy access to the information they seek. We will use our website to match the problems our customers face with the solutions we offer.

We will use the free tool, Google Analytics (http://www.google.com/analytics), to generate a history and measure our return on investment. Google Analytics is a free tool that can offer insight by allowing the user to monitor traffic to a single website. We will just add the Google Analytics code to our website and Google will give our firm a dashboard providing the number of unique visitors, repeat traffic, page views, etc.
This will help to stop wasting our company's money on inefficient marketing. Using an analytic program will show exactly which leads are paying off, and which ones to do without. We will find out what's bringing our site the most traffic and how to improve upon that.

**To improve the readability of our website, we will organize our website content in the following ways.**

1. Headlines
2. Bullet points
3. Callout text
4. Top of page summaries

**To improve search engine optimization, we will maximize the utilization of the following;**
1. Links
2. Headers
3. Bold text
4. Bullets
5. Keywords
6. Meta tags

**This website will serve the following purposes:**

| | |
|---|---|
| About Us | How We Work/Our Philosophy |
| Contact Us | Customer service contact info |
| Our Services | Specialties Benefits |
| Catering Service | Book a Party |
| Request A Stop in Your Area | Form |
| Birthday Club | Member Form |
| Place an Order | Pick-up/Delivery Form |
| Nutrition Articles | Facts |
| Our Menu | |
| Product Catalog | Online Ordering |
| Promotions | Free Coupon |
| Gift Certificates/Cards | |
| Frequently Asked Questions | FAQs |
| Newsletter Sign-up | Mailing List |
| Newsletter Archives | Foot Care Articles |
| Upcoming Events | Seminar/Cooking Classes |
| Testimonials | Letters w/photos |
| Referral Program | Details |
| Membership Club | Loyalty Program |
| Weekly Locations | |
| Truck Finder | Google Map |
| Customer Satisfaction Survey | Feedback |
| Photo Gallery | Dishes |
| Press Releases | Community Involvement |
| Latest News | |
| Strategic Alliance Partners | Links |
| Resources | Professional Associations |
| Our Blog | Diary/Accept comments |
| Refer-a-Friend | Viral marketing |
| Forums | Community Building |
| Tweets | |
| Facebook | |
| YouTube Video Clips | Seminar Presentation/Testimonials |
| Guarantees/Code of Ethics | Values Statement |
| Our Charitable Work | Cause Involvements |
| Career Opportunities | |

Live Chat
Classified Ads

**Classified Ads**
By joining and incorporating a classified ad affiliate program into our website, we will create the ultimate win-win-win. We will provide our guests with a free benefit, increase our rankings with the search engines by incorporating keyword hyperlinks into our site, attract additional markets to expose to our product, create an additional income source as they upgrade their ads, and provide our prospects a reason to return to our web site again and again
Resources:

| | |
|---|---|
| App Themes | www.appthemes.com/themes/classipress/ |
| e-Classifieds | http://www.e-classifieds.net/ |
| Noah's Classifieds | http://www.noahsclassifieds.org/ |
| Joom Prod | http://www.joomprod.com/ |

# 7.1  Website Marketing Strategy

**Our online marketing strategy will employ the following distinct mechanisms:**

1. Search Engine Submission
   This will be most useful to people who are unfamiliar with _____ (company name), but are looking for a local Mobile Food Truck. There will also be searches from customers who may know about us, but who are seeking additional information.

   **Search Engine Optimization (SEO)**
   SEO is a very important digital marketing strategy because search engines are the primary method of finding information for most internet users. SEO is simply the practice of improving and promoting a website to increase the number of visitors a site receives from search engines. Basic SEO techniques will range from the naming of webpages to the way that other websites link to our website.
   We will also need to get our business listed on as many relevant online directories as possible, such as Google, Yelp, Kudzu and Yahoo Local, write a blog that solicit comments and be active on social media sites.
   We will also try to incorporate local terms potential clients would use, such as "_____ (city) mobile food truck." This will make it more likely that local customers will find us close to the top of their search.
   Resource;
   www.officerreports.com/blog/wp-content/uploads/2014/11/SEOmoz-The-Beginners-Guide-To-SEO-2012.pdf

2. Website Address (URL) on Marketing Materials
   Our URL will be printed on all marketing communications, business cards, letterheads, faxes, and invoices and product labels. This will encourage a visit to

our website for additional information

3. Online Directories Listings

We will list our website on relevant, free and paid online directories and manufacturer website product locators.

The good online directories possess the following features:

Free or paid listings that do not expire and do not require monthly renewal.
Ample space to get your advertising message across.
Navigation buttons that are easy for visitors to use.
Optimization for top placement in the search engines based on keywords that people typically use to find Mobile Food Trucks.
Direct links to your website, if available.
An ongoing directory promotion campaign to maintain high traffic volumes to the directory site.

4. Strategic Business Partners

We will use a Business Partners page to cross-link to prominent _____ (city) area dance web sites as well as the city Web sites and local recreational sites. We will also cross-link with brand name suppliers.

5. YouTube Posting

We will produce a video of testimonials from several of our satisfied customers and educate viewers as to the range of our mobile services and products. Our research indicates that the YouTube video will also serve to significantly improve our ranking with the Google Search Engine.

6. Exchange of links with strategic marketing partners.

We will cross-link to non-profit businesses that accept our gift certificate donations as in-house run contest prize awards.

7. E-Newsletter

Use the newsletter sign-up as a reason to collect email addresses and limited profiles, and use embedded links in the newsletter to return readers to website.

8. Create an account for your photos on flickr.com

We will use the name of our site on flickr so we have the same keywords. To take full advantage of Flickr, we will use a JavaScript-enabled browser and install the latest version of the Macromedia Flash Player.
Ex: http://www.flickr.com/photos/sf2006/5816255412/

9. Geo Target Pay Per Click (PPC) Campaign

Available through Google Adwords program. Example keywords include health food, organic food, mobile catering, corporate events, catering truck, Lunch Truck Food Wagon and _____ (city).

10. Post messages on Internet user groups and forums.
    Get involved with food truck related discussion groups and forums and develop a descriptive signature paragraph.
    Resources: www.reference.com    www.deja.com    www.tracerlock.com

11. Write up your own LinkedIn.com and Facebook.com profiles.
    Highlight your background and professional interests.

12. Facebook.com Brand-Building Applications:
    As a Facebook member, we will create a specific Facebook page for our business through its "Facebook Pages" application. This page will be used to promote who we are and what we do. We will use this page to post alerts when we have new articles to distribute, news to announce, etc. Facebook members can then become fans of our page and receive these updates on their newsfeed as we post them. We will create our business page by going to the "Advertising" link on the bottom of our personal Facebook page. We will choose the "Pages" tab at the top of that page, and then choose "Create a Page." We will upload our logo, enter our company profile details, and establish our settings. Once completed, we will click the "publish your site" button to go live. We will also promote our Page everywhere we can. We will add a Facebook link to our website, our email signatures, and email newsletters. We will also add Facebook to the marketing mix by deploying pay-per-click ads through their advertising application. With Facebook advertising, we will target by specifying sex, age, relationship, location, education, as well as specific keywords. Once we specify our target criteria, the tool will tell us how many members in the network meet our target needs.

13. Blog to share our success stories and solicit comments.
    Blogging will be a great way for us to share information, expertise, and news, and start a conversation with our customers, the media, potential partners, suppliers, and any other target audiences. Blogging will be a great online marketing strategy because it keeps our content fresh, engages our audience to leave comments on specific posts, improves search engine rankings and attracts links.
    Resource: www.blogger.com    www.wordpress    www.blogspot.com

## 7.2 Development Requirements

A full development plan will be generated as documented in the milestones. Costs that ____ (company name) will expect to incur with development of its new website include:

**Development Costs**
    User interface design              $_____.
    Site development and testing    $_____

Site Implementation              $._____

**Ongoing Costs**
Website name registration        $_____ per year.
Site Hosting                     $_____ or less per month.
Site design changes, updates and maintenance are considered part of Marketing.

The site will be developed by _____ (company name), a local start-up company. The user interface designer will use our existing graphic art to come up with the website logo and graphics. We have already secured hosting with a local provider, _____ (business name). Additionally, they will prepare a monthly statistical usage report to analyze and improve web usage and return on investment.

The plan is for the website to be live by ____(date). Basic website maintenance, including update and data entry will be handled by our staff. Site content, such as images and text will be maintained by _____ (owner name). In the future, we may need to contract with a technical resource to build the trackable article download and newsletter capabilities.
Resource:    www.web.com        www.chase.com/storefront


# 7.3 Frequently Asked Questions

**We will use the following guidelines when developing the frequently asked questions for the ecommerce section of the website:**
1. Use a Table of Contents: Offer subject headers at the top of the FAQ page with a hyperlink to that related section further down on the page for quick access.
2. Group Questions in a Logical Way and group separate specific questions related to a subject together.
3. Be Precise with the Question: Don't use open-ended questions.
4. Avoid Too Many Questions: Publish only the popular questions and answers.
5. Answer the Question with a direct answer.
6. Link to Resources When Available: via hyperlinks so the customer can continue with self-service support.
7. Use Bullet Points to list step-by-step instructions.
8. Focus on Customer Support and Not Marketing.
9. Use Real and Relevant Frequently Asked Questions from actual customers.
10. Update Your FAQ Page as customers continue to communicate questions.

The following frequently asked questions will enable us to convey a lot of important information to our customers in a condensed format. We will post these questions and answers on our website and create a hardcopy version to be included on our sales presentation folder.

**What is a food truck?**
A food truck is a mobile, miniature commercial kitchen that must meet all of the same Department of Health requirements that a brick and mortar restaurant does. Depending on the type of food served, this includes having a three-compartment sink, separate hand sink and a fire suppression system. Our food trucks serve communities in _____, which have few options for affordable and diverse food choices.

**What regulations do food trucks follow?**
Food trucks follow regulations which apply to all street vendors. Like brick and mortar restaurants, food trucks are regularly inspected by the Department of Health, although, unlike brick and mortar restaurants, food trucks are billed for each inspection.
In addition to their mobile commercial kitchens, food trucks must maintain a second, brick and mortar commercial kitchen that meets Department of Health requirements where they can store and prepare food. Food truck owner-operators must pass a food manager certification test to be approved for a vending license.

**What taxes do food trucks pay?**
Food trucks pay the same taxes as other street vendors. Food trucks also pay taxes associated with their brick and mortar commercial kitchens, motor vehicle taxes, corporate/unincorporated business franchise taxes, as well as payroll taxes.

**What is organic?**
Organic food production is based on a system of farming that maintains and replenishes soil fertility without the use of toxic pesticides and fertilizers. Organic foods are minimally processed without artificial ingredients, preservatives, or irradiation to maintain the integrity of the food. In some cities, herbicides in tap water exceed federal lifetime health standards for weeks or months at a time. The organic farmer's elimination of polluting chemicals and nitrogen leaching, in combination with soil building, works to prevent contamination, and protects and conserves water resources. "Certified Organic" means the item has been grown according to strict uniform standards that are verified by independent state or private organizations. Certification includes inspections of farm fields and processing facilities, detailed record keeping, and periodic testing of soil and water to ensure that growers and handlers are meeting the standards that have been set.

**Do you offer gift cards?**
Yes, we offer a variety of gift cards in our trucks.

**What is the difference between "organic" and "natural"?**
"Natural" often is misrepresented in product labeling to imply "healthful," but "natural" only means that the product has undergone minimal processing. Unlike products that are certified organic, natural products have no certification or inspection system. Also, "natural" does not necessarily relate to growing methods or the use of preservatives.

**Are organic foods healthier?**
Organic foods are not necessarily more nutritious, rather organic food are spared the application of potentially harmful long-lasting insecticides, herbicides, fungicides and

fertilizers. Many EPA-approved pesticides were registered long before extensive research linked these chemicals to cancer and other diseases. Now, the EPA considers 60% of all herbicides, 90% of all fungicides, and 30% of all insecticides as potentially cancer-causing.

**Do organic foods generally cost more than conventional foods?**
Although many organic products do cost more, the price of organic foods is increasingly competitive as supply and demand continue to rise. It is important to remember that prices for organic products reflect many of the same costs as conventional items in terms of growing, harvesting, transportation, and storage, but organic products must meet stricter regulations governing all of these steps. Therefore, the process is often more labor and management intensive. Organic farmers have an added cost of compliance with organic certification standards and government programs do not subsidize organic farming.

**What are some of the types of events for which you provide your lunch truck service?**
The most popular types of events are Company Picnics, Casual Fridays, Health and Fitness Fairs, New Product Rollouts, Employee Appreciation Day, Anniversary Celebration, Groundbreaking Ceremonies, Birthdays, Graduations, Weddings, Rehearsal Dinners and Christmas Parties.

**Do you do catering events? If so, how do I go about reserving your truck?**
Yes we do private catering events. To get in touch with us, please e-mail us at _____ at least 72 hours before your event date. We book a lot of events in advance, which include food truck festivals as well as other catering events, so please let us know early on so that we may accommodate your requests. Thank you.

**What Discounts do you offer on your catering service?**
We offer a ____% referral discount for you when each new client (your referrals) places an order. Each new client earns 15% discount on their first order.

## 7.4 Website Performance Summary

We will use web analysis tools to monitor web traffic, such as identifying the number of site visits. We will analyze customer transactions and take actions to minimize problems, such as incomplete sales and abandoned shopping carts. We will use the following table to track the performance of our website:

| Category | 2017 | | 2018 | | 2019 | |
|---|---|---|---|---|---|---|
| | Fcst | Act | Fcst | Act | Fcst | Act |
| No. of Customers | | | | | | |
| New Newsletter Subscribers | | | | | | |
| Unique Visitors | | | | | | |
| Avg. Time on Site | | | | | | |

Pages per Visit             _____
Percent New Visits          _____
Bounce Rate                 _____
No. of Products             _____
Product Categories          _____
Number of Incomplete Sales  _____
Conversion Rate             _____
Affiliate Sales             _____
Customer Satisfaction Score _____

## 7.5 Website Retargeting/Remarketing

Research indicates that for most websites, only 2% of web traffic converts readers on the first visit. Retargeting will keep track of people who have visited our website and displays our ads to them as they browse online. This will bring back 98% of users who don't convert right away by keeping our brand at the top of their mind. Setting up a remarketing tracking code on our website will allow us to target past visitors who did not convert or take the desired action on our site. After people have been to our website and are familiar with our brand, we will market more aggressively to this 'warm traffic.'

Resource:
www.marketing360.com/remarketing-software-retargeting-ads/

# 8.0 Operations Plan

Our operations plan will present an overview of the flow of the daily activities of the business and the strategies that support them. It will focus on the following critical operating factors that will make the business a success:

1. We will enjoy the following advantages in the sourcing of our inventory: _____

2. We will utilize the following technological innovations in the customer relationship management (CRM) process: _____

3. We will make use of the following advantages in our distribution process: _____

4. We will develop the following in-house training program to improve worker productivity: _____

5. We will utilize the following system to better control inventory carrying costs. _____

**Quality Control Plan**

Our Quality Control Plan will include a review process that checks all factors involved in our operations. The main objectives of our quality control plan will be to uncover defects and bottlenecks, and reporting to management level to make the decisions on the improvement of the whole production process. Our review process will include the following activities:

    Quality control checklist
    Finished product/service review
    Structured walkthroughs
    Statistical sampling
    Testing process

**Operations Planning**

We will use Microsoft Visio to develop visual maps, which will piece together the different activities in our organization and show how they contribute to the overall "value stream" of our business. We will rightfully treat operations as the lifeblood of our business. We will develop a combined sales and operations planning process where sales and operations managers will sit down every month to review sales, at the same time creating a forward-looking 12-month rolling plan to help guide the product development and manufacturing processes, which can become disconnected from sales. We will approach our operations planning using a three-step process that analyzes the company's current state, future state and the initiatives it will tackle next. For each initiative, such as launching a new product or service, the company will examine the related financials, talent and operations needs, as well as target customer profiles. Our management team will map out the cost of development and then calculate forecasted return on investment and revenue predictions.

## Cost Control

Strict cost-control measures will be implemented. These measures will include, among others, proper and prudent purchasing practices, maximization of product distribution through strict adherence to weights, amounts and recipes (portion control), effective utilization of personnel, and the constant search for ways to reduce the cost of sales of our products without sacrificing quality and service.

To reduce the Costs of Goods Sold, which will introduce the following practices:

1. **Categorize our food expenses.**
   We will keep track of how much is spent on each food group. We will break down our food items into groups, such as meats, produce and dairy, and set guidelines that govern how much to spend in each category.
2. **Comparison shop to find better pricing.**
   We will stay informed of cost-effective alternatives, and continuously be on the lookout for more economical suppliers without sacrificing quality.
3. **Measure all ingredients in food-preparation procedures.**
   We will enforce strict measurement guidelines for our recipes.
4. **Adjust our menu or prices accordingly when using seasonal ingredients.**
   We will limit the sales of seasonal items to periods when they are plentiful and acquired at minimal price. When we sell such goods during off-season periods, we will adjust our menu pricing to offset the extra cost.
5. **Design specials that reduce waste and use slow-moving stock.**
   We will make use of soon-to-expire foods and leftovers, by incorporating them into daily specials.

## Supply Chain Relationships

We will seek to establish good working relationships with our vendors and encourage suppliers to provide more special deals, such as buy-one, get-one free to help improve sales of products. We will also encourage our suppliers to provide in-truck merchandising/marketing ideas, lower prices and other types of promotional support.

The Mobile Food Truck will be run as a team, with each employee playing an integral part in the success or failure of the business. Employees will be given whatever tools and training is deemed necessary to carry out their assignments. An emphasis on process improvement will be instilled in each of the "teammates" by offering bonuses or special privileges. Teammates will be rewarded both monetarily and non-monetarily for jobs well done. Effective communication will be stressed in the business. This will cut down on misunderstandings and miscommunications among customers, employees, and managers. Weekly meetings will be held to discuss the weekly agenda, and to give a report of last week's happenings. Teammates will be given the opportunity to add input at these meetings in the form of suggestions, comments, and complaints. Teammates will have defined tasks, but are to be receptive to doing whatever requests outside of their set guidelines need to be done to bring success to the practice. Finally, we plan to offer many perks to my employees to keep them satisfied and willing to give the business 100 percent.

We will consolidate the number of suppliers we deal with to reduce the volume of paperwork and realize volume discounts.

We will conduct a quality improvement plan, which consists of an ongoing process of improvement activities and includes periodic samplings of activities not initiated solely in response to an identified problem. Our plan will be evaluated annually and revised as necessary. Our client satisfaction survey goal is a ___ (98.0) % satisfaction rating.

We also plan to develop a list of specific interview questions and a worksheet to evaluate, compare and pre-screen potential suppliers. We will also check vendor references and their rating with the Hoovers.com.

Operations include the business aspects of running our business, such as conducting quality assessment and improvement activities, auditing functions, cost-management analysis, and customer service.

We plan to write and maintain an Operations Manual and a Personnel Policies Handbook. The Operating Manual will be a comprehensive document outlining virtually every aspect of the business. The operating manual will include management and accounting procedures, hiring and personnel policies, and daily operations procedures, such as opening and closing the store, and how to _____. The manual will cover the following topics:

- Community Relations
- Media Relations
- Vendor Relations
- Competition Relations
- Environmental Concerns
- Intra Company Procedures
- Banking and Credit Cards
- Computer Procedures
- Quality Controls
- Open/Close Procedures
- Software Documentation
- Catering Checklists

- Customer Relations
- Employee Relations
- Government Relations
- Equipment Maintenance Checklist
- Inventory Controls
- Accounting and Billing
- Financing
- Scheduling Procedures
- Safety Procedures
- Security Procedures
- Designated Route

Our plan is to automate our sales process, by developing an online registration calculator. We will develop a personnel manual. Though a time-consuming process, its purpose is to set fair and equal guidelines in print for all to abide. It's the playbook detailing specific policies, as well as enforcement, thereby preventing any misinterpretation, miscommunication or ill feelings. This manual will reflect only the concerns that affect our personnel. A companion policy and procedure manual will cover everything else.

We plan to create the following business manuals:
| | Manual Type | Key Elements |
|---|---|---|
| 1. | Operations Manual | Process flowcharts |

2. Employee Manual . Benefits/Appraisals/Practices
3. Managers Manual    Job Descriptions
4. Customer Service Policics    Inquiry Handling Procedures

Resource:
POS Nation Software    http://posnation.com/health_food_pos

## 9.0 Management Summary

The Management Plan will reveal who will be responsible for the various management functions to keep the business running efficiently. It will further demonstrate how that individual has the experience and/or training to accomplish each function. It will address who will do the planning function, the organizing function, the directing function, and the controlling function. We will also develop an employee retention plan because there are distinct cost advantages to retaining employees. It costs a lot to recruit and train a new employee, and in the early days, new employees are a lot less productive. We will need to make sure that our employees are satisfied in order to retain them and, in turn, create satisfied customers.

At the present time _____ (owner name) will run all operations for _____ (company name). _____ (His/Her) background in _____ (business management?) indicates an understanding of the importance of financial control systems. There is not expected to be any shortage of qualified staff from local labor pools in the market area.

_____ (owner name) will be the owner and operations manager of _____ (company name). His/her general duties will include the following:
1. Oversee the daily operations
2. Ordering inventory and supplies.
3. Develop and implementing the marketing strategy
4. Purchasing equipment.
5. Arranging for the routine maintenance and upkeep of the facility.
6. Hiring, training and supervision of new assistants.
7. Scheduling and planning of seminars and other special events.
8. Creating and pricing products and services.
9. Managing the accounting/financial aspect of the business.
10. Contract negotiation/vendor relations.

## 9.1 Owner Personal History

The owner has been working in the _____ industry for over ____ (#) years, gaining personal knowledge and experience in all phases of the industry. _____ (owner name) is the founder and operations manager of _____ (company name). The owner holds a degree from the University of _____ at _____ (city), and he also holds a _____ (Master's) degree in ____ (specialty) from _____. He/she began his/her career as a _____.

Over the last ____ (#) years, _____ (owner name) became quite proficient in a wide range of management activities and responsibilities, becoming an operations manager for _____ (former employer name) from _____ to _____ (dates). There he/she was able to achieve _____.
_____, owner of _____ (company name), has a ____ degree in _____.
For ____ years he/she has managed a business similar to _____ (company name). _____ (His/her) duties included _____. Specifically, the

owner brings _____ (#) years of experience as a _____ , as well as certification as a _____ from the _____ (National _____ Association). He/she is an experienced entrepreneur with ____ years of small business accounting, finance, marketing and management experience. Education includes college course work in business administration, banking and finance, investments, and commercial credit management. The owner will draw an annual salary of $_____ from the business although most of this goes to repay loans to finance business start-up costs. These loans will be paid-in-full by _____ (month) of _____ (year).

## 9.2 Management Team Gaps

Despite the owner's and manager's experience in the _____ (?) industry, the company will also retain the consulting services of _____ (consultant company name). This company has over _____ (#) years of experience in the _____ industry, and has successfully opened dozens of Mobile Food Trucks across the country. The Consultants will be primarily used for certification approval, market research, customer satisfaction surveys and to provide additional input in the evaluation of new business opportunities. The company also expects to retain the services of a local CPA to help the owner manage cash flow. Additionally, the business will make use of the following advisory board to provide support for strategic planning and human resource related issues.

The Board of Advisors will provide continuous mentoring support on business matters. Expertise gaps in legal, tax, marketing and personnel will be covered by the Board of Advisors. The owner will actively seek free business advice from SCORE, a national non-profit organization with a local office. This is a group of retired executives and business owners who donate their time to serve as business counselors to new business owners.

Advisory Resources Available to the Business Include:

|  | Name | Address | Phone |
|---|---|---|---|
| CPA/Accountant | | | |
| Attorney | | | |
| Insurance Broker | | | |
| Banker | | | |
| Business Consultant | | | |
| Wholesale Suppliers | | | |
| Trade Association | | | |
| Realtor | | | |
| SCORE.org | | | |
| Other | | | |

## 9.3 Management Matrix

| Name | Title | Credentials | Functions | Responsibilities |
|---|---|---|---|---|

## 9.4  Outsourcing Matrix

| Company Name | Functions | Responsibilities | Cost |
| --- | --- | --- | --- |

**Note:** Marketing and public relations will be handled mainly by the owner. If there is a greater need, a marketing consultant will be hired to help issue press releases and generate seminar and website content.

## 9.5.0  Personnel Plan

Employee Requirements:

1. **Recruitment**
   Experience suggests that personal referrals from contractors and manufacturer reps are an excellent source for experienced associates We will also place newspaper ads, and use our Yellow Page Ad to indicate what types of staff we use and what types of customers we serve. We will also make effective use of our newsletter to post positions available and contact local trade schools for possible job candidates. We will give a referral bonus to existing employees.

2. **Training and Supervision**
   Training is largely accomplished through hands-on experience and by manufacturer product reps with supplemental instruction. Additional knowledge is gained through our policy and operations manuals, and attending manufacturer and trade association seminars. We will foster professional development and independence in all phases of our business. Supervision is task-oriented and the quantity is dependent on the complexity of the job assignment. Employees are called team members because they are part of Team _____ (company name). To help them succeed and confidently handle customer questions, employees will receive assistance with our internal certification program. They will also participate in our written training modules and receive regular samples to evaluate.

3. **Salaries and Benefits**
   Staff will be basically paid a salary plus commission basis on product sales. Good training and incentives, such as cash bonuses handed out monthly to everyone for reaching goals, will serve to retain good employees. An employee discount of __ percent on personal sales is offered. As business warrants, we hope to put together a benefit package that includes insurance, and paid vacations. The personnel plan also assumes a 5% annual increase in salaries.

## 9.5.1  Job Descriptions

## Job Description -- Lunch Truck Operator

- Answer questions about product features and benefits.
- Circulate among potential customers or travel by foot, truck, automobile, or bicycle to deliver or sell merchandise or services.
- Contact customers to persuade them to purchase merchandise or services.
- Deliver merchandise, and collect payment.
- Develop prospect lists.
- Distribute product samples or literature that details products or services.
- Explain products or services and prices, and demonstrate use of products.
- Order or purchase supplies.
- Write and record orders for merchandise, or enter orders into computers.
- Set up and display sample merchandise at parties or stands.
- Arrange buying parties, and solicit sponsorship of such parties, in order to sell merchandise.
- Stock carts or stands.

## Job Description—General Operations Manager

Must possess proven management skills, the ability to drive sales in the truck. Must have a passion for people development and delivering excellent customer service. Must be capable of delivering performance through their teams and ultimately can drive customer service through high retail standards, availability and presentation.

Key Accountabilities:
- Exceptional customer focus.
- Excellent Interpersonal skills.
- Effective planning and organizational skills.
- Influencing and negotiation skills.
- Budget management
- Supportive and persuasive management style.
- Tactical and strategic planning and implementation skills are a must.
- Clear vision and a determination to succeed.

## Job Description -- Assistant Manager

Assists in management of Mobile Food Truck engaged in selling merchandise by performing the following duties:

1. Assist in Planning and preparing work schedules and assignments of employees to specific duties.
2. Assists and supervises employees engaged in sales work, taking of inventories, reconciling cash with sales receipts, keeping operating records and preparing daily record of transactions or performs work of subordinates, as needed.
3. Ensures compliance of employees with established security, sales, and record keeping procedures and practices.
4. Orders merchandise or prepares requisitions to replenish merchandise on hand. 5. Ensure all reports, such as purchase, inventory and sales, are accurate and timely.
5. Monitor and verify vendor activity in truck.

6. Monitor and maintain proper truck cleanliness, appearance and maintenance as per company guidelines.
7. Ensure all truck employees are trained properly.
8. Coordinates sales promotion activities and prepares, or directs workers preparing, merchandise displays and advertising copy.
9. Maintain a customer service oriented operation.
10. Perform all shift duties as required.
11. Able to perform daily duties of Truck Manager in his/her absence.
12. Assist with overall operations improvement such as increasing customer base. 13. Assist in pricing adjustments, if necessary.

## Job Description --Sales Associate

Provides quality customer service to our customers. Must be able to fulfill all responsibilities listed below when necessary. Maximizes sales through excellent customer service.

Requirements: Provides friendly, courteous, and prompt customer service. Completes proper packaging and traying of all special orders. Proper and safe use of all equipment, including maintenance and daily sanitation of all equipment. Proper stocking, pricing/labeling, and rotation of food items. Maintains proper case merchandising and allocation. Ability to safely operate all equipment, including steamer, knife, wrapper, slicer, and ice machine. Ability to reach, stoop, bend, and lift as needed to stock or pull product for processing. Ability to withstand a cold working environment (45° F or less) for long periods of time. Ability to weigh, price, label, organize, rotate and identify all varieties of food carried by truck. Other duties and responsibilities may be added to meet business demands.

## Job Description— Janitorial Staff

The janitorial staff is an outside agency that comes in daily and cleans the food truck. They are responsible for:

- Vacuuming the entire truck
- Cleaning the sinks
- Emptying trash
- Cleaning refrigeration units
- Washing truck exterior and signage
- Mopping truck floors
- Washing windows, mirrors, etc.
- Sanitizing shelves and countertops
- Cleaning truck cooking equipment

## 9.5.2  Job Description Format

**Our job descriptions will adhere to the following format guidelines:**

1. Job Title
2. Reports to:
3. Pay Rate
4. Job Responsibilities
5. Travel Requirements
5. Supervisory Responsibilities
6. Qualifications
7. Work Experience
8. Required Skills
10. Salary Range
11. Benefits
12. Opportunities

## 9.5.3 Personnel Plan

1. We will develop a system for recruiting, screening and interviewing employees.
2. Background checks will be performed as well as reference checks and drug tests.
3. We will develop an assistant training course.
4. We will keep track of staff scheduling.
5. We will develop client satisfaction surveys to provide feedback and ideas.
6. We will develop and perform semi-annual employee evaluations.
7. We will "coach" all our employees to improve their abilities and range of skills.
8. We will employ temporary employees via a local staffing agency to assist with one-time special projects.
9. Each employee will be provided an Employee Handbook, which will include detailed job descriptions and list of business policies, and be asked to sign these documents as a form of employment contract.
10. Incentives will be offered for reaching quarterly financial and enrollment goals, completing the probationary period, and passing county inspections.
11. Customer service awards will be presented to those employees who best exemplify our stated mission and exceed customer expectations.

**Our Employee Handbook will include the following sections:**
1. Overview
2. Introduction to the Company
3. Organizational Structure
4. Employment and Hiring Policies
5. Performance Evaluation and Promotion Policies
6. Compensation Policies
7. Time Off Policies
8. Training Programs and Reimbursement Policies
9. General Rules and Policies
10. Termination Policies.

## 9.5.4 Staffing Plan

The following table summarizes our personnel expenditures for the first three years, with compensation costs increasing from $__ in the first year to about $__ in the third year, based on __ (5?) % payroll increases each year and 100% enrollment. The payroll includes tuition reimbursement, pay increases, vacation pay, bonuses and state required certifications.

Table: Personnel

| | Number of Employees | Hourly Rate | Annual Salaries 2017 | 2018 | 2019 |
|---|---|---|---|---|---|
| Operations Manager | | | | | |
| Assistant Truck Manager | | | | | |

Foodservice Sales Staff _____
Cook _____
Prep Cook _____
Stocking Clerk _____
Certified Nutritionist _____
P/T Marketing Coordinator _____
P/T Bookkeeper _____
P/T Janitor _____
P/T Mechanic _____
Other _____
**Total People: Headcount** _____
**Total Annual Payroll** _____
Payroll Burden (Fringe Benefits)     (+) _____
**Total Payroll Expense**                       (=) _____

Lunch Truck Operator:   MEDIAN ANNUAL WAGE: $27,300
                        MEDIAN HOURLY WAGE: $13.13

# 10.0 Risk Factors

**Risk management** is the identification, assessment, and prioritization of risks, followed by the coordinated and economical application of resources to minimize, monitor, and control the probability and/or impact of unfortunate events or to maximize the realization of opportunities. For the most part, our risk management methods will consist of the following elements, performed, more or less, in the following order.
1. Identify, characterize, and assess threats
2. Assess the vulnerability of critical assets to specific threats
3. Determine the risk (i.e. the expected consequences of specific types of attacks on specific assets)
4. Identify ways to reduce those risks
5. Prioritize risk reduction measures based on a strategy

## Types of Risks:

_____ (company name) faces the following kinds of risks:

1. **Financial Risks**

    Our quarterly revenues and operating results are difficult to predict and may fluctuate significantly from quarter to quarter as a result of a variety of factors. Among these factors are:
    - Changes in our own or competitors' pricing policies.
    - Recession pressures.
    - Fluctuations in expected revenues from advertisers, sponsors and strategic relationships.
    - Timing of costs related to acquisitions or payments.

2. **Legislative / Legal Landscape.**

    Our participation in the foodservice arena presents unique risks:
    - Product and other related liability.
    - Federal and State regulations on licensing, privacy and insurance.

3. **Operational Risks**

    For the past __ (#) years the owner has been dealing with computers, so he is comfortable with technology and understands a wide array of software applications. However, the biggest potential problem will be equipment malfunction. To minimize the potential for problems, the owner will be taking equipment repair training from the manufacturer and will deal with basic troubleshooting and minor repairs. Beyond that, we have identified a service technician who is located close-by.

    To attract and retain client to the _____ (company name) community, we must continue to provide differentiated and quality services. This confers certain risks including the failure to:
    - Anticipate and respond to consumer preferences for partnerships and service.
    - Attract, excite and retain a large audience of customers to our

community.
- Create and maintain successful strategic alliances with quality partners.
- Deliver high quality customer service.
- Build our brand rapidly and cost-effectively.
- Compete effectively against better-established Mobile Food Trucks.

4. **Human Resource Risks**
The most serious human resource risk to our business, at least in the initial stages, would be my inability to operate the business due to illness or disability. The owner is currently in exceptional health and would eventually seek to replace himself on a day-to-day level by developing systems to support the growth of the business.

5. **Marketing Risks**
Advertising is our most expensive form of promotion and there will be a period of testing headlines and offers to find the one that works the best. The risk, of course, is that we will exhaust our advertising budget before we find an ad that works. Placing greater emphases on sunk-cost marketing, such as our storefront and on existing relationships through direct selling will minimize our initial reliance on advertising to bring in a large percentage of business in the first year.

6. **Business Risks**
A major risk to retail service businesses is the performance of the economy and the small business sector. Since economists are predicting this as the fastest growing sector of the economy, our risk of a downturn in the short-term is minimized. The entrance of one of the three major chains into our marketplace is a risk. They offer more of the latest equipment, provide a wider array of products and services, competitive prices and 24-hour service. This situation would force us to lower our prices in the short-term until we could develop an offering of higher margin, value-added services not provided by the large chains. It does not seem likely that the relative size of our market today could support the overhead of one of those operations. Projections indicate that this will not be the case in the future and that leaves a window of opportunity for ___ (company name) to aggressively build a loyal client base.

**To combat the usual start-up risks we will do the following:**
1. Utilize our industry experience to quickly establish desired strategic relationships.
2. Pursue business outside of our immediate market area.
3. Diversify our range of product and service offerings.
4. Develop multiple distribution channels.
5. Monitor our competitor actions.
6. Stay in touch with our customers and suppliers.
7. Watch for trends which could potentially impact our business.
8. Continuously optimize and scrutinize all business processes.
9. Institute daily financial controls using Business Ratio Analysis.
10. Create pay-for-performance compensation and training programs to reduce

employee turnover.

Further, to attract and retain customers the Company will need to continue to expand its market offerings, utilizing third party strategic relationships. This could lead to difficulties in the management of relationships, competition for specific services and products, and/or adverse market conditions affecting a particular partner.
The Company will take active steps to mitigate risks. In preparation of the Company's pricing, many factors will be considered. The Company will closely track the activities of all third parties, and will hold monthly review meetings to resolve issues and review and update the terms associated with strategic alliances.

**Additionally, we will develop the following kinds of contingency plans:**
Disaster Recovery Plan
Business Continuity Plan
Business Impact and Gap Analysis
Testing & Maintenance

The Company will utilize marketing and advertising campaigns to promote brand identity and will coordinate all expectations with internal and third-party resources prior to release. This strategy should maximize customer satisfaction while minimizing potential costs associated with unplanned expenditures and quality control issues.

## 10.1 Reduce New Business Risk Tactics

**We plan to use the following tactics to reduce our new business start-up risk:**
1. Implement your business plan based on go, no-go stage criteria.
2. Develop employee cross-training programs.
3. Regularly back-up all computer files/Install ant-virus software.
4. Arrange adequate insurance coverage with higher deductibles.
5. Develop a limited number of prototype samples.
6. Test market offerings to determine level of market demand and appropriate pricing strategy.
7. Thoroughly investigate and benchmark to competitor offerings.
8. Research similar franchised businesses for insights into successful prototype business/operations models.
9. Reduce operation risks and costs by flowcharting all structured systems & standardized manual processes.
10. Use market surveys to listen to customer needs and priorities.
11. Purchase used equipment to reduce capital outlays.
12. Use leasing to reduce financial risk.
13. Outsource ice cream manufacturing to job shops to reduce capital at risk.
14. Use subcontractors to limit fixed overhead salary expenses.
15. Ask manufacturer about profit sharing arrangement.
16. Pay advertisers with a percent of revenues generated.
17. Develop contingency plans for identified risks.
18. Set-up procedures to control employee theft.

19. Do criminal background checks on potential employees.
20. Take immediate action on delinquent accounts.
21. Only extend credit to established account with D&B rating
22. Get regular competitive bids from alternative suppliers.
23. Check that operating costs as a percent of rising sales are lower as a result of productivity improvements.
24. Request bulk rate pricing on fast moving supplies.
25. Don't be tempted to tie up cash in slow moving inventory to qualify for bigger discounts.
26. Reduce financial risk by practicing cash flow policies.
27. Reduce hazard risk by installing safety procedures.
28. Use financial management ratios to monitor business vitals.
29. Make business decisions after brainstorming sessions.
30. Focus on the products/services with biggest return on investment.
31. Where possible, purchase off-the-shelf components.
32. Request manufacturer samples to build your prototype.
33. Design your production facilities to be flexible and easy to change.
34. Develop a network of suppliers with outsourcing capabilities.
35. Analyze and shorten every cycle time, including product development.
36. Develop multiple sources for every important input.
37. Treat the business plan as a living document and update it frequently.
38. Conduct a SWOT analysis and use determined strengths to pursue opportunities.
39. Conduct regular customer satisfaction surveys to evaluate performance.

## 10.2    Reduce Customer Perceived Risk Tactics

We will utilize the following tactics to help reduce the new customer's perceived risk of starting to do business with our company.

|   | Status |
|---|---|
| 1. Publish a page of testimonials. | _____ |
| 2. Secure Opinion Leader written endorsements. | _____ |
| 3. Offer an Unconditional Satisfaction Money Back Guarantee. | _____ |
| 4. Long-term Performance Guarantee (Financial Risk). | _____ |
| 5. Guaranteed Buy Back (Obsolete time risk) | _____ |
| 6. Offer free trials and samples. | _____ |
| 7. Brand Image (consistent marketing image and performance) | _____ |
| 8. Patents/Trademarks/Copyrights | _____ |
| 9. Publish case studies | _____ |
| 10. Share your expertise (Articles, Seminars, etc.) | _____ |
| 11. Get recognized Certification | _____ |
| 12. Conduct responsive customer service | _____ |
| 13. Accept Installment Payments | _____ |
| 14. Display product materials composition or ingredients. | _____ |
| 15. Publish product test results. | _____ |
| 16. Publish sales record milestones. | _____ |

17. Foster word-of-mouth by offering an unexpected extra. _____
18. Distribute factual, pre-purchase info. _____
19. Reduce consumer search costs with online directories. _____
20. Reduce customer transaction costs. _____
21. Facilitate in-depth comparisons to alternative services. _____
22. Make available prior customer ratings and comments. _____
23. Provide customized info based on prior transactions. _____
24. Become a Better Business Bureau member. _____
25. Publish overall customer satisfaction survey results. _____
26. Offer plan options that match niche segment needs. _____
27. Require client sign-off before proceeding to next phase. _____
28. Document procedures for dispute resolution. _____
29. Offer the equivalent of open source code. _____
30. Stress your compatibility features (avoid lock-in fear). _____
31. Create detailed checklists & flowcharts to show processes _____
32. Publish a list of frequently asked questions/answers. _____
33. Create a community that enables customers to connect with each other and share common interests. _____
34. Inform customers as to your stay-in-touch methods. _____
35. Conduct and handover a detailed needs analysis worksheet. _____
36. Offer to pay all return shipping charges and/or refund all original shipping and handling fees. _____
37. Describe your product testing procedures prior to shipping. _____
38. Highlight your competitive advantages in all marketing materials. _____

## 11.0 Financial Plan

The over-all financial plan for growth allows for use of the significant cash flow generated by operations. We are basing projected sales on the market research, industry analysis and competitive environment. _____ (company name) expects a profit margin of over ____ % starting with year one. By year two, that number should slowly increase as the law of diminishing costs takes hold, and the day-to-day activities of the business become less expensive. Sales are expected to grow at ____ % per year, and level off by year _____.

Our financial statements will show consistent growth in earnings, which provides notice of the durability of our company's competitive advantage.

The initial investment in _____ (company name) will be provided by _____ (owner name) in the amount of $ _____. The owner will also seek a ___ (#) year bank loan in the amount of $ _____ to provide the remainder of the required initial funding. The funds will be used to renovate the space and to cover initial operating expenses. The owner financing will become a return on equity, paid in the form of dividends to the owner. We expect to finance steady growth through cash flow. The owners do not intend to take any profits out of the business until the long-term debt has been satisfied.

**Our financial plan includes:**
    Moderate growth rate with a steady cash flow.
    Investing residual profits into company expansion.
    Company expansion will be an option if sales projections are met.
    Marketing costs will remain below ___ (5?) % of sales.
    Repayment of our loan calculated at a high A.P.R. of ___ (10?) percent and at a 5-year-payback on our $_____ loan.

## 11.1 Important Assumptions

Financial Plan Assumptions
The following assumptions have been incorporated into our Proforma statements.
    All operating costs are based on the management's research of similar operating companies.
    Automated informational systems will reduce the staff requirements.
    Food and grocery inventory expense is 65 percent of revenue sales.
    Developmental start-up costs are amortized over a five-year period.
    Home office or other apartment expenses are not included.
    Overhead and operations costs are calculated on an annual basis.
    The founders' salary is based on a fixed monthly salary expense basis.
    All fixed and variable labor costs are scheduled to rise annually at ___ (5?) percent.
    All revenues are figured to rise annually at ___ (10?) percent.
    Administrative and office expenses rise at an annual rate of ____ (2.5?) percent.
    Operating costs increase at ___ (5?) percent annually.

Loan amount interest rate at _____ (9?) percent.

## Other Assumptions:

1. The economy will grow at a steady slow pace, without another major recession.
2. There will be no major changes in the industry, other than those discussed in the trends section of this document.
3. The State will not enact 'impact' legislation on our industry.
4. Sales are estimated at minimum to average values, while expenses are estimated at above average to maximum values.
5. Staffing and payroll expansions will be driven by increased sales.
6. Rent expenses will grow at a slow, predictable rate.
7. Materials expenses will not increase dramatically over the next several years, but will grow at a rate that matches increasing consumption.
8. We assume access to equity capital and financing sufficient to maintain our financial plan as shown in the tables.
9. The amount of the financing needed from the bank will be approximately $_____ and this will be repaid over the next 10 years at $_____ per month.
10. We assume that the area will continue to grow at present rate of __ % per year.
11. Interest rates and tax rates are based on conservative assumptions.

## Revenue Assumptions:

| Year | Sales/Month | Growth Rate |
|---|---|---|
| 1. | | |
| 2. | | |
| 3. | | |

**Resource:**
www.score.org/resources/business-plans-financial-statements-template-gallery

## 11.2     Break-even Analysis

**Break-Even Analysis** will be performed to determine the point at which revenue received equals the costs associated with generating the revenue. Break-even analysis calculates what is known as a margin of safety, the amount that revenues exceed the break-even point. This is the amount that revenues can fall while still staying above the break-even point. The two main purposes of using the break-even analysis for marketing is to (1) determine the minimum number of sales that is required to avoid a loss at a designated sales price and (2) it is an exercise tool so that we can tweak the sales price to determine the minimum volume of sales we can reasonably expect to sell in order to avoid a loss.

**Definition:**     Break-Even Is the Volume Where All Fixed Expenses Are Covered.

**Three important definitions used in break-even analysis are:**
- **Variable Costs** (Expenses) are costs that change directly in proportion to changes in activity (volume), such as raw materials, labor and packaging.

- **Fixed Costs** (Expenses) are costs that remain constant (fixed) for a given time period despite wide fluctuations in activity (volume), such as rent, loan payments, insurance, payroll and utilities.

- **Unit Contribution Margin** is the difference between your product's unit selling price and its unit variable cost.
  Unit Contribution Margin = Unit Sales Price - Unit Variable Cost

For the purposes of this breakeven analysis, the assumed fixed operating costs will be approximately $ _____ per month, as shown in the following table.

| **Averaged Monthly Fixed Costs:** | | **Variable Costs:** | |
|---|---|---|---|
| Payroll | _____ | Cost of Inventory Sold | _____ |
| Rent | _____ | Labor | _____ |
| Insurance | _____ | Supplies | _____ |
| Utilities | _____ | Direct Costs per Customer | _____ |
| Security. | _____ | Other | _____ |
| Legal/Technical Help | _____ | | |
| Other | _____ | | |
| Total: | _____ | Total | _____ |

A break-even analysis table has been completed on the basis of average costs/prices. With monthly fixed costs averaging $_____ , $\_\_\_\_ in average sales and $_____ in average variable costs, we need approximately $_____ in sales per month to break-even.

Based on our assumed \_\_\_ % variable cost, we estimate our breakeven sales volume at around $ \_\_\_\_ per month. We expect to reach that sales volume by our _____ month of operations. Our break-even analysis is shown in further detail in the following table.

## Breakeven Formulas:

**Break Even Units = Total Fixed Costs / (Unit Selling Price - Variable Unit Cost)**
　　　_____ = _____ / (_____ - _____)

·**BE Dollars = (Total Fixed Costs / (Unit Price – Variable Unit Costs))/ Unit Price**
　　　_____ = (_____ / (_____ - _____)) / _____

·**BE Sales = Annual Fixed Costs / (1- Unit Variable costs / Unit Sales Price)**
　　　_____ = _____ / (1 - _____ / _____)

Table:　　Break-even Analysis

Monthly Units Break-even　　　　　　　　_____
Monthly Revenue Break-even　　　　　　$ _____
Assumptions:
Average Per-Unit Revenue　　　　　　$ _____
Average Per-Unit Variable Cost　　　　$ _____
Estimated monthly Fixed Cost　　　　$ _____

## Ways to Improve Breakeven Point:
1. Reduce Fixed Costs via Cost Controls
2. Raise unit sales prices.
3. Lower Variable Costs by improving employee productivity or getting lower competitive bids from suppliers.
4. Broaden product/service line to generate multiple revenue streams.

## 11.3 Projected Profit and Loss

Pro forma income statements are an important tool for planning our future business operations. If the projections predict a downturn in profitability, we can make operational changes such as increasing prices or decreasing costs before these projections become reality.

Our monthly profit for the first year varies significantly, as we aggressively seek improvements and begin to implement our marketing plan. However, after the first ___ months, profitability should be established.

We predict advertising costs will go down in the next three years as word-of-mouth about our Mobile Food Truck gets out to the public and we are able to find what has worked well for us and concentrate on those advertising methods, and corporate affiliations generate sales without the need for extra advertising.

Our net profit/sales ratio will be low the first year. We expect this ratio to rise at least _____ (15?) percent the second year. Normally, a startup concern will operate with negative profits through the first two years. We will avoid that kind of operating loss on our second year by knowing our competitors and having a full understanding of our target markets.

Our projected profit and loss is indicated in the following table. From our research of the Food Truck industry, our annual projections are quite realistic and conservative, and we prefer this approach so that we can ensure an adequate cash flow.

Note:   IBISWorld estimates food and beverage purchases make up about 27% of all business costs. The second largest cost businesses face are primarily operating costs such as such as "insurances, telecommunications, repairs and maintenance, stationary, licenses, fuel and motor vehicle costs as well as other similar expenses. These expenses make up about 26% of business costs. If help is hired, wages can cost close to 18 % of all business costs.

## Key P & L Formulas:

**Gross Profit Margin = Total Sales Revenue - Cost of Goods Sold**

**Gross Margin % = (Total Sales Revenue - Cost of Goods Sold) / Total Sales Revenue**
This number represents the proportion of each dollar of revenue that the company retains as gross profit.

**EBITDA =Revenue - Expenses (exclude interest, taxes, depreciation & amortization)**

**PBIT = Profit (Earnings) Before Interest and Taxes = EBIT**
A profitability measure that looks at a company's profits before the company has to pay

corporate income tax and interest expenses. This measure deducts all operating expenses from revenue, but it leaves out the payment of interest and tax. Also referred to as "earnings before interest and tax ".

**Net Profit = Total Sales Revenues - Total Expenses**

## Pro Forma Profit and Loss

|  | Formula | 2017 | 2018 | 2019 |
|---|---|---|---|---|
| **Gross Revenue:** | | | | |
| Foodservice Sales | | | | |
| Other Revenue | | | | |
| **Total Revenue** | A | | | |
| | | | | |
| **Cost of Sales** | | | | |
| Products | | | | |
| Other | | | | |
| **Total Costs of Sales** | D | | | |
| | | | | |
| Gross Margin | A-D=E | | | |
| Gross Margin % | E / A | | | |
| **Operating Expenses:** | | | | |
| Payroll | | | | |
| Payroll Taxes | | | | |
| Sales & Marketing | | | | |
| Conventions/Trade Shows | | | | |
| Depreciation | | | | |
| License/Permit Fees | | | | |
| Dues and Subscriptions | | | | |
| Rent | | | | |
| Utilities | | | | |
| Deposits | | | | |
| Repairs and Maintenance | | | | |
| Janitorial Supplies | | | | |
| Office Supplies | | | | |
| Leased Equipment | | | | |
| Buildout Costs | | | | |
| Insurance | | | | |
| Location Rental | | | | |
| Van Expenses | | | | |
| Professional Development | | | | |
| Merchant Fees | | | | |
| Bad Debts | | | | |
| Miscellaneous | | | | |
| **Total Operating Expenses** | F | | | |
| **Profit Before Int. & Taxes** | E - F = G | | | |
| Interest Expenses | H | | | |
| Taxes Incurred | I | | | |
| **Net Profit** | G - H - I = J | | | |
| | | | | |
| **Net Profit / Sales** | J / A = K | | | |

## 11.5 Projected Cash Flow

The Cash Flow Statement shows how the company is paying for its operations and future growth, by detailing the "flow" of cash between the company and the outside world. Positive numbers represent cash flowing in, negative numbers represent cash flowing out.

The first year's monthly cash flows are will vary significantly, but we do expect a solid cash balance from day one. We expect that the majority of our sales will be done in cash or by credit card and that will be good for our cash flow position. Additionally, we will stock only slightly more than one month's inventory at any time. Consequently, we do not anticipate any problems with cash flow, once we have obtained sufficient start-up funds.

A __ year commercial loan in the amount of $_____, sought by the owner will be used to cover our working capital requirement. Our projected cash flow is summarized in the following table, and is expected to meet our needs. In the following years, excess cash will be used to finance our growth plans.

### Cash Flow Management:
**We will use the following practices to improve our cash flow position:**
1. Perform credit checks and become more selective when granting credit.
2. Seek deposits or multiple stage payments.
3. Reduce the amount/time of credit given to customers.
4. Reduce direct and indirect costs and overhead expenses.
5. Use the 80/20 rule to manage inventories, receivables and payables.
6. Invoice as soon as the project has been completed.
7. Generate regular reports on receivable ratios and aging.
8. Establish and adhere to sound credit practices.
9. Use more pro-active collection techniques.
10. Add late payment fees where possible.
11. Increase the credit taken from suppliers.
12. Negotiate purchase prices and extended credit terms from vendors.
13. Use some barter arrangements to acquire goods and service.
14. Use leasing to gain access to the use of productive assets.
15. Covert debt into equity.
16. Regularly update cash flow forecasts.
17. Defer projects which cannot achieve acceptable cash paybacks.
18. Require a 50% deposit upon the signing of the contract and the balance in full, due five days before the event.
19. Speed-up the completion of projects to get paid faster.
20. Ask for extended credit terms from major suppliers.
21. Put ideal bank balances into interest-bearing (sweep) accounts.
22. Charge interest on client installment payments.
23. Check the accuracy of invoices to avoid unnecessary rework delays.
24. Include stop-work clauses in contracts to address delinquent payments.

Cash Flow Formulas:
**Net Cash Flow = Incoming Cash Receipts - Outgoing Cash Payments**
Equivalently, net profit plus amounts charged off for depreciation, depletion, and amortization. (also called cash flow).

**Cash Balance = Opening Cash Balance + Net Cash Flow**
We are positioning ourselves in the market as a medium risk concern with steady cash flows. Accounts payable is paid at the end of each month, while sales are in cash, giving our company an excellent cash structure.

# Pro Forma Cash Flow

|  | Formula | 2017 | 2018 | 2019 |
|---|---|---|---|---|
| **Cash Received** | | | | |
| **Cash from Operations** | | | | |
| Cash Sales | A | | | |
| Cash from Receivables | B | | | |
| Subtotal Cash from Operations | A + B = C | | | |
| | | | | |
| Additional Cash Received | | | | |
| Non Operating (Other) Income | | | | |
| Sales Tax, VAT, HST/GST Received | | | | |
| New Current Borrowing | | | | |
| New Other Liabilities (interest fee) | | | | |
| New Long-term Liabilities | | | | |
| Sales of Other Current Assets | | | | |
| Sales of Long-term Assets | | | | |
| New Investment Received | | | | |
| Total Additional Cash Received | D | | | |
| Subtotal Cash Received | C + D = E | | | |
| | | | | |
| **Expenditures** | | | | |
| Expenditures from Operations | | | | |
| Cash Spending | F | | | |
| Payment of Accounts Payable | G | | | |
| Subtotal Spent on Operations | F + G = H | | | |
| Additional Cash Spent | | | | |
| Non Operating (Other) Expenses | | | | |
| Sales Tax, VAT, HST/GST Paid Out | | | | |
| Principal Repayment Current Borrowing | | | | |
| Other Liabilities Principal Repayment | | | | |
| Long-term Liabilities Principal Repayment | | | | |
| Purchase Other Current Assets | | | | |
| Dividends | | | | |
| Total Additional Cash Spent | I | | | |
| Subtotal Cash Spent | H + I = J | | | |
| **Net Cash Flow** | E - J = K | | | |
| **Cash Balance** | | | | |

## 11.6 Projected Balance Sheet

Pro forma Balance Sheets are used to project how the business will be managing its assets in the future. As a pure start-up business, the opening balance sheet may contain no values.

**Note**: The projected balance sheets must link back into the projected income statements and cash flow projections.

_____ (company name) does not project any real trouble meeting its debt obligations, provided the revenue predictions are met. We are very confident that we will meet or exceed all our objectives in the Business Plan and produce a slow but steady increase in net worth.

All our tables will be updated monthly to reflect past performance and future assumptions. Future assumptions will not be based on past performance but rather on economic cycle activity, regional industry strength, and future cash flow possibilities. We expect a solid growth in net worth by the year _____.

The Balance Sheet table for fiscal years 2017, 2018, and 2019 follows. It shows managed but sufficient growth of net worth, and a sufficiently healthy financial position.

## Key Formulas:

**Paid-in Capital** = Capital contributed to the corporation by investors on top of the par value of the capital stock.

**Retained Earnings** = The portion of net income which is retained by the corporation and used to grow its net worth, rather than distributed to the owners as dividends.

**Retained Earnings = After-tax net earnings - (Dividends + Stock Buybacks)**

**Earnings = Revenues - (Cost of Sales + Operating Expenses + Taxes)**

**Net Worth = Total Assets - Total Liabilities**
   Also known as 'Owner's Equity'.

# Pro Forma Balance Sheet

|  | Formulas | 2017 | 2018 | 2019 |
|---|---|---|---|---|
| **Assets** | | | | |
| **Current Assets** | | | | |
| Cash | | | | |
| Accounts Receivable | | | | |
| Inventory | | | | |
| Other Current Assets | | | | |
| Total Current Assets | A | | | |
| | | | | |
| Long-term Assets | | | | |
| Long-term Assets | B | | | |
| Accumulated Depreciation | C | | | |
| Total Long-term Assets | B - C = D | | | |
| | | | | |
| **Total Assets** | A + D = E | | | |
| | | | | |
| **Liabilities and Capital** | | | | |
| | | | | |
| **Current Liabilities** | | | | |
| Accounts Payable | | | | |
| Current Borrowing | | | | |
| Other Current Liabilities | | | | |
| **Subtotal Current Liabilities** | F | | | |
| | | | | |
| Long-term Liabilities | | | | |
| Notes Payable | | | | |
| Other Long-term Liabilities | | | | |
| **Subtotal Long-term Liabilities** | G | | | |
| | | | | |
| **Total Liabilities** | F + G = H | | | |
| | | | | |
| **Capital** | | | | |
| Paid-in Capital | I | | | |
| Retained Earnings | J | | | |
| Earnings | K | | | |
| Total Capital | I - J + K = L | | | |
| | | | | |
| **Total Liabilities and Capital** | H + L = M | | | |
| | | | | |
| **Net Worth** | E - H = N | | | |

## 11.7 Business Ratios

The following table provides significant ratios for the personal services industry. The final column, Industry Profile, shows ratios for this industry as it is determined by the Standard Industrial Classification, **SIC Industry Code: 72233**, for comparison purposes.

## Key Business Ratio Formulas:

**EBIT** = Earnings Before Interest and Taxes
**EBITA** = Earnings Before Interest, Taxes & Amortization. (Operating Profit Margin)

**Sales Growth Rate = ((Current Year Sales - Last Year Sales)/(Last Year Sales)) x 100**
**Ex: Percent of Sales = (Advertising Expense / Sales) x 100**

**Net Worth = Total Assets - Total Liabilities**

**Acid Test Ratio = Liquid Assets / Current Liabilities**
Measures how much money business has immediately available. A ratio of 2:1 is good.

**Net Profit Margin = Net Profit / Net Revenues**
The higher the net profit margin is, the more effective the company is at converting revenue into actual profit.

**Return on Equity (ROE) = Net Income / Shareholder's Equity**
The ROE is useful for comparing the profitability of a company to that of other firms in the same industry. Also known as "return on net worth" (RONW).

**Debt to Shareholder's Equity = Total Liabilities / Shareholder's Equity**
A ratio below 0.80 indicates there is a good chance the company has a durable competitive advantage, with the exception of financial institutions, which are highly leveraged institutions.

**Current Ratio = Current Assets / Current Liabilities**
The higher the current ratio, the more capable the company is of paying its obligations. A ratio under 1 suggests that the company would be unable to pay off its obligations if they came due at that point.

**Quick Ratio = Current Assets - Inventories / Current Liabilities**
The quick ratio is more conservative than the current ratio, because it excludes inventory from current assets.

**Pre-Tax Return on Net Worth = Pre-Tax Income / Net Worth**
Indicates stockholders' earnings before taxes for each dollar of investment.

**Pre-Tax Return on Assets = (EBIT / Assets) x 100**
Indicates much profit the firm is generating from the use of its assets.

**Accounts Receivable Turnover = Net Credit Sales / Average Accounts Receivable**
A low ratio implies the company should re-assess its credit policies in order to ensure the timely collection of imparted credit that is not earning interest for the firm.

**Net Working Capital = Current Assets - Current Liabilities**
Positive working capital means that the company is able to pay off its short-term liabilities. Negative working capital means that a company currently is unable to meet its short-term liabilities with its current assets (cash, accounts receivable and inventory).

**Interest Coverage Ratio = Earnings Before Interest & Taxes /Total Interest Expense**
The lower the ratio, the more the company is burdened by debt expense. When a company's interest coverage ratio is 1.5 or lower, its ability to meet interest expenses may be questionable. An interest coverage ratio below 1 indicates the company is not generating sufficient revenues to satisfy interest expenses.

**Collection Days = Accounts Receivables / (Revenues/365)**
A high ratio indicates that the company is having problems getting paid for services.

**Accounts Payable Turnover = Total Supplier Purchases/Average Accounts Payable**
If the turnover ratio is falling from one period to another, this is a sign that the company is taking longer to pay off its suppliers than previously. The opposite is true when the turnover ratio is increasing, which means the firm is paying of suppliers at a faster rate.

**Payment Days = (Accounts Payable Balance x 360) / (No. of Accounts Payable x 12)**
The average number of days between receiving an invoice and paying it off.

**Total Asset Turnover = Revenue / Assets**
Asset turnover measures a firm's efficiency at using its assets in generating sales or revenue - the higher the number the better.

**Sales / Net Worth = Total Sales / Net Worth**

**Dividend Payout = Dividends / Net Profit**

**Assets to Sales = Assets / Sales**
**Current Debt / Totals Assets = Current Liabilities / Total Assets**
**Current Liabilities to Liabilities = Current Liabilities / Total Liabilities**

# Business Ratio Analysis

|  | 2017 | 2018 | 2019 |
|---|---|---|---|
| **Sales Growth** | | | |
| | | | |
| **Percent of Total Assets** | | | |
| Accounts Receivable | | | |
| Inventory | | | |
| Other Current Assets | | | |
| Total Current Assets | | | |
| Long-term Assets | | | |
| Total Assets | | | |
| | | | |
| Current Liabilities | | | |
| Long-term Liabilities | | | |
| Total Liabilities | | | |
| Net Worth | | | |
| | | | |
| **Percent of Sales** | | | |
| Sales | | | |
| Gross Margin | | | |
| Selling G& A Expenses | | | |
| Advertising Expenses | | | |
| Profit Before Interest & Taxes | | | |
| | | | |
| **Main Ratios** | | | |
| Current | | | |
| Quick | | | |
| Total Debt to Total Assets | | | |
| Pre-tax Return on Net Worth | | | |
| Pre-tax Return on Assets | | | |
| | | | |
| **Additional Ratios** | | | |
| Net Profit Margin | | | |
| Return on Equity | | | |
| | | | |
| **Activity Ratios** | | | |
| Accounts Receivable Turnover | | | |
| Collection Days | | | |
| Inventory Turnover | | | |
| Accounts Payable Turnover | | | |
| Payment Days | | | |
| Total Asset Turnover | | | |
| Inventory Productivity | | | |
| Sales per sq/ft. | | | |
| Gross Margin Return on Inventory (GMROI) | | | |

**Debt Ratios**
Debt to Net Worth                    _____
Current Liabilities to Liabilities   _____

**Liquidity Ratios**
Net Working Capital                  _____
Interest Coverage                    _____

**Additional Ratios**
Assets to Sales                      _____
Current Debt / Total Assets          _____
Acid Test                            _____
Sales / Net Worth                    _____
Dividend Payout                      _____

**Business Vitality Profile**
Sales per Employee                   _____
Survival Rate                        _____

## 12.0   Summary

_____ (company name) will be successful. This business plan has documented that the establishment of _____ (company name) is feasible. All of the critical factors, such as industry trends, marketing analysis, competitive analysis, management expertise and financial analysis support this conclusion.

Project Description: (Give a brief summary of the product, service or program.)
_____

Description of Favorable Industry and Market Conditions.
(Summarize why this business is viable.)
_____

Summary of Earnings Projections and Potential Return to Investors:
_____

Summary of Capital Requirements:
_____

Security for Investors & Loaning Institutions:
_____

Summary of expected benefits for people in the community beyond the immediate business concern:
_____


Means of Financing:
A. Loan Requirements:           $_____
B. Owner's Contribution: $      $_____
C. Other Sources of Income:     $_____
Total Funds Available:          $_____

# 13.0 Potential Exit Scenarios

Two potential exit strategies exist for the investor:

1. **Initial Public Offering. (IPO)**
   We seek to go public within ___ (#) years of operations. The funds used will both help create liquidity for investors as well as allow for additional capital to develop our _____ (international/national?) roll out strategy.

2. **Acquisition Merger with Private or Public Company.**
   Our most desirable option for exit is a merger or buyout by a large corporation. We believe with substantial cash flows and a loyal customer base our company will be attractive to potential corporate investors within five years. Real value has been created through the novel combination of home health care services as well as partnering with key referral groups.

3. **Sale of the Business to a third party.**
   Mobile Businesses usually sell for approximately one to two times earnings given the financial strength of the business. In this event, the business would be sold by a business broker and the business loan sought in this plan would be repaid according to the covenants of the business loan agreement.

# APPENDIX

**Purpose:**   Supporting documents used to enhance your business proposal.

    Tax returns of principals for the last three years, if the plan is for new business
    A personal financial statement, which should include life insurance and endowment policies, if applicable
    A copy of the proposed lease or purchase agreement for building space, or zoning information for in-home businesses, with layouts, maps, and blueprints
    A copy of licenses and other legal documents including partnership, association, or shareholders' agreements and copyrights, trademarks, and patents applications
    A copy of résumés of all principals in a consistent format, if possible
    Copies of letters of intent from suppliers, contracts, orders, and miscellaneous.
    In the case of a franchised business, a copy of the franchise contract and all supporting documents provided by the franchisor
    Newspaper clippings that support the business or the owner, including something about you, your achievements, business idea, or region
    Promotional literature for your company or your competitors
    Product/Service Brochures of your company or competitors
    Photographs of your product. equipment, facilities, etc.
    Market research to support the marketing section of the plan
    Trade and industry publications when they support your intentions
    Quotations or pro-forma invoices for capital items to be purchased, including a list of fixed assets, company vehicles, and proposed renovations
    References/Letters of Recommendation
    All insurance policies in place, both business and personal
    Operation Schedules
    Organizational Charts
    Job Descriptions
    Additional Financial Projections by Month
    Customer Needs Analysis Worksheet
    Sample Sales Letters
    Copies of Software Management Reports
    Copies of Standard Business Forms
    Equipment List
    Personal Survival Budget

# Helpful Resources:

**Associations:**
- Organic Trade Association: http://www.ota.com
- Organic Farming Research Association: http://www.ofrf.org
- USDA's national organic program: http://www.ams.usda.gov/nop/

Convenience Caterers & Food Manufacturers Association
http://www.mobilecaterers.com/index.html

National Association of Concessionaires
http://www.naconline.org/

National Restaurant Association
http://www.restaurant.org/

National Association for the Self Employed
http://www.nase.org/Home.aspx

National Association of Specialty Food Trade
http://www.specialtyfood.com/do/Home

Southern California Mobile Food Vendors
http://site.socalmfva.com/Home.html

**Suppliers**

| | |
|---|---|
| Blenders/Mixers | www.blendtec.com |
| Restaurant Supply | www.zesco.com |
| Flavorings | www.nationalflavors.com |
| Infection Control Devices | www.brevis.com |
| Vanilla Extracts | www.lochheadvanilla.com |
| Dispensing Units | www.server-products.com |

**Miscellaneous:**

| | |
|---|---|
| Vista Print Free Business Cards | www.vistaprint.com |
| Free Business Guides | www.smbtn.com/businessplanguides/ |
| Open Office | http://download.openoffice.org/ |
| US Census Bureau | www.census.gov |
| Federal Government | www.business.gov |
| US Patent & Trademark Office | www.uspto.gov |
| US Small Business Administration | www.sba.gov |
| National Association for the Self-Employed | www.nase.org |
| International Franchise Association | www.franchise.org |
| Center for Women's Business Research | www.cfwbr.org |

# How to Get Started Marketing on Twitter

1. **Import Your Contacts**
   Import contacts from Gmail, Hotmail and your own address book. Start with a solid base of people who you consider friends, following you on Twitter.
2. **Make Sure that Your Profile is Complete**
   Fill in all the fields (both required and optional) and include your website URL. Personalize your Twitter page to match your company's branding.
3. **Understand the Dynamics of Twitter**
   Use Twitter as a social tool, not a classifieds site and follow these tips:
   - Don't spam others about your specials.
   - Follow other users.
   - Don't promote your company directly.
   - Tweet about an informative blog posting.
4. **Build Your Followers Base**
   - Put a link to "Follow Me on Twitter" everywhere (your email signature, forums, website, and business cards)
   - Every time you post on your blog, invite people to follow you on Twitter
   - Follow people who are smart in your business and look for people who follow them for you to follow. Get a re-follow will build our follower list with the right profile of followers. Make sure that you look for people who might be interested in what you have to offer and don't send a Tweet that is overtly asking for a sale.
   - Start by actually reading what prospective clients say in their Tweets and give a smart "tweetback" before you follow him on Twitter.
5. **Balance Your Followers/Following Ratio**
   - Strike a balance between people you follow and people that follow you.
   - Grow slowly by adding 30 friends at a time, and then wait for them to follow you back.
6. **Make it Worthwhile to Follow You**
   - Tweet only interesting stuff about your industry, and relate your tweetbacks to it and even post in some links.
   - Clients develop real interest and attention when they realize that the people who are meticulously maintaining the Twitter profile really want to help them.
   - Make sure that at least an hour is spent in maintaining the Twitter account, so that the profile is active, and remains interesting to people.
7. **Learn from the Best**
   - Find users with several hundred followers and learn their best practices.
8. **Twitter Uses**
   - Use twitter to extend the reach of an existing blogging strategy and to deepen or further ties. Ex: Carnival Cruise Lines.
   - Use to announce sales and deals. Ex: Amazon.
   - Increase the ability for frequent updates to blogs or web sites or news.
   - Build consensus or a community of supporters.
   - Build buzz for a blog. /Update breaking news at conferences or events.

# Sample Sales Letter

Business Prospect
Contact Information

Dear _____,

The holiday season will soon be upon us. My staff and I would very much like to help you with the planning of your next catered event. We have the expertise and experience to make your next catered party, be it an employee appreciation dinner, Christmas Party, or business luncheon, a truly special event.

_____ (company name) offers a delicious selection of themed menu items, including _____ _____
(sample of most popular menu items).

We can host your party in a rented _____ (banquet room/dining room) or provide on-premise catering at your designated location.

I have enclosed a sample menu, sales brochure, client testimonials and price list for your convenience. I do hope that you will think about us the next time you need a catered event.

Please call me at _____ or email _____ to discuss your plans.

Respectfully yours,


Your Company
Contact Information

# Sample Press Release

_____ (owner name) has big plans for his new food truck catering business called _____ (company name) in _____ (city), ___ state). If his success thus far is any indicator, then he has every reason to believe he can pull it off.

"We are very happy with the amount of business we have today," _____ (owner name) said. "It's exceeded our expectations."

Since opening in _____ (month), _____ (company name) has catered ____ (#) events, according to _____ (owner's name) estimates, and has cultivated a solid, diverse client base including big name customers such as _____, _____ and the _____ at _____ (city).

_____ (owner name) said many customers came by way of his community connections through organizations such as the _____ (Rotary Club), which he currently serves as _____ (president). He also earned a lot of valuable contacts through his ____ (#) years of experience in the hotel, restaurant, catering and hospitality industries. Most recently, he served as the _____ (director of marketing) for the _____ .

_____ (company name) specializes in corporate catering, wedding catering and special event catering. _____ (owner name) said that what sets his business apart from competitors is its comprehensive approach to service and development of themed concepts.

Presentation, for example, is emphasized. Rather than typical fruit trays, customers can get fruit "presentations," each a series of elevated marble tiles with fruit cut into artful shapes. Also, full-service catering for _____ (company name) means covering every facet of an event, from delivering the food to cleaning up the dishes afterward.

"A lot of catering companies are very good on food but not necessarily focused on the presentation, the delivery, and on the sales and marketing sides," _____ (owner name) said. With all these elements nailed down to an art form, _____ (owner name) is now working to expand his current business model.

Contact Information

# Sample Customer Satisfaction Survey

Please take the time to complete our survey. We care about your satisfaction and are always looking for ways to improve our service. We thank-you in advance for taking the time to give us your feedback on how we are doing.

Customers who complete this survey are automatically registered for a chance to win free products or services, and will receive our e-newsletters with updates and specials on products and services. Thank you.

Rating Scale:  1 = Poor   2 = Average   3 = Good   4 = Very Good   5 = Excellent

|   | | Rating |
|---|---|---|
| 1. | How would you rate the person who handled your phone inquiry? | _____ |
| 2. | Are you happy you were referred to my company? | Yes / No |
| 3. | Did you feel that I adequately explained our operating policies, menu package and party proposal? | Yes / No |
| 4. | Do you feel as though you received the party you were promised? | Yes / No |
| 5. | Are you satisfied that we completed our contractual agreement? | Yes / No |
| 6. | Was the quality of the food as good as promised? | Yes / No |
| 7. | Which dish was your favorite? _____ | |
| 8. | How would you rate the quality of staff service? | _____ |
| 9. | Did the food presentation meet your expectation? | Yes / No |
| 10. | Was the temperature of each dish correct? | Yes / No |
| 11. | Do you feel you got good value for your money? | Yes / No |
| 12. | Were there any problems you would like to have addressed? | Yes / No |
| 13. | Was your home or the party site left in satisfactory condition? | Yes / No |
| 14. | How could we have made your experience better? _____ | |
| 15. | May we use your name as a reference? | Yes / No |
| 16. | Would you feel comfortable writing us a letter of recommendation? | Yes / No |
| 17. | What did you like best about working with us? _____ | |
| 18. | Please list the names and addresses of friends or colleagues who might be interested in our services in the future? | |
| 19. | How did you hear about us? | |
| 20. | What do you like best about our business? | |
| 21. | What do you like least about our business? | |
| 22. | What products or services would you like to see added to our offerings? | |
| 23. | Other Comments | |

Thanks again. I hope that we have the opportunity to do another party for you in the near future.

Name: _____

Address: _____

Email: _____

# Advertising Plan Worksheet

Ad Campaign Title: _____

Ad Campaign Start Date: _____ End Date: _____

What are the features (what product has) and hidden benefits (what product does for consumer) of my products/services?

Who is the targeted audience?

What problems are faced by this targeted audience?

What solutions do you offer?

Who is the competition and how do they advertise?

What is your differentiation strategy?

What are your bullet point competitive advantages?

What are the objectives of this advertising campaign?

What are your general assumptions?

What positioning image do you want to project?
- ___ Exclusiveness
- ___ Low Cost
- ___ High Quality
- ___ Speedy Service
- ___ Convenient
- ___ Innovative

What is the ad headline?

What is the advertising budget for this advertising campaign?

What advertising methods will be used?
- ___ Radio
- ___ TV/Cable
- ___ Yellow Pages
- ___ Coupons
- ___ Telemarketing
- ___ Flyers
- ___ Direct Mail
- ___ Magazines
- ___ Newspapers
- ___ Press Release
- ___ Brochures
- ___ Billboards
- ___ Other

When will each advertising method start and what will it cost?

| Method | Start Date | Frequency | Cost |
|--------|------------|-----------|------|
|        |            |           |      |

Indicate how you will measure the cost-effectiveness of the advertising plan?
Formula: Return on Investment (ROI) = Generated Sales / Ad Costs.

# Marketing Action Plan

Month: _____

Target Market: _____

Responsibilities: _____

Allocated Budget: _____

Objectives _____

Strategies _____

Implementation _____

Tactics _____

Results
Evaluation _____

_____
_____
_____
_____
_____
_____
_____
_____
_____
_____
_____
_____
_____

**Lessons Learned:**
_____
_____
_____

# Viral Marketing

**Definition:** Also known as word-of-mouth advertising.
**Objective:** To prompt your customers to deliver your sales message to others.
**Strategy:** Encourage and enable communication recipients to pass the offer or message along to others.
**Benefit:** Provides an excellent advertising return on investment and builds the trust factor.

## Methodologies:
1. Encourage blog comments and two-way dialogue.
2. Use surveys to solicit feedback.
3. Use refer-a-friend forms or scripts.
4. Provide discount coupon or logo imprinted giveaway rewards for telling a friend.
5. Utilize pre-existing social networks.
6. Participate in message boards or forums.
7. Add a signature line with a refer-a-friend tagline to all posts and emails.
8. Enable unrestricted access.
9. Facilitate website content sharing.
10. Write articles and e-books, and encourage free reprints with byline mention.
11. Submit articles with 'about the author' box to article directories, such as www.articlecity.com.
12. Develop attention-grabbing product line extensions to stay connected.
13. Do the unexpected by offering a surprise benefit.
14. Deliver a remarkable offering that exceeds customer expectations.
15. Provoke a strong emotional response by getting involved with a cause that is important to your customers.
16. Provide referral incentives.
17. Get free samples into the hands of respected opinion leaders.
18. Educate customers, as to your product benefits and competitive advantages, to act as spokespersons for your company.

Explain Your Viral Marketing Program
_____
_____
_____
_____
_____

# Marketing on Social Networking Websites

1. Place banner ads or Pay-Per-Click ads on social networking sites.
2. Create an account on the website and add your company logo.
3. Encourage word-of-mouth exchanges by posting comments on friend's profiles.
4. Post surveys on your social networking pages to solicit feedback.
5. Create a profile that subtly and humbly tells everyone about you and your gift basket products and services.
6. Include links to your gift basket business website.
7. Make your profile keyword rich with keyword phases from your business specialty.
8. Use a soft sell approach, and focus on establishing your credibility and expertise as a gift basket marketing guru, to be trusted by prospective customers.
9. Name your social networking page exactly as your organization is named.
10. Have a strong presence in one channel rather than all of them.
11. Make sure you give visitors a strong call to action to supply their email address, so you can contact them later.
12. Include a signature line with your website contact info.
13. Blog often, but make certain that instead of selling, you are sharing your gift industry expertise.

Helpful Resources:
http://en.wikipedia.org/wiki/List_of_social_networking_websites

Examples:    Facebook.com        Myspace.com
             LinkedIn.com        Ryse.com


Explain Your Online Social Networking Strategy
_____
_____
_____
_____

# Integrate Marketing into Daily Operations

**Objective:** To seamlessly integrate marketing processes into daily, routine operations.

**Strategies:**
1. Develop form to ask for referrals upon new customer registration and annual renewal.
2. Present a sales presentation folder upon registration or contract sign-up with needs analysis worksheets, testimonials, new product introduction flyers, innovative application ideas, etc.
3. Develop a second sales presentation folder version for presentation upon job completion or sale, with referral program details, warranty service contract blank, and accessory suggestions.
4. Include business cards and coupons with all product deliverables.
5. Install company yard signs during job set-up.
6. Include a thank you note/comment card with all deliverables.
7. Include flyers and helpful articles in all customer correspondence, especially mailed invoices and statements.
8. Attach logo and contact info to all finished products.
9. Conduct customer satisfaction surveys while customers are waiting to be served.
10. Develop enclosed warranty card to build customer database and feed drip marketing program.
11. Provide competitor product/service comparisons that highlight your strengths.
12. Incorporate feedback cards into merchandise displays.
13. Train all employees to also be sales and customer service agents.
14. Print your Mission Statement or slogan on all forms and correspondence.
15. _____
16. _____

Indicate how you will incorporate marketing into daily operations.

| Sales Stage | Business Processes | Opportunities to Incorporate Marketing Techniques |
|---|---|---|
| Pre-sale | | |
| Transaction | | |
| Post Sale | | |

# Monthly Marketing Calendar

Instruction: Use to plan your monthly marketing events or activities and evaluate individual event results and marketing lessons learned for the month.

Month/Year: _____

| Event/ Activity | Responsibility | Cost | Comments | Date | Results Evaluation |
|---|---|---|---|---|---|
| | | | | | |

Monthly Evaluation of Lessons Learned:
_____
_____
_____

# Form Strategic Marketing Alliances

**Definition:** A collaborative relationship between two or more non-competing firms with the intent of accomplishing mutually compatible and beneficial goals that would be difficult for each to accomplish alone. Also referred to as 'Collaboration Marketing'.

**Note:** Usually, potential alliance partners sell distinct or complementary products and/or services to the same target market audience.

**Advantages:** Improve marketing efficiency by achieving synergy in resource allocation with strategic partners.
Improve marketing effectiveness by creating a one-stop or wraparound shopping experience.
A way to inexpensively test the market for growth potential.

## Types of Co-Ventures:
1. Informal Strategic Alliances
2. Contractual Relationships (Attorney review recommended)
3. New Business Entity (Set-up by attorney)

## Informal Strategic Alliances
1. Most involve consultations regarding:
    a. Mutual Referrals
    b. Research for product improvements
    c. Promotion of products or services (affiliate programs).
    d. Creative product bundling arrangements.
2. May or may not require a written agreement.
3. May or may not require compensation.

## Topics to be Covered:
1. The specific strategic goals and objectives of the alliance.
2. The performance expectations of the parties.
3. The scope of the alliance.
4. The period of performance.
5. Termination and renewal procedures.
6. Strategic marketing plan to promote the alliance.
7. Dispute resolution procedures.
8. Performance tracking methods.
9. Periodic evaluation of reciprocal benefits realized.
10. Website pages/links to promote alliance partners.

**Example:** The mutual referral relationship between a sports bar and a fitness club or physical fitness trainer.

# Strategic Marketing Alliance Worksheet

## Methodology:
1. Identify the assets and capabilities you can provide to the alliance.
2. Identify the assets and capabilities that the proposed partner will bring to the alliance.
3. Determine the benefits you are seeking from the alliance.
4. Determine the gaps in your offerings that the alliance partner can fill.
5. List any conflicting relationships with other businesses and benefits received.
6. Research the potential alliance for strategic fit and other opportunities.
7. List the ways in which your customers will benefit from this alliance.
8. Assess any alliance risks.
9. Determine the ongoing actions needed to maintain the alliance.
10. Design a marketing plan to promote the alliance.
11. Develop a Mission Statement for the alliance.
12. Develop the Management Plan for the alliance.
13. Design the alliance appraisal and renewal procedures.

| Potential Alliance Partner | Partner Strengths Offered | Your Offering Gaps Filled | Customer Benefits | Alliance Risks |
|---|---|---|---|---|
| | | | | |
| | | | | |
| | | | | |
| | | | | |
| | | | | |
| | | | | |
| | | | | |
| | | | | |
| | | | | |
| | | | | |

# Referral Program Tips

**Objective:** To formalize your referral program so that it can be easily and consistently integrated into your operating processes.

1. Define the stages in the sales process when you will ask for a referral. Ex: Registration, Renewals, Annual Drive, etc.)

2. Document your referral asking script (include objection handling responses).

3. Include a request for referrals in your customer satisfaction survey and your registration forms.

4. Stress the dependence of your business on referrals in all your marketing communications.

5. Set-up a follow-up procedure and tracking form to convert referral leads into actual customers.

6. Publish your referral incentives, awards criteria and timetable for settlement.

7. Customize your referral program to the motivational needs of a select number of potential 'Bird Dogs' or 'Big Hitters'.

8. Educate potential referral agents as to the characteristics of your ideal prospect. (Develop Ideal Prospect Profile)

9. Set-up special, mutual referral arrangements with strategic business alliance partners and track the reciprocity of efforts.

10. Join or start a local lead group.

11. Set-up 'thank-you note' templates to facilitate your expression of gratitude.

12. Use logo imprinted giveaways, such as T-sheets, as referral thank you expressions.

# Seminar Outline Worksheet

**Objective:** To establish your expertise on the subject matter, and produce future possible networking contacts by offering a newsletter sign-up and/or business card exchange.

**Warning:** Make seminar information rich and not a sales presentation.

1. Start with Attention-Grabbing Headline
   Ex: Hard-hitting Quotation, Thought Provoking Question, Startling Fact

2. Introduce Yourself and Establish Your Credentials

3. Present Seminar Overview

4. Discuss Attendee Participation Guidelines

5. Solicit a sampling of attendee interests, backgrounds and concerns.

6. Establish Learning Objectives

7. Preview the Bulleted Topics To be Covered

8. Share a Relevant Success Story (Case Study).

9. Use analogies and comparisons to create reference points.

10. Use statistics to support your position.

11. Conclusion: - Summarize Benefits for Attendees / Appeal to Action

12. Hold Question and Answer Session

13. Final Thoughts
    - Appreciation for Help Received
    - Indicate after-seminar availability

14. Handout A Remembrance
    - Business Cards
    - Seminar Outline
    - Glossary of Terms
    - Feedback Survey

Made in the USA
San Bernardino, CA
16 October 2018